TOUT SOUL

TOUT SOUL

The Pursuit of Happiness in Rural France

Karen Wheeler

CHIVERS

British Library Cataloguing in Publication Data available

This Large Print edition published by AudioGO Ltd, Bath, 2013.
Published by arrangement with the Author.

U.K. Hardcover   ISBN 978 1 4713 3061 2
U.K. Softcover   ISBN 978 1 4713 3062 9

Printed and bound in Great Britain by
TJ International Limited

For Luis

Contents

Note from the Author

This is a true story. I have changed only some minor details and names, including that of my village, in order to protect the innocent (and the not so innocent). The timing of Travis's party and the reopening of the café in Puysoleil have also been altered slightly in order to make for a better narrative.

Chapter 1

September

'I cannot miss this flight. I *cannot* miss this flight,' is the mantra that I repeat to myself as I sprint the five miles—at least that's what it feels like—from the HMV shop in Stansted's departure lounge to the gate where, if the tannoy is to be believed, my bag is about to be removed from the plane.

With a second enormous bag containing ten kilos of organic vegetables slung over my shoulder, I negotiate two sets of stairs, jog along a moving walkway and run down a long corridor, barging past fellow travellers and possibly mowing down small children and pensioners in my wake. I don't stop to check. *I cannot miss this flight.*

Breathing heavily, and drawing odd looks from the passengers dawdling towards passport control on the other side of the glass wall, I stop to adjust the black nylon bag, dangling like a small bungalow from my shoulder. I'm tempted to ditch my blueberries and broccoli florets in favour of one last push towards the departure lounge, but organic vegetables are hard to find and expensive in rural France. Plus, I don't want to be escorted away in handcuffs for triggering a security alert.

I cannot miss this flight. I really can't. Up another escalator I go, relieved when the departure lounge looms into view. I leg across that, too—not easy in my new cherry-red Prada shoes with tower block heels. But there is no sign of Gate 48. Have I run past it, I wonder? Wild-eyed, I run towards the desk for Gdansk. 'Gate 48?' I plead and a woman in a blue and yellow uniform indicates a small sign pointing towards yet another escalator. I clatter down it, my way suspiciously clear now—where is everyone?—cursing the fact that Ryanair's planes always depart from gates so far away that you almost need a visa and vaccinations to go there.

Finally, I see the sign: *GATE 48.* But there is no queue. My fellow passengers are probably all buckled into their seats listening to Ryanair jingles. Please don't let it be too late. *Please, don't let me miss this flight.* But (hallelujah!) I spot a member of staff still at her station, frowning at a list. I jog up with my boarding pass and breathe a huge sigh of relief when she lets me through—albeit with a tut and a 'You'd better hurry up: they're waiting to close the doors'. Then it's just a short sprint across the tarmac in the autumn sunshine to board at the rear, my face as pink as the tropical blooms on my Marni dress. I haven't missed my flight but it was pretty close.

I've been on a work trip to London—

this time to interview the scientist behind a 'revolutionary' new anti-aging cream involving some rare berry, hand-plucked at dawn, the morning after a full moon on a remote Himalayan mountainside. Now I am (literally) running back to rustification—to my darling black-haired dog, my Portuguese boyfriend, and my idyllic, rural lifestyle.

Breathless, I put my bag into an overhead locker as the door is closed behind me. Now that the summer holiday season is over, the plane is almost empty. As I survey the brash yellow and blue interior, wondering which empty row to make my own, a familiar voice booms out a greeting from somewhere behind me.

'I MIGHT HAVE KNOWN IT WAS YOU,' exclaims the voice. I turn around and am delighted to see Jocelyn, friend, fellow expat and (ahem) my former line-dancing teacher, sitting in the window seat, looking tanned and freckled. She is wearing dark denim jeans with turn-ups, a navy polo shirt and a cheeky grin.

Hers was a hard won friendship. When we met at a line-dancing class—an activity, I should point out, that bears no stigma in rural France—I liked her immediately, thanks to her blunt manner and northern sense of humour. But for the best part of a year she eyed me with extreme suspicion, as if I were an acquired taste, like Guinness or Lady Gaga.

Only very recently has she started to warm to me.

'I looked out of the window and saw someone running past the wing,' she says, her blue eyes twinkling. 'And I thought to myself, who could this be, arriving so late? Then I thought, I *recognise* that face.'

'You know me,' I say, flopping into the seat next to her. 'Never knowingly on time.'

'So what have you been doing in the UK?' she asks.

'Oh, just work stuff,' I reply. This seems like the easiest way to describe the frantic forty-eight hours, into which I've packed half a dozen work meetings, two hours of Pilates, a visit to the dentist, and three glasses of Pinot Grigio with my former flatmate.

'Oh, look. They're doing the safety demonstration,' says Jocelyn, focusing her attention on the stern-faced Croatian flight attendant standing before us in a limp lifejacket. She waits until the plane starts to move down the runway to strike up a conversation again. 'And how's your Portuguese boyfriend. What's his name, Louis?' (She pronounces it *Loo-ee*, like one of the French kings and the X-Factor judge.)

'*Loo-eee-sss,*' I say, pronouncing it softly, as the Portuguese do, so that it rhymes with 'peace' with three syllables and the emphasis on the hissing 's'. Several of his compatriots actually pronounce it with a hint of a 'shh' at the end. *Loo-eee-sh*. Even the mention of his name has an effect on me like a tequila shot, sending swirls of happiness through my brain.

'Yes, it's going really well,' I say. My face breaks into an involuntary smile at the thought of my bilingual builder with jet hair and eyes as black as a rural night. He is the reason that I am so keen to get back to France. Now, I am less than two hours away from his strong brown arms. I know his Sunday morning routine so well. No doubt he will have slept as late as possible, after a week of working fifteen hour days, and he will have made it to Intermarché—which closes at noon on Sunday —- with five minutes to spare. Right now, it's just after midday in France. He will be sitting on the *terrasse* of the café in the early autumn sunshine, dragging on a cigarette and scowling in that super-macho way of his. And if he is not scowling, he will be laughing—a deep, sonorous laugh, electrifying the air around him. My closest French friend, Delphine, the mayor of a nearby village, describes him as 'very electrical', which is most apt, as an erotic charge seems to spark from him. When Luis enters a room, pulsating with life and vitality, everyone is aware of his presence.

As the plane soars into the pale blue sky, I picture him sitting outside the café, dressed in jeans and a long-sleeved orange T-shirt, layered over another in a clashing shade—he loves bright colours—and running his hands

5

through his lush black hair. There is so much that I love about Luis—or The Lion, to use the nickname I gave him when he lived next door. I called him this partly because of his proud demeanour and partly because he seemed to be the leader of the pack of Portuguese builders living there. To begin with, I regarded him as the enemy and for over a year we were at war. Several times, I reported him and his friend Piedro to the gendarmes for disturbing the peace with their loud music and laughter. But everything changed when, in the middle of a very hot summer, my dog Biff jumped out of the window and The Lion brought him back to me.

I took one look at him standing on my doorstep, holding Biff in his arms like a little black lamb, and it was as if a switch had flicked inside me. Suddenly, I saw my nuisance neighbour with new eyes, noticing his charismatic smile and magnetic black eyes for the first time. I invited him into my courtyard for a drink and everything started from there. If I'm honest, the initial attraction was purely physical, but it wasn't long before I had fallen for his larger-than-life personality. There is so much to love about my builder boyfriend: the fact that he notices the colour I've painted my toenails, that he tells me all the time that I am *'beaucoup jolie'* (lots pretty) and that he doesn't mind that I'm nearly ten years older than him.

6

I love the fact that he works so hard—sometimes leaving with his compatriots at dawn and returning at midnight from a job over 100 kilometres away, only to depart again four hours later—and that he never, *ever* complains. I love it that he is super fit and strong—he can scoop me up in his arms and carry me upstairs as easily as if I were a small child—and that he smells of lemons and green ferns. And that even though there is something wild and untamed about him, his fingernails are always clean and his table manners refined. It makes me smile that, despite his macho persona, he has vibrant pink sheets on his bed and a pimento-coloured sofa, and that his new apartment, a few minutes' walk across the square from my house, is always spotlessly clean. I even love the way that he slices an onion, holding it in the palm of his hand and using a knife to unravel it like a corkscrew.

I've learnt to love the fact that his musical tastes are so eclectic, ranging from heavy metal to salsa. (The reason I almost missed the plane was that I had stopped to buy him the latest Kings of Leon CD.) I love him so much that I'm prepared to overlook the fact that he likes Metallica and Dire Straits—or, as he pronounces it, *Dear* Straits.

As a member of the cabin crew reminds us to keep our seat belts fastened in case of turbulence, I think of the funny, unexpected twists that life takes. Five years ago, I limped

7

across the channel, an injured soul, on the run from misery and a relationship that had ended unexpectedly in my mid-thirties. I could never have imagined that I would end up falling for a Portuguese neighbour. Nor could I have envisaged the wonderful summer evenings that we'd spend together, laughing and chatting in my jasmine-scented courtyard; and the winter nights eating candle-lit dinners at midnight at the kitchen table or sharing a bottle of wine—or occasionally champagne—in front of the roaring fire.

It hasn't all been plain sailing. We actually broke up for two months last autumn, but that seems a long time ago now. There is also the fact that Luis is very unpredictable. I never know what time of the day or night he is going to turn up at my door. Sometimes, if he is working away from home, I don't see or hear anything of him for days. This means that weekends take on a heightened sensibility, where every minute counts—the reason I was so desperate to catch this flight. At least I will get to spend this afternoon with Luis.

'Karen!' Jocelyn is saying, as the plane levels out in the blue organza sky. 'Take that soppy look off your face.'

'Oops, sorry, I was miles away,' I say.

'I can see that. I was asking about Travis?' she replies smiling.

Travis, a mutual friend—I met him at an expat dinner party in a nearby village—

moved to France six months ago after being made redundant from his job as a TV producer in London. He's been busy blowing his redundancy money on building works ever since. 'Travis is fine,' I say. 'Still looking for Mr Right and still battling on with his renovations.'

An hour later, we disembark to a delphinium blue sky and coppery autumn sunshine. 'Not bad for late September, eh?' says my companion, as we cross the tarmac to the small, satsuma-painted arrivals hall, where we say goodbye. I am happy, as always, to be back in the land of sadistic French bureaucrats, suicidal drivers and hapless Brits bravely attempting to turn their barns into habitable abodes. I'm proud of the fact that I have built a life here from scratch. My house is now fully renovated. I have an adorable dog, a hot builder for a boyfriend, and an extended family of French and English friends. My life, I think to myself as I drive out of the airport, is almost perfect.

There is only one thing that could make it more perfect. Earlier this year Luis asked me, without being prompted, if I would have an *enfant* with him. Initially, he was vague on timing—'perhaps next year, *chérie*,' he said—but a few months ago, he asked me again, without any implied delay this time. I can't think of anything I have ever wanted more but, since time is no longer on my side, we need to

9

get a move on.

I drive out of the airport and onto the N10, listening to Lily Allen singing *Smile*. My village is 30 kilometres from the airport, but the drive home takes me through a lush, golden landscape of sunflowers and maize. The Poitou-Charentes does not offer the romance (and exorbitant house prices) of Provence or the allure of Bordeaux, but it's known for its sunny climate, juicy cantaloupe melons and world-renowned goats' cheeses. It also produces a butter called Échiré, said to be the best in the world, thanks not to the breed of cow that produces it but the quality of the grass that they eat.

My village is not the prettiest in France. In fact, some would say that Villiers is not picturesque at all, that it is rather lacking in cobblestones and quaintness, but it boasts three cafés, two bakeries, an organic grocery, a hunting shop and several clothing boutiques—all laid out around the *mairie*. Villiers, like much of the Poitou-Charentes, is the real rural deal. In the summer, tractors, combine harvesters and agricultural convoys crawl along the nearby country roads, while wheat, oats, rapeseed and sunflowers grow in abundance in the surrounding fields. Whenever I see a farmer ploughing his furrows late at night, I always feel grateful, because it is thanks to their efforts that much of Europe is kept in porridge, bread and sunflower oil.

I didn't really choose the region; rather, it chose me when I went to visit an English friend for the weekend and ended up buying my house. It might not be the most fashionable area in France but the Poitou has been my home for the past five years and I wouldn't have it any other way.

*   *   *

As always on a Sunday afternoon, Villiers is deserted when I arrive back. I drive into the square and turn into rue St Benoit, pulling up in front of Maison Coquelicot, or 'house of the wild poppy', as I have named my little cottage. The first thing I do on arriving home is to call Luis. I noticed that his pale green shutters were tightly closed as I drove past his apartment, but his white Renault Clio was parked outside, so he must be at home. His mobile goes straight to voicemail.

'Darling, I'm back. Come over as soon as you get this message,' I say in French, the language in which we communicate. The Lion is probably in his lair sleeping off a hangover. Or he may be watching a DVD with his new flatmate Sergio, a fellow worker and Brad Pitt lookalike, in his early twenties. Sergio recently replaced Luis's best friend and sidekick, Piedro, who has just moved out of the apartment to live with his new girlfriend. It's possible that Luis is away on a job. After all,

11

it's not unknown for him and his compatriots to work entire weekends. He hasn't replied to the messages that I've left over the past two days, but I know that his phone often remains uncharged for days if he has been working away from home.

I throw open the pale blue shutters of the *petit salon* and bring my bags in from the car. Then, because I'm not very good at waiting, I call Luis again. '*Chéri*, maybe it's better if I go and collect Biff now. I'll be back in an hour, so call me on my mobile when you get this message.' I jump back in the car for the twenty-minute drive to the little hamlet, surrounded by fields of sunflowers and maize, where Steve and Sarah, Biff's former owners, live. The sun reappears on the way, forcing its way through a gap in the clouds like a spotlight, illuminating the stalks of maize, which are bleached gold now and ready to be harvested.

I'm impatient to get there and back as quickly as possible, but I get stuck behind a tractor and then a Sunday driver, who is dawdling along the narrow, winding road that leads to Sarah's hamlet at 30 kilometres an hour. (In France, if someone is driving so slowly, it's usually because they've been drinking.)

Biff is waiting for me when I arrive, his hairy black face peering through the gaps in the wooden gate that Steve, a carpenter, has

12

specially reinforced to keep him in. He gives a bark of excitement, but he is a proud little creature and tries not to look too delighted to see me. Milou, Sarah and Steve's snowy white terrier comes running out to see what the fuss is about. In the large terracotta kitchen, Steve, tall and thin, is standing near the sink shelling walnuts for his homemade walnut bread, while Sarah is sitting at the dining table sewing a tentacle back onto Biff's toy octopus. Their home is like a dog kindergarten, with toys and stuffed animals strewn across the garden and kitchen floor. I love visiting their house.

Sarah gets up to greet me and then runs through the highlights of Biff's forty-eight hour mini-break. Apparently, he's chased the neighbour's cats, shredded a kitchen roll on the front lawn and dug up the leeks in their vegetable patch.

'He probably thought he was being helpful,' says Sarah who, despite all the mischief, is still smiling.

'So he's had a good time then,' I say. 'Has he shown any signs of missing me?'

'None whatsoever,' says Steve, absolutely deadpan, without looking up from his walnuts. 'In fact, I think he might want to move back in with us.'

I know that Steve is joking, but it would be an ironic twist if it were true, since I effectively stole Biff from them. (I volunteered to look after him for a fortnight and fell in love with

13

him. And when it became obvious that Biff felt the same way, bless them, they gave him to me.)

'Of course he's missed you,' says Sarah. 'He's just too proud to show it right now. Have you got time for a coffee?'

'Actually, Luis is on his way over.'

'Well, you'd better get going then,' she says, with a wink. 'I'll get his things.' She pads off down the hallway in her Ugg boots and returns carrying Biff's doughnut and the straw basket containing his other possessions. Steve helps me out to the car and Biff races down the path ahead of us, no longer able to hide his joy that I'm back. He jumps in the car and curls up like a comma in his usual position behind the driver's seat.

I race home, so busy thinking about Luis that I don't notice the 2CV stopping suddenly in front of me in order to make a right turn. I slam on the brakes at the last moment and then reach round to reassure the little dog curled up behind me. In the years that I've lived in France, I've solved many of the mysteries of my host nation. I know, for example, that the reason why Frenchmen prefer Speedos is because surfer-style shorts are banned in French swimming pools. (But it still doesn't explain why they wear them two sizes too small.) I also understand that the point of all the bureaucracy is to keep *fonctionnaires*, or civil servants, in jobs. But I

14

still can't get my head around French drivers. Why, when they drive so audaciously on the autoroute, tailgating at 130 kilometres an hour while holding a phone to their ear, do they exercise such extreme caution when turning left or right?

As we approach Villiers, I make a small detour so that I can drive past Luis's building again. Looking up at his first floor apartment with its decorative iron balcony, I see that the shutters are still closed. Back home, I unpack my organic vegetables, paint my toes pink and wait for Luis to arrive. And wait. I wash my hair and switch from my London clothes to my rustic uniform of jeans and flip-flops. I water the plants in the courtyard garden and throw a ball around for Biff. And then I wait some more.

I've learnt to give Luis space and a long leash. But even so, loving him is like being in a high-speed elevator, the sort that you find in Manhattan skyscrapers, which whizz you up from the basement to the penthouse in a matter of minutes. Sometimes, when I haven't heard from him for days, I am emotionally in the basement. Then suddenly, he'll be standing outside my door, installed in my kitchen making a salad dressing, or lying in my bed wearing a big smile and I'm catapulted back up into the sky. Sometimes, I wonder if I'm addicted to these highs and lows.

I think back to a recent weekend where he

failed to surface until late on Sunday evening. I was sitting at my desk, listening to *Carey* by Joni Mitchell and writing a 'To do' list for the coming week. Furious that he hadn't called all weekend, I refused to let him in. He rang my doorbell, threw pebbles up against the tightly closed shutters and made alternate calls to my landline and mobile for over half an hour. In response, I turned up the music, while outside I could hear him calling my name and telling me that he loved me.

Suddenly, everything went quiet and I assumed he had gone next door to visit his friend and fellow worker Ruigi, the only Portuguese worker still living at 7 rue St Benoit. But then I heard a plaintive voice, sounding mystifyingly close.

'*Ka-renne, ma chérie . . . je t'aime . . . je t'aime beacoup.*'

It sounded like he was on the other side of the thin partition wall that separates my bathroom from the apartment next door. I turned up the music again but his voice sounded even closer, as if he were in the same room. I turned around from my computer screen, only to find that he *was*.

'*Chérie*,' he said, holding out his arms and looking very pleased with himself.

'How did you get in?' I demanded, shocked, alarmed and thrilled in equal measure.

'Love let me in,' he replied, before changing his story to, 'It was Biff who let me in. He

16

opened the door with his paws.' (I doubted it: Biff had been hiding under the bed for the past half-hour, wide-eyed at the sound of the stones hitting the shutters and the loud music.)

At first, I thought that Luis had somehow managed to pick the lock or force the front door. But the open skylight in the bathroom and the black footprints on the white walls told a different story. Still, it took me a while to work out that in order to drop into my house SAS-style, he first had to access the roof via his former bedroom next door. It was an impressive feat, and thrilling to know that someone would go to such lengths to see me— even if he didn't bring me a box of Milk Tray or a red rose between his teeth.

'You are mad,' I said, as he fell backwards on to my bed, a big grin on his handsome face, his eyes shining like black glass. 'That was a really mad thing to do.'

'I know, *chérie*,' he replied. 'But you are mad, too. That's why I love you.'

I'm beginning to wonder if there is some truth in this. I know that breaking in through a skylight is not normal behaviour, but after the initial shock had worn off, I couldn't help but laugh. It was also a little ironic. When my friend Delphine predicted that the love of my life would arrive when I least expected it, I replied, 'Well, since I spend most of my time home alone working, he'll have to drop in through the roof.' Which is exactly what Luis

17

did that night.

But although I was laughing, alarm bells were also ringing. Luis could provide no meaningful answer for where he had been all weekend. And only much later did it occur to me that he could have fallen off the roof with disastrous consequences.

As the church bells behind my house ring out the fact that it is 4.00 pm, I decide to confront matters head-on. I set off across the square, smelling of rose and frankincense, hair still damp from the shower, to ring Luis's doorbell.

Chapter 2

The End

It's disconcerting to find that the bedroom shutters are now slightly ajar. Luis is obviously up but he hasn't bothered to call me. I ring the bell but there is no answer. I call his mobile and ring the doorbell several more times. Even if he is still in bed, why isn't his flatmate Sergio answering? In rural France there is nowhere to go on a Sunday afternoon. And anyway, Luis must be at home because his car is parked outside.

I throw some coins up against the shutters, using the tactic Luis once used, before he had keys to my house, to wake me when he returned home late from work. It's demeaning to have to resort to this to get him to open the door. Even if he's hung-over, he could at least come to the window and let me know. Sitting beside me, Biff looks up at the closed shutters with sad eyes.

'Come on, darling, let's go for a walk,' I say. 'We can't hang around waiting for naughty Luis any longer.'

Troubled, I walk down towards the river on the outskirts of the village and then follow a narrow track alongside it for a couple of kilometres. The radiance of the late September sunshine does nothing to improve my mood. Instead, it's a horrible contrast to the dark clouds gathering in my mind. As I crunch through yellow, mottled leaves, twigs and newly minted green acorns, I try to think of innocent explanations for Luis's elusive behaviour, but none spring readily to mind.

As I stop to check my mobile to see if I've missed any calls, Biff runs along the track ahead, nose to the ground, on the scent of something delicious. The hedges and burrows of the French countryside are to Biff what Bond Street was to me when I lived in London: full of tantalising but largely unobtainable treats. Biff, thankfully, is never quite fast enough to bring home the object of his desire. I watch as he attacks a molehill in the same way I once attacked the shoe racks in the Selfridges sale, and then suddenly he is gone, disappearing into a hedgerow. I carry on walking, but ten minutes pass and there is still no sign of him, so I retrace my footsteps, calling out his name.

'Biff, you are a *naughty* boy!' I yell, wondering if I'm destined to spend my life hanging around for errant males. It's a while before he reappears, looking sheepish. We walk back up the hill, stopping to ring Luis's doorbell again. I am hoping that his handsome, grinning face will appear at the window and that he will throw the keys down. But all is silent within.

Back home, I suddenly feel very tired. I climb into bed with a book. Even for a Sunday afternoon in rural France, the hours are passing very slowly. I can't stop wondering what Luis is up to. As the church bells chime the passing of another hour, I can stand it no longer. I throw on a jacket and head back out with Biff.

Sitting on the doorstep of 7 rue Saint Benoit I see Ruigi, smoking a cigarette. The quietest and most sensitive of the Portuguese workers, he nods a curt *'bonjour.'*

'Do you know where Luis is?' I ask. 'I haven't seen him all weekend.'

He shakes his head and shrugs. 'Neither have I,' he says.

As I reach Luis's building, my nervous system switches to a state of red alert. All three sets of pale green shutters are tightly closed again and loud rock music is blasting out from the sitting room. Luis is *so* not lying in bed with a hangover. This time, I ring the bell and keep my finger on it, for a full minute. But there is still no reply. The Lion is up to no good behind those shutters, I know it.

Feeling sick and shaky, I ring the bell to the flat below on the ground floor. It takes a few minutes for a young, red-haired woman to come to the door and I feel guilty when I see that her legs are in callipers and she is walking with crutches.

'I'm very sorry to bother you,' I say, trying to sound casual, calm and completely sane. 'I'm trying to visit my boyfriend but the music is so loud, I don't think he can hear me.'

She nods and lets me into the hallway. Dry-mouthed and with my heart thumping, I climb the wooden staircase to the first floor. Biff scampers along beside me with excitement as if we are going to a party, which in a way we are—just not one that we are invited to. I hesitate in front of the door. It will probably be unlocked and I could, if I wanted to, barge straight in and take Luis by surprise. Instead, I wait a few seconds and knock. No reply. I rap on the door again, more loudly this time and I hear movement within. Then the door opens slightly and Luis appears, dark and furtive in black jeans and a black shirt. For a Sunday afternoon at home, he's made quite an effort.

21

The last time he wore black was on Valentine's Day, when *I* was the person he was trying to impress.

'So what's going on here?' I ask, fighting the usual tug of attraction. 'A party?'

'Sort of,' he replies, surprise and panic in his devil-black eyes. This, I realise, is almost the exact exchange of words we had when I discovered him cheating on me last autumn. Then, the confrontation took place on the terrace of the café and I could see my love rival, a Portuguese girl with long, dark hair. (He claimed she had followed him back from Portugal.) This time, the girl with whom he is betraying me remains a mystery. But I know from Luis's demeanour that she is in there.

'Open the door,' I say, putting my foot over the threshold.

'No, no, it's not possible,' he says, blocking my entrance with his strong, muscular body. His voice is low and urgent, as if he is desperately trying to think on his feet—which, I notice, are bare. He has probably pulled on his pants in a hurry. At that moment, he seems as dark and cruel as the Marquis de Sade.

'OPEN THE DOOR!'

'Ssshh,' he says, putting his finger to his lips, as if to protect the person inside from upset. 'Quick! Come with me!' Suddenly, he grabs me by the wrist and pulls me down the stairs, He is far too strong to resist.

'What's going on?' I shout, furiously, trying

to twist myself free of his grasp and pulling Biff, who is too stunned to bark, down the stairs behind me. 'You've got someone in there, I know it!'

'No, no,' Luis is saying, scarcely making sense. 'It's just Sergio's ex-girlfriend . . . a problem . . . difficult to explain . . . I'll call you later.'

'You're a liar. You've got someone in there!' I shout, angered and insulted by the pathetic explanation and the speed with which he is trying to dispatch me. 'Why haven't you answered my calls all weekend?'

In the hallway, the woman with the red hair is going through her mail. She looks up as Luis practically pushes me out of the front door with Biff at my heels. I feel so humiliated. And angry and foolish—so many emotions, all of them toxic, swirling around like poison in the pit of my stomach. I've lost all dignity and self-respect but I don't care.

'TELL ME THE TRUTH!' I shout, trying to stop him from closing the door.

'Ssshh,' he says again, as if dealing with a fractious child. 'I'll call you later.' The door closes in my face and he is gone—back up the stairs to resume whatever he was doing, without so much as a backward glance.

I stare mutely at the glass-panelled door for a few seconds, feeling utterly shaken. Biff looks up at me with sad, uncomprehending eyes. I'm so angry . . . not just with Luis, but

23

with myself. I should have put up a greater fight. Instead, I've allowed myself to be put onto the street like a bag of recycling. I walk back across the square in a state of shock, not sure what to do next. I sit on the sofa taking some solace in the presence of Biff, cuddling my faithful little dog close to me and watching through the sitting room window as something very odd happens. As if out of nowhere, a solid band of cloud appears on the horizon and starts to spread across the sky like a big black bruise. It grows until the radiant blue sky has been obliterated. And suddenly, I decide I'm not going to sit at home feeling like a victim. I'm going to tackle this head-on. Most people would probably just walk away from this situation, but I'm not that sort of person. I need to know.

I switch on the evening news to keep Biff company, and then walk back towards Luis's building. I'm halfway across the square when hail starts to fall. Icy pellets hammer down from the sky with a violence that takes me by surprise. The hailstorm is shocking in its suddenness, sucking all of the light out of the sky. I think about turning back. I don't need to put myself through this, but I'm so hurt, so humiliated, that I have nothing to lose.

I know I shouldn't bother the poor woman in the ground floor flat again, but I'm ashamed to say that I do. This time, I don't offer an explanation and she doesn't ask for one. Instead, she simply shoots me a look of sympathy and holds the door open.

'*Merci*,' I say, pathetically grateful. '*Merci beaucoup.*'

Shaking and covered in hailstones, I climb the stairs to the first floor landing. I feel sick at the thought of what I'm about to discover, but it's better than sitting at home, not knowing. When I arrive in front of the sage-green door, I pause, not sure if I can go through with this. Despite the loud heavy metal music, I can hear giggling and a female voice inside. I'm too upset to knock on the door again and too shocked to go home. I slump to the floor, silently devastated. There is no longer room for doubt: Luis is betraying me behind that door. It hurts so badly that I would take all the physical pain I've ever experienced—torn knee ligament, blinding migraines, root canal treatment and Venezuelan food poisoning included—in one intensive hit, rather than suffer the emotional pain I am feeling now.

I sit on the staircase, knees pulled up to my chest, hailstones melting on my jacket and in my hair, feeling like I've been the victim of an emotional hit and run. I hear the sound of plates and glasses chinking in the kitchen and wonder if Luis is making dinner for his date? Have they, I wonder, spent the entire weekend together? This, I realise with horrible certainty, is it: The End.

Immobilised by shock, I stay there, shivering

25

in the darkness and with a terrible list of questions racing through my mind. Probably it would have been better if I'd barged in the first time and discovered the truth immediately. I can hear Luis walking about the flat, followed by more giggling and low voices—all set to the same soundtrack of hard rock. Too scared to knock on the door again, I call his mobile and can hear it ringing, followed by heavy footsteps as Luis walks into the sitting room to turn it off. The realisation that he can just flick me away so carelessly causes another wave of angst, corroding my self-esteem. *He doesn't give a damn.* This is the man who told me he loved me, with whom I've been trying to have a child. It just doesn't add up.

Then I hear Sergio emerging from his bedroom. The music is turned off, and the television switched on. I hear Luis and his female companion retreating along the narrow corridor towards his bedroom. It's now or never. Hardly breathing, I get up, summon all my courage and knock on the door. As expected, Sergio answers. He looks taken aback when he sees me and immediately tries to bar my entry. 'Luis isn't here,' he says.

'Don't lie to me,' I say, forcing my way into the flat. Sergio, like Luis, is strong and powerfully built but he is no match for me this evening. He steps in front of me and tries to take hold of my wrists. How dare he collude in Luis's treachery! Furious, I push him out of the way with a sharp stab of my elbow and an angry, *'Arrêtes tes conneries!'* (Stop the bullshit!) and run along the narrow passage to Luis's bedroom.

The door is closed. There is giggling within. I burst into the dimly lit room—the shutters are drawn against the outside world—and see Luis, bare-chested and in the process of undoing his jeans, standing on one side of the fuchsia-covered bed. He looks as if he has probably spent most of the day undressed. I notice a fat pillar candle—a new and romantic addition to his bedroom—flickering in a corner. And, sitting languidly on the other side of the bed, a coy expression on her face, is a girl with long blonde hair, fully dressed in jeans and a navy sweater. (Ironically, I'm wearing a khaki military-style jacket, which seems appropriate for my flat-storming mission.)

Despite knowing that I wasn't going to find Luis playing Solitaire, I am still unspeakably shocked at what I've found. But not as shocked as Luis. He freezes on the spot as I crash his carefully orchestrated scene of seduction. Then horror, disbelief and grudging admiration flash across his face in rapid succession. The girl on the bed gasps, also taken by surprise. I notice that she is in her early thirties and has a hard, angular face.

On the mantelpiece, I see the statue of the Madonna that Luis gave me in the early days

27

of our relationship. I left it on his doorstep at 7 rue St Benoit, the first time he was unfaithful to me, but now I feel strangely possessive towards it: it's *my* Madonna and she shouldn't have to witness this.

'*Alors, une explication, s'il te plaît,*' (so, an explanation please), I shout.

Luis looks at me aghast. He throws his hands up in the air as if to say 'what the f***?', purses his lips, flashes his dark, amber-flecked eyes in my direction and runs a hand through his thick black hair.

'UNE EXPLICATION, S'IL TE PLAÎT,' I shout, twice as loudly this time, surprised at how strong my voice sounds, when inside I am falling apart. The pain is so intense, so blisteringly awful, that I can't even cry.

He shrugs his bare shoulders, at a loss for words, and moves towards me. At first, I think he is going to try to physically remove me from the room, so that he can carry on as planned, but instead, he storms out and along the corridor to the sitting room, presumably to take Sergio to task for letting me in. Hands on hips, in the time-honoured pose of the wronged woman, my hair wild and still damp, I turn to my rival who is sitting calmly on the bed.

'So, where did you meet him?' I ask. 'In a night club?'

She shakes her head as if in disbelief and eventually tells me with great reluctance, that they met on the street, when he gave her a light for her cigarette. Did she ask or did he offer, I wonder? There is something about her—perhaps the sly, catlike eyes—that suggests the former.

'Where do you live?' I ask.

'Here. In Villiers.'

'Where?'

She points vaguely towards the square. I wonder why I have never seen her before.

'Just tell me one thing and then you are welcome to him,' I say, even though I know he is not mine to give away. 'How long has this been going on?'

She shrugs, looks away.

'How long? That's all I want to know.'

'And who are you?' she asks, in a disdainful way which makes me want to slap her.

'I'm his girlfriend.'

'Since when?'

'Since over a year.'

'I had no idea,' she says (unconvincingly) and gets up to leave. A few minutes later, a door slams. It's gratifying that she has gone but, deep down, I know it won't be long before she is back.

Heart racing, I return to the sitting room, pathetically grateful that Luis hasn't gone after her. Instead, he looks resigned to the fact that he's been caught out. *'Excuse-moi,'* he says with a shrug, as if he were apologising for accidentally stepping on my toe or some

29

other minor misdemeanour. He goes into the kitchen and reaches for a bottle of whisky while Sergio, with admirable sang-froid, continues to watch a game show in the sitting room.

'Would you like a drink?'

Shaken, I accept and sit down in the clean, tidy kitchen. I know that our relationship is going to end here, this evening, at the kitchen table, with its flowery plastic covering.

'I just want to know one thing,' I say, as he puts two glasses down and pours the whisky. 'How long has this been going on?'

He sits down opposite me, bare-chested, and shakes his head, as if unable to answer.

'*How long*?'

'I met her this morning,' he replies, looking away.

'*Arrêtes tes conneries,*' I say, furious that he should insult my intelligence in this way, continuing to lie even when he has been found out.

'I swear,' he says.

'TELL ME THE TRUTH!' I yell in French, sounding so fierce that I frighten myself. In the sitting room, Sergio keeps his eyes fixed on the television.

'Where were you yesterday?' I say. 'TELL ME THE TRUTH!'

'In Poitiers, shopping,' he says. 'And then I stayed at home.' Probably with her, behind closed shutters, I think. I take a gulp of the whisky, noticing that my hands are trembling. Really, I'm lost for words, a situation that does not come naturally to me. There is silence for a few seconds.

'Why?' I ask, shaking my head. 'Why have you done this?'

He is silent, puts his head in his hands.

'WHY?'

'I don't know. I'm sorry,' he says, with another shrug.

'You have problems in the head,' I say.

'I know. I miss Portugal,' he replies, as if this is somehow an excuse for serial adultery.

Silence again.

'So, have you slept with her?' I ask. It's a ridiculous question. I already know the answer.

'No,' he replies, without even trying to sound convincing. I can't believe that he's still lying to me even though he has been caught seconds away from the act. There is so much to say . . . and yet so little. The bottom line is that it's over. I can't possibly take him back now, even if he was begging, which he's not. I down the remaining whisky in one gulp.

'Thanks for everything, Luis, and goodbye,' I say, getting up to leave.

He makes no attempt to follow; he doesn't even get up from the table. He shouts one half-hearted *'Ka-renne'* after me and then it's all over. I clatter down the staircase and exit his life with a minimum of fuss—no crying, wailing or histrionics—leaving him free to

31

pick up his evening where he left off. Perhaps I should have been more Latino about it? I could have screamed the place down, thrown the whisky over his head, or even smashed up the white porcelain dinner service that he once showed me with such pride. Instead, I've just walked away from the thing that I wanted most in the whole world.

As I cross the square in the darkness, I realise that he's probably already on the phone to the French girl, begging her to come back over. No doubt she'll make him suffer for . . . ooh, all of ten minutes. He'll swear that he wants her, that I am history; and she will be back in his candle-lit bedroom, lying between his hot pink sheets within the hour. In matters of love, I've noticed, many French girls like to cultivate an attitude of languid indifference—to pretend that they are always the one being pursued—but they can be much more devious than their British counterparts.

I walk home reeling from the events of the past few hours. There are so many questions spinning round my head. Why? When? Where? How many times? And above all: how long?

As I walk back down rue St Benoit, I spot Ruigi standing outside his house, chatting to a neighbour. He looks guilty when he sees me. I stop in front of him, making no attempt to hide the pain I am feeling. 'So you knew?' I say, 'That Luis was cheating on me?'

He shrugs his shoulders. Of course he knew. What a fool I've been.

'How long has it been going on?' I ask, even though I know he won't tell me. These macho Portuguese men always stick together.

'Shoo pas,' he says, which is the local dialect for *'je ne sais pas'* or 'I don't know.'

As I open the door, Biff comes to greet me, his head hung low and tail wagging sheepishly as if he is to blame for my misery. I sit down on the sofa again, at a complete loss as to what to do with myself. Biff climbs up next to me and puts his head on my knee, his dark eyes looking up at me. But there is nothing that could happen tonight, this week, or probably for the rest of this year, that would make me feel any better about this. Life with Luis has been a series of wonderful highs and terrible lows, but my emotional elevator has now hit the basement and broken down.

The phone rings. For a stupid second I think it might be Luis, to plead for forgiveness, to say that he's made a terrible mistake, but it's my friend Delphine calling to see if I still want to go the *marché des producteurs*, the evening market of local food producers, later this week.

'I'm not sure I'm going to be up for that,' I say.

'Are you OK?' she asks. 'Shall I call back another time?'

'Sorry, I've just had a bit of a shock.'

I tell her what has happened.

'Oh my goodness. I am so sorry to hear this,' she says. 'Was he drunk?'

I tell her that no, he was sober. He knew exactly what he was doing and he had gone to considerable effort to do it.

'I am very surprised by this news,' she says. 'When I saw you together, it seemed to me that he was very in love with you.'

'That's what he told me, many times, but I guess it wasn't true. I feel such a fool.'

'No,' says Delphine. 'When he told you this, I am sure that he meant it. And it doesn't sound like he has been cheating on you for long. This girl probably means nothing to him.'

'Maybe,' I say. 'But I can't take him back now, even if he wanted me to. And I have to say that he didn't exactly come running after me.'

'He is probably very ashamed,' says Delphine.

'I'm not sure about that. Mostly, he just looked annoyed that I'd interrupted his evening. I doubt very much that he is giving me a second thought.'

Delphine offers to come over but I tell her that I'm probably just going to go to bed.

'OK, my friend, I will call you tomorrow to see how you are,' she says.

Later, I take Biff for his nightly walk around the *mairie*, noticing that the full moon is veiled

34

in a strange mist. When I get back, the phone is ringing again. It's Travis.

'Hello darling, just calling to see what you've been up to?' he says, sounding cheerful, as always.

'You really want to know?'

'What's happened?'

I tell him.

'Oh. My. God.'

'Yeah, it's pretty bad. I'm still in shock, like it hasn't really sunk in.'

'What did he say?'

'Not a lot. There is surprisingly little to say in a situation like that. His actions had already said everything.'

'I just can't believe you'd put yourself through something so traumatic,' he says.

'Well, what would you have done?'

'I think I'd have just walked away the first time.'

'I had to know.'

'But darling, you *did* know,' he says. 'It was obvious when you knocked on his door the first time that he had something to hide.'

'Yes, but I wanted to know exactly *what* he was hiding. This way, I know everything. I don't have to torture myself forever, wondering what she looked like.'

'Honestly,' says Travis. 'What a wanker!'

'I know. But if I hadn't barged into the flat and been confronted by the horrible reality, I might have carried on giving him the benefit of the doubt.'

'Well, there's no way you can ever take him back now,' says Travis.

That, I think to myself, is the awful thing.

After talking to Travis, I switch off the red lamps in the sitting room and, still in a state of shock, go up to bed. Biff follows—I don't try to stop him—and jumps up on the bed, curling his body around my feet. His presence is quite comforting. I lie there unable to sleep, looking at the hazy, mist-covered moon through the window. All I can think of is Luis and *la Française*, who are probably in bed together across the square, while I lie here with just a little black dog for company.

'It will end in tears,' one of my (married) friends predicted when I first told her about Luis. But it doesn't. It ends in shock, anger and bitter disappointment. How, I wonder, will I ever find peace in Villiers again?

*   *   *

The following morning, a Monday, I wake up to the stark realisation that I'm single again. My first thought is to go back to sleep, rather than face this new reality and the week stretching ahead like a long black tunnel. The only reason to get up is that I have to take Biff to a 10.00 am grooming appointment. I'm tempted to just stay in bed anyway, but his shaggy coat is matted from all his muddy cross-country exploits and desperately in need of a cut. At the very last minute, I throw on some clothes and drive to the veterinary clinic on the outskirts of Villiers, on the same industrial estate as Luis's employer, Supodal.

Biff refuses to get out of the car when we arrive, so I have to carry him up the steps into the specially equipped grooming van. Madame Calin, the *toilettage* lady is deaf and signals for me to put him on the grooming table. As always, I stay to help, patting and reassuring Biff, telling him what a good boy he is, while she works. It's never easy, as he immediately goes into flight mode when the clippers appear, but this time I've left it too long between appointments and his fur has practically turned into dreadlocks. Madame Calin is not impressed and signals that she'll have to shave him to remove the knots. Poor Biff. He's about to be deprived of his furry coat just in time for winter.

As Madame Calin sets to work, he yelps in agony and tries to make a suicide leap from the table. I feel his pain. Normally, I would try to soothe him, but today my mind is elsewhere—in Luis's bedroom, with the blue-robed Madonna and the sly-looking blonde, replaying scene-by-scene yesterday's awful dénouement. Madame Calin is waggling her finger, scolding me and giving me the usual lecture about how the knots tug at his skin and cause him pain. Usually I try to defend myself,

x

37

explaining that he has a great life, swimming in stagnant pools of water, rolling in mud and sticking his head down rabbit holes, but as a result he will never be perfectly groomed. Today, I just nod dumbly, while poor old Biff shakes like a sonic toothbrush, in obvious distress.

'Speak to him!' commands Madame Calin. 'Say some words to reassure him.'

As she takes the clippers to his pale pink belly, Biff is crying with pain. And suddenly, I am crying too. Like a wounded animal, I just want to crawl into a corner and die. The tears fall, along with chunks of Biff's matted black fur onto the grooming table.

'*Ça va?*' mouths Madame Calin.

I nod, but the tears keep falling. I can't use my hands to wipe them away as I'm using them to restrain Biff. Madame Calin puts the clippers down and squeezes my wrist. Feeling guilty for neglecting my little dog, I try to reassure Biff, telling him not to worry, that the pain will be soon over. If only the same could be said for me.

When Madame Calin has finished, Biff looks sweet and vulnerable. He arrived like an amiable, long-haired hippy; he exits the van looking lean and super-fit, his tail wagging. It takes more than a savage haircut and a dunking in tepid water to dampen his spirits, I think, envying him his optimism. In the car I hug him close. 'At least I've still got you,

38

darling,' I say.

Back home, I catch sight of my reflection in a mirror. My eyes are the colour of prawn shells and all puffed up, my hair wilder than Biff's before his cut and blow dry. I sit down at my desk, trying to summon up the will to answer some emails. The phone rings. It's the editor of a glossy magazine in the UK, for whom I've recently written an article about my life in France, entitled *My French Love Affair*.

'Hi there, Karen! I was just wondering if you could give us a little more detail about your Portuguese boyfriend?' she says, sounding very enthusiastic.

'What do you want to know?' I ask, feeling nauseous at the reminder that I have boasted about Luis in several national newspapers.

'How old is he? What does he do? And how did you meet him?'

This would be a good moment to tell her that he is now my ex-boyfriend and suggest renaming the piece *My Failed French Love Affair*, or *The End of the Affair*, but it's way too humiliating. And anyway, they've probably already done the layout.

'He's thirty-one,' I say. 'And I met him when he was living next door. He brought my dog back after he escaped.'

I console myself that, whatever has happened since, these facts remain true.

'Sounds wonderful,' she says. 'Everyone in

the office is very jealous.'

After I've hung up the phone, I put my head in my hands in despair and embarrassment at my own stupidity. Anyone reading about my 'idyllic' life in France would be stunned if they knew the reality. This is the very worst possible ending.

Chapter 3

The Cheek of The Devil

It's Saturday afternoon, almost a week since I discovered Luis and *la Française*, and I'm sitting outside a local café with Delphine. As always, she is wearing red lipstick, Chanel No 5 (her winter fragrance) and a big smile, along with a pink ruffled skirt and a necklace of ruby-coloured orbs. (Overstated necklaces and large, colourful handbags being very much her thing.) Of the three cafés in my village, today we've chosen to sit in the autumn sunshine outside the Bar de l'Hôtel de Ville on the corner of the square, owned by the jovial Jean-Luc and his wife, Marguerite. On the table in front of us are two pink *diabolos*—drinks made with lemonade and a dash of strawberry syrup—and Delphine's red patent bag, put there to avoid Biff's probing nose.

Like me, Biff is always happy in Delphine's

presence. I often joke that it's because they both have black curly hair—which today Delphine is wearing piled up on her head—and even share a birthday: Delphine was born on May 1, the birthday allocated to Biff by the animal shelter in Bergerac where he was found.

Delphine and I met in a local café shortly after I moved here four years ago. I count her friendship as one of the best things about my life in France. In her jolly, upbeat presence, it is hard to feel anything other than optimism. Like many of her constituents, I value her calm wisdom and her easy-breezy approach to life. Only very recently, a resident who had seen Delphine's smiling face in a local newspaper, sent her the following note:

Dear Madame,

Permit me to congratulate you on the happiness that you bring to the residents of Puysoleil, by your knowledge and your smile . . . it's reassuring. I'm always very happy to see you in the newspaper.

With my respectful greetings,
Mme Lenoir.

I couldn't have expressed it better myself. Delphine is not without her own problems: her husband asked for a divorce shortly after

41

she became mayor—a common problem for lady mayors, apparently, as Frenchmen don't take kindly to their women having more power than them—and a year later, she is still waiting for her share of the house. Fortunately, she was able to move back into the small farming hamlet owned by her family, where she and her brother and sister all have houses.

Delphine also has problems with her 'sceptic' [sic] tank at the moment, as well as two warring farmers and an 18th-century stone bridge that is badly in need of repair after a combine harvester crashed into it. But she never dwells on her own setbacks. Instead, she devotes a great deal of her time to helping other people—not just the residents of Puysoleil, but hapless expats who've missed their hospital appointments, lost their passports, or suffered at the hands of France Telecom. If you were in a plane that was going down, you'd count yourself blessed to have Delphine sitting next to you.

Today, she has some good news. The café in Puysoleil will reopen at the end of October. It closed last August following a scandal that few could possibly have predicted for the sleepy little village. Until that point, the café, favoured by local hunters, was best known for its *tête de veau* or veal's head—an offal dish that is popular in rural France. But it seemed that Didier, the proprietor, was cooking up more than roe deer pâté in his little rural restaurant, with its red lamps and cluttered, shabby-chic interior. Last summer, strange rumours started to circulate about the bar, the decor of which I once described as very 'bordello chic'—a description that was to prove strangely prescient.

At first, Delphine ignored the talk of naked dancing and other late-night activities. But the rumours persisted and following allegations that it was being used as a brothel, the gendarmes subsequently raided the Café de la Paix. It being August, when nothing much happens in France—everyone is either at the beach or in the mountains—the story made the national news and journalists and TV crews besieged the rose-covered mairie. Fortunately for Delphine, a cannabis plantation was discovered in a nearby *commune* the following month and the media swiftly moved on.

Delphine was very worried about the bad publicity but, as a former newspaper journalist, I could see only potential. 'This could put Puysoleil on the map,' I said and sure enough, the *mairie* subsequently received three applications to rent the bar, proving that there is no such thing as bad publicity. The reopening, however, had to be delayed until the gendarmes had finished their investigations. Didier is currently residing in the shiny new prison in Vivonne, and since the charges against him have yet to be proved, Delphine has been forced to *faire pattes de velours* (proceed with velvet paws). This being France—why fill in one form when a dozen will do?—there was also a landfill of paperwork to complete. But finally, the lawyers have given the green light and the lease on the café has just been signed over to two sisters for a year. The bar is currently being given a makeover by Puysoleil's trusty council workers, Bruno and Rémi, and the reopening party will take place at the end of October.

'And how are you doing, my friend?' asks Delphine.

'Well, I'm just about managing to get out of bed in the morning. Which feels like a major achievement, all things considered.'

'I am still very shocked by this news. Have you heard from him?'

'This is the question that everyone is asking, but the answer is no.'

'What about the girl? Do you know anything about her?'

'No. Apparently she lives in Villiers but I haven't seen her since. She seems to have disappeared. Either that or she's still in his bedroom.'

'This story is very strange. I saw myself how he was with you at the Celtic festival just a few months ago.'

'I know.' I think back to the Saturday evening at the height of the summer, when we drove to Delphine's village for the annual outdoor concert. All the way to Puysoleil he

44

had protested his love for me, his hand on my thigh, as we drove past fields of smiling sunflowers.

'*Ka-renne*, she is the most beautiful woman here,' he said to Delphine about a million times that night. I should point out that he'd had a lot to drink and, with hindsight, maybe he was protesting too much, but as Delphine said at the time, '*in vino veritas.*' Now I'm not so sure. Sunday's discovery has cast everything in a new light.

'He really is a big devil,' says Delphine referring to the nickname, The Devil, that we coined for him the first time that he betrayed me; although, by pronouncing it 'divil', Delphine still makes him sound endearing.

Suddenly, the expression on her face changes. I look to my left just in time to see Luis and his sidekick, Sergio, coming round the corner in our direction. There are several tables free outside the café but, to my surprise, they sit down at the one closest to us. This means that The Devil is directly in my line of sight and I in his. My first thought is to be pleased that he is not with the sly-eyed blonde. But still, the audaciousness, the absolute shamelessness, leaves me momentarily speechless. Any other person would have slunk past into the café and tried to avoid me, but The Devil seems to have no sense of regret or shame. Perhaps he thinks that by sitting there, in his red board shorts and black T-shirt, I'll find him so irresistible that I'll just start talking to him again as if nothing has happened.

'My goodness,' says Dephine, in English, 'I can feel those devil eyes boring into us.'

'I just can't believe it,' I say. 'What's going on in his head?'

Even though I avoid looking, I know that he is staring in my direction. Marguerite comes to take their order, and I see her flash him a coquettish smile.

'Are you OK? Do you want to leave?' asks Delphine.

'No,' I say, making no attempt to hide the anguished expression on my face. He might as well see how hurt I am. And anyway, The Devil has always been able to read my mind like a Google map. I'm quite sure that his antennae are picking up my unspoken distress signals, as the longer he sits opposite me, the more subdued he becomes. He and Sergio drink their coffee in silence. The Devil then throws some coins on the table and gets up to leave, looking over in our direction one last time. I detect a note of resignation—could it even be guilt?—as they walk back towards their apartment.

'What was that about?' I say, once they have gone.

'I don't know, but his eyes, I have not seen anything like them. They were flashing orange at the edges,' says Delphine, who has sniper-like vision.

Later that afternoon, I drive over to see Travis, who lives in a small hamlet called St Romain, on the outskirts of a village called St Hilaire. There is a weak autumn sun in the pale blue sky and copper leaves dance across the road in front of the car. The countryside reminds me of a Gustav Klimt painting; with the trees lining the roadside cloaked in a rich patchwork of ochre, gold, orange-red and aubergine.

Until recently, autumn was my favourite season in France, but now I've started to equate it with sorrow and loss. Still, I'm sure that Travis, whom I met at an expat dinner party over a year ago, will cheer me up with tales of his latest disasters. Despite all evidence to the contrary—his nearest neighbour is a goat farmer—Travis has convinced himself that he is living on the Côte d'Azur and is busy transforming his house into the sort of villa you would expect to find in St Tropez, rather than a rural farming community.

The first stage of his renovation plan was to build a fancy path through his garden, based on a design he'd seen in a five-star hotel in Dubai. The path, inlaid with decorative stones and featuring a border of spiky cactus plants, was not a success. Shortly after the (British) builder had laid it, sections of the concrete started to crack and detach from the ground. Fortunately, he hired French artisans to do his roof and had better luck with that.

Mystifyingly, given that his only cooking facilities are a portable electric ring and a microwave oven, Travis then decided that his next project would be a wraparound terrace.

'You've sorted out your priorities then?' I said. 'You've got no kitchen and an avocado bathroom suite, but at least you'll have a lovely patio just in time for Christmas.'

'Well, I like to think I'm bringing a bit of glamour to St Romain,' he replied. 'Or SAN-TRRRO-mahn,' as I prefer to call it.' He rolled the R dramatically so that until the final syllable, it sounded like he was going to say St Tropez.

But Travis is a happy-go-lucky character and just what I need right now. I turn into his driveway, which currently resembles Glastonbury after everyone has gone home: an expanse of churned mud. I fix a cheerful expression on my face as I knock on the door. Travis has spent hours on the phone with me in the past week dissecting the 'whys' and 'what ifs' of the Luis situation and I can't bore him with it any longer. He's also got problems of his own—though his are of the cheating builder rather than the boyfriend variety. He opens the door in cut-off jeans and a grey Abercrombie & Fitch T-shirt and gives us a big, upbeat welcome.

'Hello, darling! Hey Biff!' he says. 'Lovely to

see you both. And Biff, I hope the next time you see that nasty Luis, you're going to take a big bite out of his ankle.'

'Only his ankle?' I say, as Biff bolts into the house ahead of me. 'I'd much rather it was something else.'

'Well, that too,' says Travis, reaching in the cupboard where he keeps a box of dog treats. One of the things I love about Travis is that he is always very playful with Biff. After making him sit for a couple of biscuits, he leads the way into the large *salon*, where ambient music is playing and a Diptyque candle diffuses the scent of sandalwood into the air. A log glows incandescent orange behind the glass door of the wood burner, the focal point of the space. Dotted around the room are many photos of Travis in his younger days when, in both looks and dress, he could easily have been mistaken for the Ross character in *Friends*.

If it wasn't for the silver MacBook Pro open on a desk and the blue gym ball and yoga mat in another corner of the room, Travis's *salon* could easily be in the chill-out room of a nightclub. There are two white sofas in front of the fire, scattered with black sequinned cushions, and two matching sequinned poufs beside them; while large modern art canvases hang on the walls, some of them painted by Travis himself. I've always admired the terracotta-tiled floor, but Travis is planning to replace it with something 'pale and glossy'. I'm pretty sure he's thinking white marble.

'So how's the building work going?' I ask.

'Well, between you and me, I've had a bit of a crap week, too,' he says. 'Though nothing compared to what you've been through.'

'Why, what's happened?'

'Well, you know the new door?'

'Yes,' I say, remembering that Travis recently paid a builder €3000 for bespoke French doors from his sitting room to the new terrace.

'I asked for a curved arch. I even drew pictures of a curved arch and what have I got?'

'Not a curved arch?'

'A *rectangular* arch.'

'It looks quite nice, though. And when all is said and done, it's an arch.'

'It's not what I wanted. It's all too . . . straight.'

'Well, it's the only thing in your house that is,' I say with a wry smile. 'And how's the patio going?'

Travis pulls a face of mock pain. 'Don't ask. And please don't call it a patio. It's a *terrasse*.' He opens the new French doors onto a grand sweep of lustrous white flagstones, with steps down to the garden and an unbroken view of green fields. '*Voilà!*' he says.

'Travis, it's AMAZING,' I say.

'Yeah, the problem is the steps. They go straight down.'

'Isn't that what steps are supposed to do?'

He pulls a face. 'I wanted them to fan out. Sort of like a Roman coliseum.'

'Travis, you live in rural France, not ancient Rome.'

'Honestly, I thought I was going to come out here to lie in the sun and hang out with friends by a pool, not have to deal with an endless parade of problem builders.'

'It will get better,' I say, remembering my own renovation dramas. They included a log burner that melted the paint on the fire surround, filling the house with toxic fumes, and a decorator who misunderstood my French and painted every inch of the sitting room in white gloss paint so that it felt like I'd fallen into an icy crevasse.

'For every bad day, there'll be wonderful days when everything goes right.'

Travis looks doubtful for a second but then rallies. 'Yes, you're absolutely right,' he says. 'Now, would you like a cup of herbal tea?'

'Go on then, let's live dangerously. It's been a horrible week.'

'All the more reason to watch what you put into your body,' says Travis, lighting a cigarette. 'Please tell me you are not crying any more tears over that Portuguese builder?'

'No,' I lie.

'Good. The best thing you could do right now is throw yourself into a health and fitness regime,' he says, as he disappears into the kitchen.

51

'Can't I just throw myself off a cliff instead?' I say.

Travis pretends not to hear. Instead, he launches into the details of his own daily routine hoping, I imagine, to inspire me. I've heard it many times before. He gets up at 7.00 am and starts the day with a cup of hot water and lemon juice, followed by half an hour's exercise with weights. He then jumps on his bike and cycles around the countryside for up to an hour. What he doesn't mention is the cigarettes that he smokes in between. I know that he is doing his best to be motivational, but the idea of waking up to hot water and lemon rather than Luis and pastries from the local *boulangerie*, is profoundly depressing.

Suddenly, I hear the unexpected pop of a cork and Travis, bless him, reappears with two glasses and a bottle of champagne in an ice bucket. 'Well, that's certainly an improvement on herbal tea,' I say. 'What's the occasion?'

'When the going gets tough, it's time to crack open the Veuve Cliquot,' he says, filling up the glasses. 'There is no situation that cannot be improved by a glass of champagne. And anyway, it's got grapes in it, so it sort of counts as a fruit.'

'I like the way you're thinking,' I say, clinking his glass. I might have crap judgement when it comes to men, but at least I have wonderful taste in friends.

We sit in front of the fire, talking about

Travis's other plans for his house (a sweeping gravel driveway and a new kitchen next, followed by a swimming pool and a hot tub in time for summer). He also tells me that two friends of ours have just split up after twenty years of marriage. 'Honestly, so many couples have problems when they move here,' says Travis, whom I can see is really trying hard to make me feel better, 'that I sometimes feel quite lucky to be single.'

What he is saying is true. I know of several couples that have moved to France to live the dream, and split up a few months later amid acrimony and recrimination. The wife might have moved in with the postman, or the husband run off with an expat yoga teacher. Then, before you know it, one of them is on the ferry back to the UK, while the other is left trying to sell the house and—according to one sorry tale on a blog recently—eating cold curry for breakfast.

'One day our prince will come,' says Travis.

'Well, let's just hope it's not the same guy.'

'And then there's all the excitement and surprise of meeting someone new,' he says, sounding wistful.

'Yeah, well, I've had enough surprises recently,' I say. 'I don't think I want any more. I've notched up more than my fair share of failed relationships.'

'There is no such thing as a failed relationship,' says Travis. 'The term is an oxymoron. To have had a relationship at all, whether it lasted one night or twenty years, means you connected with someone on some level. Just because a love affair has run its course or ended badly, doesn't mean it wasn't an achievement.'

'I guess.'

'The thing is, when life gives you lemons, you have to make lemonade.'

I nod while secretly thinking that I'd rather make gin and tonics.

'So what are you doing tomorrow?' he asks.

'No plans,' I reply, dreading the thought of the blank Sunday ahead. But somehow, after a glass of champagne and a chat with Travis, things don't seem quite so bad. 'Well, I guess I ought to go home. Thanks for the champagne.'

'Are you sure you won't stay for dinner and *The X-Factor*?'

'I'm tempted but I have to walk Biff before it gets dark.'

'I'll call you tomorrow,' says Travis as he follows me to the door. Suddenly, he puts his arms around me and gives me a big hug. 'Listen gorgeous, I know you're going through a horrible time right now, but hang on in there. It will get better, I promise. And remember: what doesn't kill you makes you stronger.'

I drive home, thinking that this is not necessarily true: what doesn't kill you can also leave you in a coma.

The next morning, I wake to find a mop of black hair on the adjacent pillow, and a face staring at me with dark, besotted eyes. Unfortunately the face belongs to Biff, who no longer sleeps in his beige suede doughnut but has annexed my bed as part of his domain. His first move was to position himself at the bottom of the bed, curled up by my feet. Then he gradually contrived it so that he was sleeping in the crook of my knees; next thing, he was lying with his back nudged up against mine. Now, he is propped up on a neighbouring pillow, looking down at me. He is taking full advantage of my fragile emotional state.

'*Aaagh*!' I shout, sitting up with a start. 'Get off the pillow!' But he merely rolls onto his back with his paws in the air, revealing his pink belly. I guess this is a glimpse of how Sunday mornings are going to be from now on: me sharing my bed with an over-entitled dog. Luis and I used to take it in turns on Sundays to throw on some clothes and walk up to the *boulangerie* to buy breakfast. The Lion would always return with a box of cakes, my favourite being the *Tropézienne*, a bun made of crème patisserie sandwiched between two layers of brioche. But that was then and this is now. I drag Biff off the bed, then bundle him into the car. We drive out of the village by a back road, thus avoiding the café and Luis's building. I've decided that we will do 'the emerald walk', as I've termed the grassy, tree-lined track that meanders for many kilometres between farmers' fields, with not a soul in sight.

Divided by untamed hedges or trees, the fields unfold like huge outdoor film sets as we walk, each one a different colour and texture. I had no idea that so many shades of green existed until I moved to the Poitou. Many of the fields are fallow now, some roughly churned into mounds of red-brown earth, others a pale beige and ploughed as smoothly as a beach. I used to associate the French countryside with the primary greens, blues and yellows of summer, but in autumn the colours are much more subtle. At dusk, for example, I've noticed a mauve-like cast to the red-brown fields; and I love the contrast of the rose-gold maize against a gunmetal sky.

The track eventually takes us through a sleepy hamlet where the farmyard smells and piles of old hay send Biff into a frenzy of excitement. While he sticks his head down rabbit holes and digs for mice, I feel reassured at the sight of dilapidated barns, distressed shutters and houses with peeling paintwork. Not everything in the French countryside has been bought and renovated by a Brit. So many buildings and old houses have been turned into airtight boxes, their old wooden window frames replaced with characterless double-glazed windows from Castorama (the French equivalent of B&Q), that sometimes I worry that there will be no barns left for the British to renovate.

We walk until lunchtime and then return home, where I wonder what to do next. Sunday afternoons are going to be really difficult now. I try to remember what I did before Luis burst into my life like a million Roman Candles set off at once. The answer, when I think about it, was DIY, but there are no floors left to sand now, no walls in need of paint, so there is only one thing for it: I sit down at my desk and type the words, *Prepare To Flare!* And so I kill a couple of hours writing about the return of the wide trouser.

Later that afternoon, I call Travis. He tells me that he has spent the day ripping out kitchen cabinets—an act of great folly in my opinion, since he has nothing and no one lined up to replace them. It could be years before he has anything remotely resembling a kitchen again.

'Well, I've got to keep busy while waiting for my prince to come,' he says. 'Though I wish he'd get a move on.'

Me, I no longer believe in princes. But, on the bright side, at least I haven't sunk so low as to be eating cold curry for breakfast. Not yet, anyway.

Chapter 4

Arnaud

I have a new neighbour. The narrow house next door has been empty since the lease expired a couple of weeks ago. The owner, no doubt influenced by the seventeen different complaints that had been lodged at the *mairie* during the course of the Portuguese tenancy, declined to renew. As a result, Ruigi, the last of Luis's colleagues to remain, has moved to a studio apartment further along the street, and the house has been quiet ever since. The only reason I know that someone is living there is because a red organza curtain has appeared in the upstairs window, and a straw mat with a picture of a cat has been placed outside. I'm convinced that my new neighbour is a little old lady who spends her days in a floral overall, stroking her cat and boiling up great pots of bouillon.

But one damp and dismal morning in mid-October, I return from walking Biff and see a small, wiry man emerging from 7 rue St Benoit with his *sac jaune,* or yellow recycling bag. In his early fifties, he is smartly dressed in corduroy trousers, a chunky-knit sleeveless pullover and a striped shirt rolled up at the elbows—a style that in my fashion editor days,

I would have described as 'grandad chic'. He has abundant grey-brown hair that flops over his forehead, a somewhat wily appearance and a twinkle in his hazel eyes.

When he sees me, he drops his recycling and throws open his arms, as if he has been waiting for me forever. Then he turns his attention to Biff and swoops down to waggle his ears with a cry of *'Bonjour, toutou,'* (Hello, doggy). He introduces himself as Arnaud and asks if I would like to take a coffee with him in the café.

'Now?' I ask.

'Yes. If you would like to.'

'Pourquoi pas?' I reply, thinking it would be good for neighbourly relations.

He beckons for me to come out of the rain and I stand in the small white kitchen, which now boasts a profusion of pots, pans and cooking equipment, while Arnaud rummages around for his coat in a cupboard under the stairs. It's weird to see the little space, once occupied so exuberantly by Luis and his compatriots, now taken over by someone else.

Arnaud pulls on a Barbour-style jacket with a corduroy collar and we walk up to the Bar de l'Hôtel de Ville in the wind and the rain. Winter has descended with a ferocity and suddenness that has taken everyone by surprise, and the *terrasse* outside the bar is now bare, stripped of its plastic tables and red parasols.

Inside the café, Arnaud seems to know most of *les vieux gars* (old boys) sipping their early morning rosé in sherry-size glasses.

'*Bonjour, jeune homme,*' (Hello, young man), he cries to several of them, all comfortably past retirement age, with a hearty slap on the back. Arnaud laughs a lot and very loudly. His presence is like a lightning rod in this quiet little bar.

'*Bonjour, Marguerite,*' he cries to the wife of the proprietor, twirling his wrist in the air. '*Deux cafés, s'il vous plaît.*' He gestures for me to sit at a small table with another expansive sweep of the hand, and sits down opposite.

Over several shots of coffee, he then proceeds, in French, to ask many questions. What do I do? (A fashion and beauty writer, I tell him, and he looks impressed.) How long had I lived in Villiers? (Over four years.) Why did I move here? (A long story, I say, but fate had a lot to do with it.)

'I've been told that the Portuguese blokes who lived in the house before me were very noisy,' he says, with a sideways glance.

'Yes, very noisy,' I say, trying not to look wistful for the days when the thin wall that divided our two houses reverberated to the sound of Metallica and Meat Loaf.

Arnaud asks if I have a *copain*. I shake my head. And then, because I don't want my neighbour to think that I've been loveless for a long time—a Frenchman would almost certainly feel duty bound to do something about it—I tell him that I had one until a few weeks ago.

'Really? What happened?'

'I found him with a French girl in his bedroom.'

'*Oh, la, la,*' says Arnaud, shaking his head. 'Was he French, this boyfriend?'

'No, Portuguese.'

'Is it one of the *mecs* (blokes) that lived at number seven?' he asks, and it occurs to me that my new neighbour has already done some research.

'Yes.'

'Which one?'

'You know them?'

'Yes.'

'He was called Luis,' I say, looking miserable.

'The tall, strong one?' says Arnaud, knowingly.

'Yes, that's him,' I say, thinking that everyone seems to be acquainted with The Lion. 'How do you know?'

'The boss of the company he works for is a friend of mine.'

'Fernando?' I say, thinking of Luis's sharply dressed *patron*.

'Yes. I used to run a bar in Veron and the Portuguese would come in there late at night. Sometimes we would go to a nightclub together. Fernando is a good friend.'

'Really?' I say, finding it difficult to imagine

Fernando in his snakeskin boots and dark jeans, hitting a nightclub with my grandfatherly neighbour.

'*Oh, la, la,* he really knew how to party, that one,' says Arnaud, twirling a hand in the air to emphasise the point.

'Really?' I say, knowing full well that the Portuguese in my village practically have PhD's in partying.

'Yes. But then he met his wife, a French girl. He stopped partying overnight—became a different man.'

'Oh,' I say, pained that the sly-looking blonde might similarly tame The Lion.

'You need to forget this bloke,' says Arnaud, as if reading my mind.

'I know,' I say. 'But it's a bit difficult to forget him when we both live in the same village. I keep bumping into him.'

Only last weekend, as I was returning from a shopping trip to Poitiers, Luis leaned out to open his bedroom shutters at the exact moment I was driving by. He was wearing a navy T-shirt, the long sleeves rolled up to the elbows, revealing his strong brown arms and his hair was tousled as if he'd just emerged from a particularly vigorous session between his pink sheets.

'Luis always looks like that,' said Delphine when I told her, but it didn't make it any easier. The only way I can completely avoid The Lion is if I stay inside my house at weekends, which would be an option if I didn't have a dog.

Arnaud sighs, leans forward suddenly and takes my hand. 'Listen! I know it's not easy. Because I am in the same situation.' He goes on to explain how his girlfriend, whom he lived with in the nearby village of Liard, dumped him unexpectedly a few weeks ago. 'We'd been out for a meal at her cousin's place,' he tells me. 'There was no indication that anything was wrong. But when we got home, she told me she didn't want to live with me any more and asked me to leave.'

'That's awful,' I say. 'Did she give a reason?'

'No. It was completely unexpected.' He shakes his head sadly and tells me that, like me, he is *'très blessé'* (very injured).

'So why Villiers?' I ask.

'I was actually on the train to Paris,' he says. 'But I got as far as Tours and realised I didn't know anyone there. So I came back and found the house next door to you.'

I feel a huge wave of empathy at this sad tale of displacement. Like Arnaud, the reason I first came to live in Villiers was because I was on the run from a failed relationship. After splitting up with my French boyfriend, I couldn't bear to carry on living in my West London neighbourhood, as it was too full of memories. Then, by chance, visiting a friend in France for the weekend, I found Maison Coquelicot, a small village house in need of love and renovation and costing less than some people would spend on a car. Having spotted my escape route, I ran towards it faster than a roe deer fleeing the hunt. How ironic, then, that Maison Coquelicot, the house that I worked so hard to restore, is starting to feel like a prison. Despite having filled it with colour, and pattern and Laura Ashley prints, it seems like a very dark place now that Luis's larger-than-life presence will never fill my courtyard again.

'So, have you heard from Luis since you found him with the other one?' asks Arnaud, as if once again tapping into my thoughts.

'No,' I say. 'Nothing.' The truth is that every time Biff barks, I dare to hope that it might be The Devil. Even though I cannot possibly take him back, it would be nice to have the satisfaction of telling him so. But he is not exactly beating down my door.

Arnaud shakes his head again. 'You need to forget him,' he says. 'What we both need is to go out and dance.' He jiggles his upper body— he seems to have a lot of nervous energy— and twirls his hands in the air. I nod and try to look enthused, even though I can't think of anything I'd like less.

'Listen,' I say. 'It's been very nice to meet you but I must give my dog his breakfast.'

Suddenly, Arnaud grabs my hands. 'Don't worry,' he says in a heartfelt way. 'Everything is going to be fine. For both of us.'

'Let's hope so,' I say, reaching for my wallet. Through the lace curtains of the café, I can see that it is pouring with rain outside. I try to pay for our coffees, but Arnaud won't let me. 'Next time,' he says, waving me away. *'Allez!'*

As I walk home with the wind and rain whipping my hair across my face, I'm struck by the coincidence that Arnaud and I both found ourselves dumped at the same time. It's as if fate has intervened to bring two injured souls together to commiserate with each other.

The house is very cold when I get back and I can't be bothered to haul wood in from the dwindling supply in the garage. Instead, after giving Biff his breakfast, I crawl under the Laura Ashley floral eiderdown in my bedroom and set to work on an article about the allure of French labels. As I type the first sentence on my laptop, Biff pads slowly up the stairs and jumps up onto the bed next to me, curling up against my legs. Outside, the wind bangs against the windows and the shutters, while rain slams down intermittently on the bathroom skylight.

In matters of dress, as in love, many French girls like to cultivate an air of casual indifference, I type. *To give the impression that they haven't made any effort at all, when the reality is often rather different.*

I pause, as an unwelcome image of the blonde in Luis's bedroom pops into my mind. I wonder how hard she had to try to get there. Or how hard Luis tried to lure her in? I sigh. Your own mind can be so inventive, so endlessly creative in summoning up new ways to torture you. But, in a moment of sudden clarity, I realise that I don't have the energy to run away again. This time, I will just have to brave it out in Villiers with the support of my friends.

Suddenly, there is a loud bang as a particularly strong gust of wind blows open a casement window. I get out of bed to close it and as I do so, a panel of glass in the bottom of the old wooden frame shatters, scattering shards of thin glass over the floor. *Marvellous.* Those lemons that Travis was talking about, they just keep coming. Soon I'll have enough to open a lemonade factory. But, on the bright side, I guess I should count my blessings that Biff and I have not been maimed.

I'm tempted to get back into bed and ignore the broken window, but a gale is now blowing through the bedroom. So, with a supreme effort of will, I go downstairs and find a dustpan and brush. I then sweep up the lethal-looking pieces of glass, while Biff watches with interest from the bed. I can almost read his mind: *What's my crazy pet doing now?* (For I'm quite sure he thinks that I am his pet, rather than the other way round.)

'If only you could do useful stuff like DIY,' I say, as I stare at the void in the window-frame. 'And then we'd be entirely self-sufficient, you and I.' Eventually, inspiration strikes and I patch up the hole with a piece of cardboard and some brown parcel tape. It's not ideal but it will have to do. I have no idea who I should call to fix a broken windowpane, and right now it feels like an insurmountable obstacle to find out.

I climb back into bed, thinking of a Winston Churchill quote—the one that defines success as 'going from failure to failure with no loss of enthusiasm.' It's a pretty apt description of my relationship history to date. But, after so many failures, this time I feel like I've lost my enthusiasm for life itself. My definition of success right now is to see Luis in the local café, or opening his bedroom window, and to feel nothing.

Apart from a brief foray into the freezing kitchen to make lunch (a piece of stale baguette with chocolate spread), I stay in bed for most of the afternoon, listening to the rain falling as I write flattering words about French fashion. But focusing on the timeless appeal of the Breton stripe shirt and the understated allure of the well-cut trench coat at least gives my mind a break from Luis.

Later in the afternoon, I drag myself out from under the eiderdown to walk Biff before it gets dark. We drive to an isolated farm track a couple of kilometres from the village. Then I sit in the car for at least a quarter of an hour, cuddling Biff as the rain beats down on the windscreen and I try to motivate myself to get out and start walking. It takes another supreme effort to open the door, but eventually I manage it. Then, head down against the horrible weather, I tramp along the soggy farm track, past fields of kale trembling in the wind, until darkness falls.

Back home, I give Biff canned dog food for dinner in place of his usual cooked meal—yes, things are that bad—and I have a glass of red wine and a handful of crisps for mine. And so ends another day without Luis.

The following morning brings another struggle to get up. It's difficult when the day ahead offers so many possibilities for misery. But Biff is sitting next to the bed, looking up at me with pleading eyes. Feeling guilty, I throw on some tracksuit bottoms, a jumper, a woolly hat and a wholly unflattering duvet coat and we set off towards the river. Biff dances along beside me, unembarrassed by my repellent outfit and the fact I haven't bothered to brush my hair. As we cross the square, I spot a slightly-built figure waving from outside the café on the corner, throwing his arms in the air, so pleased is he to see us. As I get closer, I see it is Arnaud.

'*Ça va?*' he shouts, advancing towards us with enthusiasm and squatting down to greet Biff. 'Look at that! He is so handsome, your dog. And so proud, the way he walks across the square with you.' Arnaud does a rather camp impersonation of Biff's walk, moving his shoulders and holding his head aloft in a snooty, poodle-like fashion. Biff, unimpressed by the flurry of compliments, eyes him with a mix of tolerance and suspicion.

'Come on,' says Arnaud, putting his arm around my shoulders and ushering me towards the steamed-up café door. 'Let's go and have a coffee.'

'I've got to walk him first,' I say. 'Maybe on the way back.'

'OK,' says Arnaud. 'I'll be here. See you in a while.'

The ground is frosty down by the river and the air smells of decay, like damp clothes that have been left too long in a gym bag. Undeterred by the cold, Biff slips into the river and paddles in a determined fashion towards a family of ducks. They toy with him, taking flight at the very last moment and Biff swims back to the river bank, standing in the green slime like a mini-hippopotamus before wading out of the water and shaking himself down.

Arnaud emerges from the café and calls out to me as I walk home. He has a friend with him. 'This is Basile,' says Arnaud, introducing me to a dark-haired man in his fifties, with a small moustache and perceptive brown eyes.

'*Enchanté*,' says Basile, who is fashionably dressed—for Villiers, anyway—in jeans, a dark shirt and a brown leather flying-jacket. (Most men in my village dress in blue overalls and flat caps.)

'He's all wet,' says Arnaud, bending down to pat Biff.

'Yes, he's been in the river chasing ducks.'

'*Really?*' says Basile, looking interested. 'Does he ever catch one?'

'Never,' I say.

'That's a shame. I was thinking that Arnaud here could make a nice duck *à l'orange*, I will bring the candles and wine and we could come to your house for dinner,' he says, in such a deadpan way that I can't figure out if he is joking or not. Either way, I laugh.

'Listen!' Arnaud says suddenly, grabbing my hand. 'Do you like *moules frites*?'

'Yes. Why?'

'Because the café in Puysoleil is reopening next week and soon they will be having an evening of *moules frites*.'

'You know Puysoleil?' I say.

'Yes. I lived there for many years,' he says. 'Before I moved to Liard.'

'So do you know my friend Delphine, the mayor?' I ask.

'Ah, Delphine!' he says, throwing his arms in the air. 'Of course I know Delphine. Everyone knows Delphine. She is a friend of yours?' Arnaud looks impressed.

'Yes, a very good friend.' And then, because I know that Arnaud does not have a car, I say, 'Listen, I'm going to the opening of the bar next week. We can go together if you like?'

'Super,' says Arnaud, pronouncing it *soup-AIR*, the way the French do.

'*Moules frites*—very nice,' says Basile, with a drag on his cigarette. 'But duck *à l'orange* is better. You need to teach your dog to swim faster.'

Chapter 5

Welcome to Puysoleil

Before the week is out, Arnaud has established himself as an avuncular figure in my life. He refers to me as '*ma petite puce*', or 'my little flea', which according to Delphine is a term of endearment. Some might be suspicious of the speed with which Arnaud has befriended me, but I have always made friends fast, so it doesn't bother me.

Over countless cups of coffee in the days that follow our first meeting, he tells me his life story. It turns out that my new neighbour is a chef by profession. Until a few months ago, he was working in a café a couple of kilometres away, but at the moment he is signed off work with a repetitive strain injury in his upper arm caused, apparently, by too much chopping. He also tells me that he is a reformed alcoholic and hasn't touched alcohol for at least three years. He now chain-smokes and drinks coffee instead.

He must be drinking about twelve cups a day and as a result, he's in a constant state of hyper-caffeination. Whenever I walk by the café, Arnaud emerges and waves his arms like a wind turbine, inviting me to come and join him. Often I decline for fear that one more espresso might send him over the edge. I also wonder how he can afford all these coffees when he is not working. Soon, he is knocking on my door or tapping on the window at least once a day, to see if I want to join him in the café where he practically lives, along with Basile, a retired physiotherapist.

The joke in the village is that they are like an old married couple, huddled together smoking and gossiping about everyone who passes by. Some mornings, Basile is standing outside the café alone and looking lost without his friend. Invariably, he asks if I know where Arnaud is, as if I should be keeping tabs on my neighbour's activities. 'Relax, your wife will be here soon,' one of the old boys will tease him and sure enough, Arnaud comes sashaying across the square, performing a camp little dance when he sees us.

Arnaud is relentlessly cheerful. When autumn suddenly reverts temporarily back to summer—according to Delphine, the weather is so mixed-up that local farmers can no longer predict it—and tables once again reappear outside the café, my neighbour sets up camp there. As a result, he manages to fast track his way into the life of the village. He is interested in everyone and everything and pretty soon knows the name, marital status and life synopsis of almost everyone in Villiers.

Some might find Arnaud's manner a little loud and overbearing, his non-stop good mood irritating. I notice that some villagers look very suspicious when he accosts them with a cheery greeting or jocular comment, but they seem reassured when they see me with him.

One afternoon, Arnaud stops me in the square to ask if I like Toulouse sausages.

'Um, yes. Why?'

'This evening, I will bring you some,' he says.

'That's really very kind of you, Arnaud,' I say, touched.

Shortly after 7.00 pm, the doorbell rings and there is my neighbour grinning in the darkness, holding a foil-covered dish in each hand. He doesn't wait to be invited in but marches straight through the *petit salon* and into the kitchen, placing the dishes on the refectory table.

'Sorry about the mess,' I say, pointing to the pile of unwashed dishes and coffee cups in the sink.

'It's not important,' he says, dismissing the domestic chaos with a wave of the arm. 'There are more important things to do in life than clean.'

Biff jumps up so that his front paws are on the kitchen table, checking to see if our neighbour has brought any dinner for him. Thanks to his long body, when he stands on his hind legs he is almost as tall as Arnaud, who laughs and bends down to waggle Biff's ears.

'*Tu es très coquin*,' (you are very cheeky) he says. Then, with a cry of '*Bon appétit*' he marches back next door, leaving behind a delicious dish of fat Toulouse sausages and lentil purée. For dessert, there is a slab of homemade apple tart with chocolate custard. There are worse things, I think to myself, than having a lonely chef living next door.

A few nights later, touched by his kindness, I make a Gordon Ramsay recipe for lasagne. Happy to have someone to cook for other than Biff, I divide it into two dishes and take one next door, along with a crisp green salad and alcohol-free trifle for dessert. Arnaud is delighted. The following morning, I'm relieved to see that not only is he still alive, but he doesn't seem to be suffering from any digestive malady. Instead, he jumps up to thank me as I walk past the café, where he is sitting with Basile in the autumn sunshine.

'Thank you, my little flea,' he says, taking both my hands in his and declaring last night's gesture to be '*super gentil*', or super-nice. I notice the old boys on the terrace watching him, like the chorus in a Greek tragedy, with a look that is half suspicion and half reluctant admiration.

'Don't forget,' he says, loudly enough for everyone to hear. 'We are going out this evening. Time to dress up, my little flea. We need to go out and dance.'

'We'll see,' I say. My heart still feels like it has been the victim of an emotional hit and run. It's going to be a long time before I dance again.

*   *   *

At 5.00 pm, I knock on Arnaud's door as arranged. He jumps out immediately, as if he has been hovering behind it. *'Bonjour! Bonjour!'* he cries, flapping his arms around by way of a greeting. He seems almost as excited as Biff to be going out for the evening. Wearing dark, tailored trousers and a crisply ironed shirt with his Barbour-style jacket, he seems to have made quite an effort.

'So did you know Didier?' I ask as we set off in the direction of Puysoleil, a fifteen-minute drive away.

'Yes, I knew him well. If the stories are true, he was stupid to do what he did. But these two new girls will be a disaster.'

'Why do you say that?'

'They are cousins of mine. Pauline, she is not a bad cook. But neither of them is agreeable. If you run a bar, you need to look happy, smile, make the customers feel you are happy to see them.' He puts his fingers to the corners of his mouth and pulls his lips up into a forced smile. 'It will be a catastrophe, I'm sure of it.'

'Well, Delphine seems to think they will do a good job,' I say.

Arnaud makes a snorting sound. 'We'll see,' he says.

We drive along in silence for a while, passing the occasional combine harvester reaping the last of the golden stalks of maize. Most of the crops have been harvested now, the fields reduced to a bleached stubble or *les chaumes* as the French call it.

Eventually, we pull up in front of Puysoleil's ivy-covered church. There is a small crowd outside the bar, which is glowing in the sweet caramel light of autumn. A *tricolore* ribbon has replaced the police tape that sealed the pink-beige building until recently, and I can see that Bruno and Rémi, Delphine's trusty council workers, have repainted the shutters a glossy shade of ox-blood. There is also a new wooden sign above the door: the Café de la Paix will henceforth be known as Bienvenue à Puysoleil, or Welcome to Puysoleil. It doesn't exactly trip off the tongue.

Arnaud jumps out of the car like a coiled spring. *'Allez le Biff!'* he cries and taking Biff with him—or rather, the other way round—they head towards the small crowd, a combined energy force that's impossible to ignore.

Delphine approaches, wearing a purple ruffled skirt and a poppy red smile. *'Bonjour,'* she says, looking very surprised to see Arnaud, even though I'd mentioned that I might bring my new neighbour. *''Allo Arnaud, how are you?'* she says.

'Bonjour, ma belle blonde,' (Hello, my beautiful blonde) he yells to Delphine, who has raven-coloured hair, stepping backwards to admire her like a painting. He seems delighted to be seen with the mayor. I notice him glancing towards the crowd a couple of times to see if anyone is looking.

'It's a very long time since we last saw you in Puysoleil. What have you been doing?' asks Delphine.

Arnaud runs through the story of the ex-girlfriend in Liard, his job in the restaurant and his arm injury. 'And now I am living in Villiers. Next door to *Ka-renne*,' he concludes.

Delphine tells us that she has been in the *salle des fêtes* all afternoon making canapés, which strikes me as rather odd. 'Shouldn't the two sisters be doing that?' I say.

'Pauline and Odile are . . . a little *stressed*,' she says, choosing her words carefully. 'They have done some bowls of nuts and crisps but I was worried that there might not be enough. And anyway, I didn't mind. Bruno and Rémi helped me.'

I sometimes wonder what Delphine's

77

commune would do without Bruno and Rémi, who can turn their hand to almost anything. They grit the roads in winter, water the flowers in summer and do everything from maintaining municipal buildings to disposing of the occasional dead boar. They are versatile in their duties and willing in attitude. To thank them for their efforts on behalf of the *commune*—which often surpass those that they are paid to perform—Delphine takes them out for a nice lunch at least twice a year.

'Well, it's a good turnout,' I say.

'Yes, I'm very honoured because several of my mayor colleagues have come this evening, even Stephan Barbe,' she says, referring to the heart-throb mayor of a nearby *commune*. 'The two girls were so excited when I told them. Pauline said she was going to wear a miniskirt.' She nods towards a large, stern-faced woman. Arnaud snorts and mutters something disparaging, before allowing himself to be dragged away by Biff, who is eager to check out the local cats.

'My goodness,' says Delphine, when Arnaud is out of earshot. 'I had no idea he was your neighbour. Arnaud is, how shall I say it . . . very well known in Puysoleil.'

'He told me about his drink problem.'

'Well, what a transformation.'

I look over to the trestle tables, which are being set up outside the café by Bruno and Rémi. Arnaud is talking to them, throwing

78

his head back and laughing theatrically at his own jokes. 'Look at him! What an old rogue,' says Delphine—'old rogue' being her term of endearment for any flirtatious man of a certain age.

She gives a short speech saying how delighted she is to be reopening the bar. Many people nod when she describes the café as 'the soul of a small village' and very important to the rural community. The two sisters meanwhile, stand either side of her with their arms folded like sumo wrestlers, as if trying to warn customers away.

Delphine concludes by presenting each of them with a bouquet of roses. Then, with a big smile and an *'et voilà,'* she snips the *tricolore* ribbon and pushes open the glossy red door to the café.

Bruno and Rémi have worked very hard to scrub away any signs of the bar's scandalous past. The red lamps, stag heads and horns jutting out from the wall have all been eradicated, along with the oil painting of the large-breasted nude. In their place are clean white walls and simple wooden tables, the only decoration being a few leather-bound books in a shelved alcove. 'Bordello chic', as I once termed it, has now been replaced by 'monastic chic'.

The two sisters retreat behind the tiny bar, where they appear to be having a heated discussion by the beer pumps.

'Odile is a little unhappy because we were unable to put her name on the lease,' whispers Delphine. 'She hasn't done the necessary training course in food safety. The two girls got into a bit of a fight about it this afternoon.'

Oh dear. This does not bode well.

'Excuse me, are you a friend of Monsieur Fillon?' A Frenchwoman with a chic grey bob and an Hèrmes scarf around her neck, is looking me up and down. She's wearing tan-coloured tailored trousers, a white shirt and a navy blazer with gold buttons—the uniform of the posh, postmenopausal Frenchwoman. She nods towards Arnaud, so I assume that he is the Monsieur Fillon she is referring to.

'Yes. Arnaud is my neighbour. In Villiers,' I reply in French.

'It is very good for his rehabilitation that he is seen here with you. Everyone knows that you are a friend of *Madame le Maire*. It will make him seem more respectable.'

'More respectable?'

'Yes. I'm afraid to say it but he had a very bad reputation here in Puysoleil. He was the worst drunk in the village. He once drove his car along the pavement for a good 500 metres and we had to confiscate his car keys.'

'*Ah bon?*' I say, employing the phrase that the French use when being told something that they don't want to hear.

'Yes. It was not good to be seen in the company of this man. But maybe people don't know about his past in Villiers.'

She pushes her grey bob behind her ears and narrows her eyes, while I look around for a means of escape. I spot Delphine bringing out two plates of canapés from the kitchen and use this as an excuse, saying that I must help. Outside, the long table set up for *le cocktail* remains bare, as Pauline and Odile act like diffident guests at their own party and seem in no hurry to serve the drinks.

Eventually, Pauline emerges with a punchbowl of *pamplemousse rosé* (rosé wine with grapefruit juice), which she starts to ladle slowly and reluctantly into wine glasses. Arnaud watches with disapproval. A few minutes later, he has rolled up his shirtsleeves and taken over, ladling out the fuchsia pink liquid in generous measures, while Biff, who is tied to a table leg, watches. All the time, Arnaud keeps up a cheerful banter with the waiting crowd. He is really enjoying himself. His cousins, on the other hand, look as if they want to kill him.

But thanks to Arnaud, the party has finally started. Laughter, rather than the embarrassed murmur of conversation, now fills the evening air.

'Look at him,' says Delphine. 'He really knows what he is doing.'

Arnaud winks at me and beckons me over. He hands me two glasses.

'Extra large ones,' he says. 'For you and

Madame le Maire.'

'By the way, Delphine, who is the lady over there with the grey bob and the Hèrmes scarf?' I ask, as I hand her the cocktail.

'Oh, that is Madame Mabillon. She is married to a local businessman and very . . . how do you say . . . very correct.'

By 7.00 pm, it is dark and the party is over. 'I give it till Christmas,' says Arnaud as we walk back to the car, 'before they close.' Based on tonight's performance, I have to agree. As we follow the twisting road back to Villiers, I see the headlights of a combine harvester moving stealthily across a dark field like a huge beast with big, illuminated eyes. It's a common sight at this time of year: a lone farmer working as late as midnight to gather in the maize before the rain comes. The life of the French farmer is not an easy one.

'It's no wonder so many of them go mad,' says Arnaud, as if reading my thoughts. 'Ploughing the same furrows day after day, all on your own. It must be so boring.'

'Do they really go mad?' I ask.

'Oh yes,' says Arnaud. 'They are always flinging themselves down wells or shooting themselves. It happens all the time. Usually in winter.'

Cheery! But just the thought of the long French winter, which officially begins next weekend, is enough to sap the soul. Whereas in previous years I've found things to love about each of the seasons in France, I'm now dreading the cold and darkness ahead. This year it feels like it is going to be an endurance test.

'*Bonne nuit, ma puce,*' says Arnaud, as we turn our respective keys in the locks in rue St Benoit. '*À demain.*'

'Yes, see you tomorrow,' I say, thinking how reassuring it is to have Arnaud living on the other side of the wall.

Chapter 6

The Pursuit of Happiness

I limp into November with a new resolution: I am going to devote myself to the pursuit of happiness. Nothing overly ambitious, you understand. I'm not looking for deep joy or everlasting love. Instead, I'll settle for peace and a low-key kind of contentment and not wanting to throw myself off a cliff. Inspired by Travis and another cosy pep talk in front of his log fire, the plan is to count my blessings and be grateful for the small pleasures of everyday life in France (other than the patisserie and the Pouilly-Fumé). Even in the dark days of winter, they exist. The secret is to be able to identify them at the time, rather than with hindsight.

Many of my most delightful moments, I realise, revolve around my little dog. Watching Biff gobble down a chicken and basmati rice dinner, or feeling his warm body pushed up against mine on the sofa, provides a big hit of happiness. (Watching him wriggle in a festering pile of hay doesn't.) Other unexpected pleasures occur while out walking in the countryside at the end of the day. A salmon pink sun setting in a white winter sky and framed by the black branches of a tree creates a warm glow in the soul. So too does the sight of two deer standing together in a copse as if having a conversation, before flitting across the horizon, graceful as prima ballerinas, with Biff in hot pursuit.

There is, in fact, a lot that I can learn from Biff and how little it takes to make him happy. It warms my heart to see how thrilled he looks, clutching a little pile of my stolen socks in his doughnut bed as if they were a glittering prize. His other great pleasures in life are long walks, home-cooked food and the occasional roll in fox poo, along with some social interaction with other animals. Apart from the fox droppings, maybe this could be the basis for my happiness, too. What I really envy, though, is Biff's eternal optimism—the enthusiasm with which he snuffles down a rabbit hole or chases hare and deer, despite never having come close to catching anything.

As Travis is always telling me, the secret

of happiness is to appreciate what you've got, rather than focusing on the things that you lack. So I'm going to stop envying friends who seem to have everything and wonder instead what secret unhappiness or unfulfilled wish they might be carrying around. It seems to me that almost everyone is dragging some kind of invisible cross behind them. It's just that some are better at hiding it than others.

My pursuit of happiness will begin with cleaning the house for, as Travis points out, happiness requires self-discipline. 'Crank up the music and treat it like a workout,' he says. (Hmm, for me, that would mean feigning a knee injury and slacking at the back.) But I throw on some old clothes that I once wore to Pilates and prepare to get busy with a mop and some microfibre cloths.

I start in the hallway, picking up the money pot on the small table. It's heavy, and so stuffed with money that £20 notes are sticking out of the wide slot near the neck. The Terramundi money pot, to give it its proper name, was a birthday gift from a friend just before I moved to France. It has always made me smile, partly because of the cheeky red and yellow spotted design and partly because of the charming concept behind it. The idea is that you write a wish and drop it in with the first coin. When the pot is full, you smash it open and give half the money to a good cause, which in turn, is supposed to bring you luck.

I estimate that it contains £800-1000, as I've mostly stuffed it with £20 notes and pound coins left over from trips to London. Each time I manage to avoid taking a taxi or buying something I don't need, I put the money in the pot instead. There is only room for a couple more coins, which means that it is almost time to smash it open. The thought makes me feel sad, since the wish I made five years ago died on the day I discovered Luis with *la blonde*.

Still, I mustn't dwell on the negative. Instead, I mop the hallway, scrub the bathroom to a gleaming white, vacuum up the dust and ashes from the wood burner, and pick up the clothes and shoes that Biff has ferried downstairs from my bedroom to the *petit salon*. (Not so long ago, my clothes were scattered around the sitting room for a more exciting reason.) It takes nearly four hours to blitz the house. Do I feel better? Actually yes, I do. Being miserable in a clean house is a marginal improvement on being miserable in a messy one.

Later that morning, Arnaud knocks on my door clutching a small cardboard box. 'A present for you,' he says. 'I've been doing a little clear-out and thought you might like these.' Inside the box is a set of six glass beer tankards, emblazoned with the Holstein Pils logo. Much as I appreciate the thought, I don't drink beer—nor do any of my friends—and it's hard to see how such a gift would fit into my life. But then I realise that, as a reformed alcoholic, he needs six beer glasses even less than I do, so I grab them off him and pretend to be delighted. He then disappears next door and returns with a slab of socialist magazines.

'I thought you might also be interested in these,' he says and my heart sinks. The sort of French magazines that I read feature pictures of charming country houses, not creepy politicians. But I accept them graciously, while planning to put them in the recycling bin later.

'Do you want to go for a coffee, my little flea?'

'I can't, Arnaud. I don't go to the café at the weekend in case I bump into Luis.'

'Luis, he is away working. He won't be back until tomorrow morning.'

'How do you know?'

'I keep my ear to the ground on your behalf. And I saw Fernando, *le patron*, who told me they are working on a big job in Cognac. They've been away all week.'

This is good news as it means I won't have to worry about bumping into The Devil in Intermarché or at the cash point. As I've discovered, breaking up with someone in a small village is much more traumatic than in a big city. It's a bit like being stuck permanently in a lift with them.

'It's very kind of you, Arnaud, to carry out reconnaissance on my behalf.'

'It's nothing. I can find out more if you like.'

I laugh and tell him that I'm going to call him 'Agent Arnaud' from now on.

I get my coat. There is a cold nip in the air now and Villiers once again smells like Diptyque's *Feu de Bois* (a candle I used to burn in my flat in London to create the smell of woodsmoke). Over two *café crèmes* Arnaud tells me that I need to stop hiding away at weekends. 'The best thing you can do is completely ignore Luis. If you see him, act like he doesn't exist,' he says. He tells me that he bumped into his own *ex-copine* outside the *mairie* earlier in the week and blanked her completely. He mimes cutting a throat with a knife. 'As far as I am concerned, she might as well be dead,' he says.

Arnaud certainly hasn't wasted any time crying over his former love. Instead, he's been busy 'draguing' the locals ('draguing' is a hybrid word that Dephine and I jokingly use, based on the French verb *draguer* which means to try to pick up or literally, 'to dredge'). He is audacious and confident in his approach, striking up conversations and flirting with every woman in the village between the ages of eighteen and eighty. I can only admire his resilience. He is like a soldier who has been sent home to have his wounds patched up, but who cannot wait to get back to the frontline.

Later that evening, I drive to Puysoleil for a *moules frites* evening, an event which is 'by reservation only' since Pauline and Odile apparently need to 'plan' the food. (Strictly speaking, the *moules frites* season in France is from July to November but increasingly the dish is offered all year round.) Arnaud has had to back out because of an important political meeting—or at least that's what he said—but I have agreed to go as Delphine, bless her, is very keen to drum up support for the café.

Only two other tables are occupied when we arrive, but when a couple turn up without a reservation, Odile's response is so fierce—shaking her head and blinking at them with a look of defiance—it's as if they'd asked her for a vital organ rather than a table for two. Delphine and I hover in the doorway until Pauline deigns to seat us. Dressed in leggings and a pumpkin-coloured top, she looks like a Halloween lantern, but without the smile. With a minimum of greetings and warmth— not even for Delphine who is spending the best part of her salary here, coming for coffee and lunch most days—she seats us in the small white dining room.

'You remember my friend *Ka-renne*?' says Delphine.

Pauline stares at me for a few seconds and gives a barely discernible nod. 'Would you like an aperitif?' she asks.

I ask for tonic water, but Pauline just glares at me and does not say anything. I ask again and this time she shakes her head. She doesn't have tonic water, so I settle for Perrier instead.

'Well, this is nice,' says Delphine casting her eyes around the room. 'It's good to see some other people here.' She lowers her voice. 'The big group behind you is their family,' she says. I look around, wondering what kind of men have been mad enough to marry Odile and Pauline, but their husbands look surprisingly normal, as do their teenage children.

'Are you ready to eat?' asks Pauline, when she returns with the drinks. It's not so much a question as a command. We've barely got our coats off but we both nod. She reappears immediately with a copper dish of mussels, their glossy black shells glistening in the white wine sauce, plonking it down like a sour-faced school dinner lady, along with a small bowl of chips.

The food is good but there isn't very much of it. Delphine would like a carafe of water and I would like some bread. Unfortunately, Odile and Pauline have both disappeared.

'Maybe we can ask for another bowl of chips?' I suggest, but when we finally get Odile's attention—I flag her down as she's stepping outside for a cigarette—she says something in rapid-fire French that I don't understand.

'They have run out of chips,' says Delphine. 'Odile's husband is about to drive home to fetch some potatoes.'

'How far away is home?' I ask.

'About 10 kilometres,' says Delphine. 'But

at least it proves the chips are homemade.'

'*R-i-g-h-t,*' I say, amazed at their *modus operandi*.

Unconcerned that several customers are still waiting for food, the sisters fetch themselves beers and sit down with their family. This would be fine if it were the end of a long night in a crazily-busy restaurant, but chilling out in the middle of service just seems plain wrong in these circumstances. I don't know much about running a restaurant, but I've eaten in lots of them and it seems to me that this pair lack the intuitive skills necessary to the hospitality trade, most notably a sense of timing. Whenever we want anything, they are nowhere to be seen. It would be nice to have a coffee and dessert but it seems like too much trouble to ask. When Delphine finally manages to get their attention, she asks for the bill instead, which is a relief.

'Was everything OK?' asks Pauline, in a way that suggests she has no doubt that it was.

'Delicious,' says Delphine. I am tempted to list the areas where there might be room for improvement but instead we pay the bill, nod goodbye to the other diners and step into the dark winter night. It's cold outside but not as cold as the atmosphere inside.

'So is the café proving very popular with the locals?' I ask, as we walk towards our respective cars.

'Not really,' says Delphine. 'They say that

whenever they go there, it is as if they are bringing bad news.'

I glance back at the café, which looks so charming under the starry winter sky. Something tells me that Bienvenue à Puysoleil—such irony!—might soon be Au Revoir, Puysoleil. I do have some sympathy for Pauline and Odile, as it is notoriously difficult to make a living from a bar in rural France. Not only are there crippling social charges to pay—several thousand euros before you've even switched on the lights—but the hours are long and unsociable. And if, like Puysoleil, your café is in a quiet backwater, you can wait a whole morning for a single customer to walk through the door.

But having twice witnessed the sisters in action, I do think that they're the architects of their own downfall, which seems assured if they've alienated the locals.

It's just after 9.00 pm when I arrive home in Villiers. I throw a log on the fire, which fortunately hasn't gone out, and take Biff out for his bedtime walk. Normally, we do a circuit of the square, avoiding the main road and Luis's apartment. But tonight, reassured by the knowledge that The Devil is in Cognac, I break my own rules and walk past his building. When I see that the lights are on, I panic and turn around. He must have returned early. Then I hear loud sobbing and realise that there is a major drama unfolding in the building next door. The front door is open and a thin blonde woman is bawling her eyes out on the stairs, while an embarrassed-looking friend tries to comfort her. My natural instinct is to stop and see if I can do anything to help. Before I can say anything, the blonde turns her tear-stained face towards me, with a venom that takes me by surprise.

'Go away, Englishwoman with your stupid dog,' she rasps in a harsh, gravel-like voice. Her face, which is equally hard, looks familiar. Just as I'm wondering why she would be so nasty, or how she even knows that I am English, a red emergency vehicle pulls up outside. It's the *sapeurs-pompiers*—the first port of call for any crisis in France, be it medical, fire, or road traffic emergency. Two men in navy uniform run inside the building, one of them carrying a medical bag. And then it hits me: the blonde on the staircase is the woman that I found in Luis's bedroom.

I walk home shaken. Now it all makes sense. She, too, was the 'girl next door', just like I was. Luis didn't need to look very far. Oh, the irony—and the convenience! I wonder if he 'dragued' her in the same way that he did me, knocking on her door to borrow a bottle of tomato sauce? I feel sick at this discovery—it must have made it very easy for him to cheat on me—but also somewhat vindicated since the blonde, I am quite sure, was crying over Luis. I wonder if they have had a row? If so, it was a pretty nasty one judging by the state of her. The candle-lit love-in that I imagined taking place behind those green shutters was not necessarily the reality.

The following morning, Sunday, I bump into Arnaud outside the *boulangerie*. 'What's the matter, my little flea?' he asks.

'I know who Luis's girlfriend is,' I say, before telling him about the scenario that I stumbled upon last night.

'You mean the tall blonde woman, who lives in the building with the brown shutters?' says Arnaud. 'Everyone says she is crazy.'

'It helps if you're going out with Luis.'

'Don't worry, my little flea. He is only using her for sex and will soon cast her aside like a used tissue.'

'Yes, like he did me.'

'Listen. What are you doing this evening?'

'I have to work on an article that is due in tomorrow.'

'I will bring you dinner,' he says. 'So you can get on with your work uninterrupted.'

Travis calls when I get home, sounding even more upbeat than usual. Has he finally found his prince tucked away somewhere in the French countryside, I wonder?

'Sadly not,' he says. 'But last night one of my neighbours took me to *the* most wonderful restaurant—fab food, really good ambiance. Amazing!'

I know how picky Travis is when it comes to

94

restaurants—if they don't have candles on the table, he won't even consider eating there—so this sounds promising.

'Where is it?' I ask.

'It's called L'Auberge de L'Écurie—not that far from you, actually, in Usson-du-Poitou. It's run by a really lovely gay couple called Franck and Frédéric.'

'Oh, please let's go,' I say.

'Well, I'm hoping you're free on Thursday, because I've already made the booking.'

This is cheery news. It would be wonderful, after so many gastronomic disappointments, to find a great French restaurant on my doorstep. Later that day, I realise that I already do have a great French restaurant on my doorstep. It's called Chez Arnaud. Just after 7.00 pm, my neighbour knocks on the door with a cassoulet, potatoes dauphinoise and a chocolate mousse.

'Listen,' says Arnaud before he leaves. 'I saw Luis in the café this morning.' He mimes a long face. 'He was on his own and looked very miserable.'

'Good,' I say. Small moments of happiness seem to be popping up at every turn today.

As I eat the delicious dinner in front of the *X-Factor* results show, I mentally log my neighbour's kindness as another small and unexpected happiness.

* * *

November drags on, dark and damp, with five days of rain—not the dramatic kind that makes you feel cosy and happy to be indoors, but the constant, monotonous rainfall that saps the morale. It's even getting Travis down. He calls regularly, his voice sounding smaller and more demotivated by the day. Despite numerous trips to the DIY stores around Poitiers, he still hasn't decided on his kitchen cabinets and is going to be living on microwaved food for the foreseeable future. 'My God, is this rain ever going to end? I haven't been out for FIVE days and I think I'm going MAD,' he says.

I feel the same and at least I can take refuge in my work. Writing 500 words on *Seeing Spots* (the return of the polka dot—again!) acts as a welcome diversion, whereas Travis, I know, is worrying about what to do when his redundancy money runs out. Thank goodness we have dinner at L'Auberge de L'Écurie to look forward to. In order to boost our morale, we both agree to dress up, as if we were visiting a posh restaurant in London. Wearing a dark tailored jacket with a designer T-shirt and jeans, Travis picks me up on a Thursday evening—a week night, which in rural France usually means that we will be the only people in the restaurant. But I'm excited to be going somewhere new and have pulled out all the stops in a short black dress, purple cardigan and red Prada shoes. Biff senses that we are going somewhere nice and attempts, via some fancy footwork, to come with us, but for once I insist that he stays at home.

'Did you choose this music especially?' I ask as we set out for the 15-kilometre drive, with Lady Gaga's *Bad Romance* playing on the sound system of his convertible BMW.

'Well, technically speaking it's now no romance, isn't it?' says Travis. 'Unless—please tell me this is not the case—you're back with him?'

'No chance of that,' I say and tell him about the blonde crying on the staircase.

'You know what? I actually feel really sorry for her,' says Travis. 'In my opinion you've had a lucky escape. Luis seems to leave a trail of destruction behind him.'

I say nothing, as 'lucky escape' is not how I would sum up the misery of the past couple of months.

'The thing is,' says Travis, 'you have to ask yourself why you are attracted to men like Luis. Why do you choose them?'

'Um, I don't choose them. They choose me. He knocked on my door, remember? He pursued me.'

'Well, let yourself be chosen by them.' Travis turns to look at me. 'You know, when you make the effort, you look amazing,' he says.

'Gee thanks! I won't ask what I look like the rest of the time.'

'Well, I'm just saying. Recently, you haven't

been making much of an effort. And you should, because you've got so much going for you. That's all.'

We pass through Usson-du-Poitou and then suddenly, in the middle of nowhere, an old building lights up the road ahead. With red-orange lamps glowing in the windows, it looks like one of the old-fashioned inns that you see on Christmas cards. I know immediately that I will love it.

'Here it is,' says Travis, as he pulls up in the adjacent car park. 'Prepare to be delighted and amazed.'

'I already am,' I say.

As we step in from the freezing night air, all senses are immediately engaged. There is warmth, thanks to a roaring log fire, music (the fashionable lounge variety) and a delicious smell of slow-cooked meat filling the air. In place of the Formica top tables and strip lighting usually found in French rural restaurants, fat red pillar candles flicker on the wooden dining tables, casting the room in a soft, flattering light.

Within seconds, a jovial, smiling man appears and clutches hold of Travis like a long-lost relative. *'Ah, bonsoir Trav-eece,'* he cries with a big smile and then turns his attention to me, introducing himself as Frédéric. He takes our coats and leads us to a table near the large stone fireplace. To my surprise, at least half a dozen other tables are occupied, which immediately makes this restaurant in the middle of nowhere seem like an insider secret. Frédéric asks if we would like a cocktail. *Cocktails?* On a Thursday evening, in rural France? This is an unexpected delight.

'I think we could be persuaded,' says Travis.

'The house cocktail?' says Frédéric.

'Oh, I think so,' he replies.

Almost immediately, our friendly proprietor returns with our drinks, a mix of champagne and apricot brandy served ice-cold and in old-fashioned champagne *coupes*. I am already won over. This man could now serve me frozen pizza from Lidl and I would still love his restaurant.

'What do you think?' says Travis, basking in the glow of candlelight and the knowledge that he's done well.

'Totally impressed.'

'I knew you would be. Isn't it nice to go somewhere that doesn't feel like a school canteen?'

'It's actually very romantic,' I say, looking around at the cleverly placed screens and potted palms, which help to create an intimate ambiance around each table.

'Don't go getting any funny ideas,' says Travis.

'I'll try not to.'

At exactly the right moment, Frédéric reappears with the menu—three courses for €25. It's written on a blackboard in chalk, which he props up on our table before explaining the various dishes. Eventually, I decide on snails in a garlic sauce as a starter, followed by *bavette à l'échalote*. (Bavette is a lean, flank cut of beef that is very popular in France but not so well known in the UK.) The snails are delicious and the steak cooked perfectly *saignant* (bloody) and surprisingly tender, falling apart in the mouth in soft, delicate threads.

For dessert I order a chocolate mousse, which is as light as organza and overlaid with the flavour of lychee. Later, as we sip peppermint tea, Frédéric's partner, Franck (pronounced 'Fronc') emerges from the kitchen, his manner modest and unassuming, to ask if we enjoyed our dinner. We thank them both for a wonderful evening. The food was as good as anything I've eaten in London or Paris, the service was warm and efficient without being bombastic or overbearing, while the music and the lighting were perfectly pitched.

As we drive back to Villiers, I count the day's blessings. The discovery of this wonderful restaurant definitely counts as one of them, as does Travis's friendship. As I inch my way into the bed that Biff has now made his own, for the first time in ages I experience a feeling of gratitude.

Chapter 7

Champagne and Black Ice

Christmas knocks on the door like an unwelcome guest. Happy or sad, the festive season always seems to amplify my mood. This year I decide that I won't bother with a Christmas tree, as I don't feel much like celebrating, but at the last minute I relent and buy the only tree left in Intermarché, as it looks so lonesome on its own. Later that afternoon, I climb the rickety wooden stairs to the freezing cold attic to dig out the decorations.

Then in the evening, with the fire lit, and fortified by a glass of a chilled Château Graves, I unpack the tinsel, the naughty-looking fairy and the posh icicles bought from Le Bon Marché department store in Paris several years ago, while Biff watches from the sofa with big, intrigued eyes. When I've finished, the *petit salon* is lit only by the orange glow of the fire and the dancing white fairy lights. *Voilà,* instant Christmas!

The following morning, I wake to find that, right on cue, several inches of snow have fallen. Sunlight and snow make for a beguiling combination and Villiers suddenly looks spotless and pure. Feeling energised by the brilliant white view from my window, I walk Biff down to the *plan d'eau*, a rustic park with a lake on the outskirts of the village. All is calm and still, everything glistening white under a radiant blue sky, while the partially frozen lake looks like a pool of mercury. As we crunch along in the virgin snow, I feel exhilarated. I take a moment to breathe in the pure air, to look around at the little blades of grass poking up through the snow like green shaving stubble, and to feel grateful for the gifts of Mother Nature.

On the way home, I stop at Intermarché to buy firelighters and, noticing that there is a special offer on champagne, I buy a bottle for Christmas lunch. As I turn into the snowy square, I see Arnaud and Basile standing outside the café smoking, while stamping their feet and rubbing their hands together to keep warm. They wave wildly when they see me.

'For me? You shouldn't have!' says Basile, seeing the bottle of champagne. 'Over to your place later, then? Be sure to have the candles lit so that it's nice and romantic.'

It's too cold to hang around, so I wish them *'Bonne journée'* and head home, still smiling at the 'old rogues', as Delphine would call them. Then I freeze. Coming across the square towards me are The Devil and his boss. Usually there is no danger of seeing Luis on a Friday, but there he is, looking in my direction, moving—reluctantly, it seems—towards me.

He's wearing red fleece tracksuit bottoms and a grey Supodal body warmer—an unlikely outfit for the Don Juan of Villiers, I know—but even in this outfit there is a force field around him that is hard to ignore. But I'm more than up to meeting him today. Cheeks flushed pink from the bracing walk and the orange box of Veuve Cliquot swinging by a rope from my wrist, I look happy. For once, I'm not wearing my shabby dog-walking gear, but a smart navy coat and brown leather knee boots.

Following Arnaud's advice, I act as if The Devil does not exist and keep walking towards them, head held high and an enigmatic smile on my face. I know he has seen me. He looks embarrassed and at the very last moment, he ducks into the shoe shop to avoid me. His boss swivels around in surprise and follows him, but not before making a feeble joke about the potentially dangerous combination of champagne and snow. The Veuve Cliquot, I hope, has hurt. Luis and I once shared a bottle of it at midnight at my kitchen table, for no other reason than he'd had a hard day at work (or at least that's where he said he'd been). Hopefully, he'll wonder whom I'm planning to drink this with. Yep, champagne definitely sends the right message. Mentally, I give myself a high-five. Childish I know, but this is the most successful of our post break-up encounters.

The snow hangs around for three more days before being swept away by a downfall of rain. Then Christmas Eve arrives. It turns out to be an unexpectedly lovely day. After taking Biff for a long walk, I switch on the fairy lights, get the fire going and spend the morning wrapping presents, including a red Guerlain lipstick for Delphine, a scented candle from posh French candle maker Cire Trudon for Travis, and at least half a dozen presents for friends' dogs. I gave Arnaud a box of handmade chocolates before he left to visit his sister in Bordeaux a few days ago. *'Merci, ma puce,'* he said, squeezing my hand. For a moment, I thought he might cry.

No sooner have I finished wrapping the presents than the doorbell rings. It's Steve and Sarah dropping off presents for Biff (a little Barbour style jacket) and me. They sit down by the crackling fire, while Biff jumps up behind them on the sofa and tries to drape himself around their shoulders. As I'm putting the kettle on, the doorbell rings again. This time it is Travis, who's been on one of his regular visits to the DIY stores around Poitiers. He looks exasperated.

'Well,' he says. 'I never thought I'd do an 80-kilometre round trip to buy a shelf bracket, only to find that they didn't have it in stock.'

I laugh. 'Welcome to the reality of renovating a house in France,' I say, remembering my own daily visits to

Castorama, 30 kilometres away.

As I serve the coffee by the glittering lights of the Christmas tree, I'm glad I bothered to buy it after all. The point of the tinsel and baubles and putting on a good show, I've realised, is that it's as much for other people as yourself. When I lived in London, the idea of guests showing up unannounced on Christmas Eve would have been unthinkable. But here in my French village, I've somehow managed to recreate the cosy, suburban Christmas of a BBC sitcom, where middle-class neighbours pop into each other's houses for a glass of sherry and a mince pie—or in this case, coffee and a slice of *bûche de Noël* (Christmas log).

Christmas Day itself is thankfully quiet and uneventful. Travis and I spend it with English friends, who have kindly invited several other expats to their farmhouse for a traditional Christmas lunch. We drink chilled champagne by a roaring fire, walk Biff over nearby fields after lunch and then settle down to watch the *Dr. Who* Christmas special (our host is an avid fan). Afterwards, I drive home along the dark, frosty roads, glad that Christmas is out of the way for another year.

The next hurdle to negotiate is New Year's Eve. I've booked a group of French and British friends including Travis and Delphine into The Mad Hatter's Kitchen, a farm restaurant in a charming rustic setting near Chaunay, 40 kilometres away. There is a brief moment of panic when Biff, who has been lying quietly at my feet, suddenly makes a break for the buffet table, but fortunately, Travis jumps up and manages to catch my little black terrier just before he sinks his teeth into the chicken liver terrine. At midnight, we clink champagne glasses, kiss cheeks and wish each other wonderful things in the year to come. Then, with New Year's Eve ticked off without tears or trauma—always an achievement, I think— we head home. As Delphine drives us along the foggy winding roads, I wonder what the year ahead will bring.

*　　　*　　　*

The year starts on a sobering note. One morning, early in January, I leave the house in darkness to catch a train to Lille and then London, relieved to see that it hasn't snowed. Instead, the road is glistening as if it has just rained. In high-heeled boots and pulling my case behind me, I march out of the house— and immediately receive a nasty shock. Suddenly, my heels seem to have a momentum of their own and are moving downhill at double-speed, one slippery step after another. It's as if the road has been sprayed with a mixture of water and olive oil.

I make it to my car without sustaining major injury and after thawing the weird-looking frost on the windscreen—it's clear rather than opaque—I set off for Poitiers, somehow imagining that the roads will be less slippery on four wheels. I don't make it very far. Just half a kilometre out of Villiers, my car slides across the road and swerves to a terrifying halt, narrowly avoiding a ditch. I'm too scared to go any further and turning around is too dangerous. The cars coming towards me are crawling along at about 20 kilometres an hour—in France!—which gives you some idea of how bad the conditions are. Behind me, it's a different story. In my rear mirror I can see the headlights of vehicles travelling at normal speeds, unaware of the treacherous conditions ahead. If they slide out of control, I will be first in line to be hit. Shaking, I get out to speak to the driver in front, who tells me that the problem is black ice, a phenomenon I've never encountered before. It seems that it has rained lightly on frozen ground, turning the main road into the proverbial skating rink.

'What's the best thing to do?' I ask.

'I don't know,' he shrugs.

Right now, catching the 8.20 am train couldn't seem less important. I sit in the darkness waiting for I don't know what. A gritting lorry? Daylight? I think about abandoning the car and walking home, but since there isn't a pavement to walk on, that would be even more dangerous. I'm relieved when, a few minutes later, I see the blue lights of the gendarmes in my rear window. 'What's happened?' they ask, drawing up alongside me. 'Has there been an accident?'

'The road is too bad to go any further.'

'Well, you can't stay here. It's too dangerous.'

They tell me that there is a small side road 500 metres ahead, where I will be able to turn around safely. Adrenals in overdrive, I restart the engine and manage to crawl home in first gear. I am forced to abandon the London trip but it feels like I've had a lucky escape.

As January limps on, it's hard to be jolly. Even the landscape looks depressed: the sky is a flat grey, the fields a dull brown. When I walk Biff in the mornings, there is a mournful mist hanging over the land and the grass is silvery with frost. I spend most of the day in front of my iMac and only venture out to go to the café or walk Biff. By mid-January I've got cabin fever, so when Delphine asks if I would like to go to a *steak frites* evening at the café in Puysoleil, I don't need to be persuaded. Even a soirée with sulky Pauline and scary Odile is preferable to sitting home alone.

I figure that the sisters in Puysoleil might have warmed up since the *moules frites* evening, which will at least have taught them how to calculate chip quantities. And anyway, it's hard to screw up steak and chips, which despite all the talk of snails and exotic animal entrails, is pretty much the French national dish. Delphine, eager to recruit custom for the café, suggests that we invite Arnaud along, but when I mention it to him he rolls his eyes and pulls a face of mock horror. Anyway it's not possible, he says, because he'll be attending another socialist convention in Poitiers.

By the time Saturday comes around, I'm really looking forward to the soirée. All day, I visualise a pile of crisp golden *frites* and a rose pink steak cooked to tender perfection. Delphine has also organised a small night market of local food producers in order to draw customers to the café. She collects me at 6.00 pm and, as we drive towards Puysoleil in her sedate green Rover, she tells me that she is 'ever so slightly miffed' because Pauline and Odile no longer want to open at weekends.

'Really? That's mad.'

'I know. I've told them and I'm absolutely perturbated [sic] by this, but they just shake their heads and say that they cannot work all hours; they need to have family time.'

'But the weekend is exactly when people are likely to go to the café,' I say. 'Sunday morning is the busiest time of the week at the bar in Villiers.'

'They say that no one was going, so it was not worth the petrol to go there to open up,' says Delphine, slowing down as we approach Puysoleil. 'We 'ave to be very careful as there are lots of wild boar in the woods and it can be very dangerous if you run into one.'

Wild boar and black ice: who knew that life

in France would involve so many hazards?

As we turn into the small village, I see a white butcher's van parked at the side of the café and a handful of stallholders stamping their feet to keep warm, their icy breath visible in the darkness. Even though it is mid-January, fake Christmas presents are still swinging from the municipal trees (I've noticed that many villages keep their decorations and *Joyeux Noël* banners up until the end of January, or even longer).

'Bruno and Rémi have been too busy gritting the roads to take those down,' says Delphine, as we pull up in front of the *mairie*.

'Perhaps when they've finished in Puysoleil, you could send them over to Villiers,' I say. 'There hasn't been much gritting going on there.'

Shivering, I wrap my scarf round my neck as we head towards the impromptu market.

'This butcher, Vincent, he is very good. He used to be a student of mine,' says Delphine. Through her part-time job as an English teacher at the agricultural college in Clussay, she has taught many of the region's hunters and farmers to discuss the weather and Barack Obama—on whom Delphine has a big crush—in *anglais*.

The butcher, who is in his late twenties, is delighted to see his former teacher. He talks us through his produce with enthusiasm, pointing out that his farm-reared chickens and guinea fowl, his beef and pork, have all been sourced locally from farmers that he knows personally. He was probably even on first name terms with the animals, who I'm quite sure have known grass, sky and Poitevin sunshine, rather than the interior of an industrial shed.

To support the local producers I spend lavishly, buying chicken breasts, a guinea fowl and some steak for *boeuf bourguignon*. At another trestle table, the butcher's (much older) girlfriend is selling a selection of Bordeaux wines from years that I know to be excellent—2003, 2006 and 2009. Delphine and I sample a few and again, to support the market (any excuse!), we each buy a couple of bottles of the 2003, the most expensive. And then finally, I buy several kilos of vegetables that I don't need from a young couple who are selling garden produce. It's a costly business visiting local markets, especially if other customers are thin on the ground, as I always feel obliged to step in and compensate.

Odile is standing in the doorway of the bar looking displeased. Delphine quietly explains that she is unhappy with the butcher. Not only is he using electricity from the café to power his van but, by offering wine tastings— even eggcup-sized ones—his girlfriend is discouraging people from buying drinks in the bar.

'Hmm. It's probably got more to do with the fact that Odile has stationed herself in the doorway like a pit bull,' I say.

'All the same, it might be diplomatic if we go inside and order some drinks.'

Odile steps aside reluctantly, like a nightclub bouncer, to let us in. Inside, her sister, who is standing guard over the bar, greets us with a half-grimace, half-smile. Only one other table in the restaurant is occupied— by an elderly French couple that look like they'd rather be checking into the Dignitas clinic in Switzerland, than dining here.

Pauline seats us at the table closest to them and then Rémi, a polite and gentle character, joins us along with the butcher, who is carrying a bottle of wine and a corkscrew. 'I have something else I would like you to taste' he says. Odile glares in our direction. If looks could kill, the butcher would be in intensive care right now.

Rémi and Vincent speak in a thick local dialect so I have to rely on Delphine to translate. 'Rémi is asking 'im if he 'as any pigs' ears,' explains Delphine.

'Pigs' ears? What do you do with those?' I reply in French.

'You simmer them for about five hours,' says Vincent. 'And then you can serve them hot or cold.'

'Cold pigs' ears?' I repeat, trying not to look appalled.

'Yes, they're very good with a little salad and vinaigrette dressing,' he replies.

'Aren't they a little . . . *crunchy?*'

'*Oui,*' says Rémi, rubbing his hands together in delight at the thought of the crunchiness.

'But they are cleaned out first, *non?*' says Delphine.

'Oh yes,' says the butcher. 'And when you boil them you can, if you like, add a carrot, onions, thyme and parsley. It is also possible to make a good pig ear pâté.'

'*Tout est bon dans le cochon,*' says Rémi. Everything is good in the pig.

'Oh yes,' says Delphine. 'This is what we say in France.'

'Nothing goes to waste apart from the nails,' says Vincent. 'Would anyone like to taste my pig ear pâté?'

Rémi nods vigorously, Delphine says '*Pourquoi pas?*' and I try to share everyone's enthusiasm. (What yummy dish, I wonder, do they make with the reproductive organs? Pig penis pâté?) Vincent disappears and returns with a plate, earning mega-glares from the sisters. On the plate is a large slab of pâté consisting of four layers, each a different colour and texture.

'What is that, exactly?' I say, pointing to the white outer edge, which looks like lard.

'That's the ears,' says Vincent, and then, pointing at the various sections of the pâté, 'that's the groin and those are the cheeks.'

Yum! They taste exactly as you might imagine—crunchy and gristly, just like munching on . . . ears.

'Here, have another slice,' says Vincent, as soon as I've managed to swallow the last chewy morsel. Fortunately, I'm saved by Pauline who marches over, with her hands on her hips, to ask if we are ready for our food. Vincent takes the hint and stands up to leave, along with Rémi.

'Are you sure you won't join us?' Delphine asks.

'Ah, *non*,' says Rémi, shaking his head with surprising vehemence.

Later, I wonder if he knew something that we didn't, for what follows is the most memorably awful meal of my life. The steak is not a delicate, juicy pink, but ash grey. I can only assume that the animal it came from had a terminal disease and a tortured life. It was probably on suicide watch. The chips— how can anyone go so wrong with chips?—are flaccid and pale and look like boiled potatoes that have been sliced up and smeared with grease. But by far the worse thing is the thick yellow sauce that has been dolloped over them.

Perhaps, I persuade myself, it tastes better than it looks. I put a small quantity into my mouth, which makes my taste buds squeal with shock and my throat tighten. The sauce is sweet, before evolving into something cloying and sour. It manages to violate several senses at once: the taste, the sickly smell, the hideous colour. It's the intense yellow of rancid butter, which, it suddenly dawns on me, is what it might be—and not just slightly 'off', but centuries old. It has probably been decomposing since the Revolution.

Delphine asks for salt, causing Odile to shake her head in surprise. 'No one else has asked for salt,' she says. I'm tempted to ask for an enema. I imagine the forkful that I've just eaten sitting in my stomach like a spent nuclear rod, releasing toxic waste for the rest of my life. Delphine is silent as she soldiers valiantly on.

'Are you OK?' she asks.

I nod and down a glass of water. Without even trying to be discreet, I scrape away the sauce and feed bits of the mouse-coloured meat to Biff under the table. Even he seems reluctant, so I leave the festering pile of dead animal on my plate. Twenty or so nauseous minutes later, Pauline reappears. Arms folded and oozing self-satisfaction, you'd think that she had served up a Michelin-starred meal rather than something close to baby vomit.

'I hope it pleased you,' she says, ignoring all evidence to the contrary. Delphine manages a smile but her face looks pained. Pauline then asks if we would like dessert. Honestly, what kind of mugs does she take us for? We each hand over €15 euros and leave. As we drive home, my stomach rumbling with hunger, I wish I'd eaten more of the pigs' ears.

The following morning, a Sunday, I take Biff for a long walk and decide to go out for a coffee in the café before bunkering down for a solitary day of work. I can't stay in my house like a prisoner at weekends forever. Anyway, I haven't seen The Devil since the pre-Christmas encounter and I'm beginning to wonder if he's still in the village. But just in case, and as a matter of pride, I head to the café in skinny jeans with knee boots. I'm even wearing make-up, though cleverly applied to look like I'm not. The overall effect is very French: making an effort to look like you haven't.

I push open the door to the café and am instantly engulfed by the steam, the screech of the espresso machine and the inviting aroma of ground coffee. On Sunday mornings the café is always buzzing. It's the social high point of the week, with everyone piling in before lunchtime. The Portuguese community, including several of Luis's macho colleagues and their wives, have commandeered a table at the very back, but Luis, I'm relieved to see, isn't with them. I order a *petit crème* and sit at a small table facing the door.

I haven't been there long when the door opens and Luis slips in, clean-shaven and dressed in dark grey jeans and a denim jacket. It's obvious that he has just stepped out of the shower. He's alone, which is unusual as he normally travels in a pack, and he's not his usual swaggering self. He seems chastened, almost humble. Why, I wonder, is his girlfriend not with him? As he stands at the bar with his back to me, I notice his underwear, a flash of turquoise cotton, visible above his jeans and against the brown skin of his back. I'm ashamed to say that I feel nothing but lust.

He nods *'Bonjour'* to several people, says something to Marguerite who is behind the bar and then heads towards the back of the café. I keep my eyes down, with Arnaud's words ringing in my ears: 'Act like he doesn't exist! Don't acknowledge him in any way!'

As soon as he passes my table, I jump up as if I've been poked with an electric cattle prod and gulp down the remainder of my coffee standing at the bar. I need to put as much distance as possible between The Devil and myself. I'm worried that to spend even a few minutes in close proximity is to be pulled dangerously back towards him. As I stand at the bar, my hand shaking as I lift my coffee cup, it feels like a bomb has gone off again in my heart. Marguerite flashes me a sympathetic smile as if she knows what is going on. Luis and I don't have to talk to each other or make eye contact. Delphine says that people can just feel that there is, or rather *was*, something between us.

I walk home feeling, as Delphine would say, 'perturbated.' 'Get a grip,' I tell myself. I'm over forty years old and acting like a teenager.

The truth is, I can't believe how pathetically pleased I am to have seen Luis and to know that he is still in the village. I'm ashamed to admit it, but months after discovering him with the blonde, I still feel attracted to him, which is *so* wrong. I've never been good at bearing grudges, but now I'm starting to wonder if I'm missing a microchip in my emotional circuitry.

That evening, Arnaud knocks on my door, high on the experience of having met Ségolène Royal, the President of the Poitou-Charentes, at a socialist convention over the weekend. He's carrying several foil-covered dishes, apparently left over from the event.

'*Tout bio,*' (all organic) he declares, for he's noticed my obsession with organic vegetables.

I invite him into the *petit salon*. '*Excuse-moi, c'est le bordel ici,*' I say, using the slang phrase for 'it's a mess in here.' I point at Biff, who is sitting in his doughnut looking quite saintly. 'It's his fault.'

This makes Arnaud laugh. My neighbour can normally be relied upon to laugh loudly at almost anything, but this is laughter of the deepest and most genuine kind.

'*Oh, la, la,*' he says, in paroxysms of unstoppable mirth.

'I'm not joking. It really is his fault,' I say, mystified as to why this is so funny.

'*Biff, tu es très vilain,*' (you are very naughty), says Arnaud, wagging his finger at him with more loud laughter.

Biff fixes him with regal black eyes, surveying his kingdom as if it were filled with precious jewels rather than bits of shredded paper, shoes, socks and other random items stolen from my bedroom. The wood burner, meanwhile, seems to be oozing ash—I haven't swept it out in a week—and there is a thick layer of dust over everything. Upstairs, the bedroom window is still patched up with a piece of cardboard. It's fair to say that I'm not on top of things. Most mornings, it feels like a gargantuan feat to just get myself out of bed and into the shower, where I've taken to washing my hair with Biff's anti-flea shampoo as I've run out of my own. I have so little energy that even the simplest tasks are beyond me.

'Look!' says Arnaud. 'There is a carrot salad, some chicken pâté and *farci poitevin*.' (The latter is a regional delicacy consisting of stuffed cabbage leaves.)

'I brought this back for you, my little flea,' he says. 'Because I know you are working very hard on your articles.'

'Well, it's very kind of you to think of me,' I say.

Before my neighbour leaves, he tells me that he has found out some information about *la blonde*. She and Luis are still together, he tells me. 'But from what I hear, they're always fighting and shouting. He doesn't love her, that's for sure.'

The following morning, I wake to find that the temperature has plunged below zero again, highlighting the fact that I'm down to my last few logs of wood. Back in September, lulled into a false sense of security by all the talk of global warming, and imagining that the winter would be a mild one, I made the rash decision not to order any wood. I figured that once the small stash of logs from the previous year's delivery had gone, I would tough it out by wearing an extra jumper or two and by judicious use of the (very) expensive oil-fired central heating. As an extra precaution, I bought a few thermal vests. But this strategy is not going to get me through February and March. I need the comfort of a real fire to take the edge off the biting cold and the long nights alone.

Galvanised into action by the glacial wind that is blowing through the kitchen, I phone Monsieur Rousseau, the farmer who usually supplies the wood. He informs me that sadly he has none left. And anyway, his tractor has broken down. As an emergency measure, I go up to the attic and locate my extreme weather kit, which includes a pair of sheepskin snow boots by Sorel, a Canadian brand good for temperatures of up to minus 20 degrees. They were acquired on expenses over a decade ago, during my tenure as fashion editor of a national newspaper. A few weeks before Christmas, I was called into the deputy editor's office and given a very special assignment: the chairman's son had written a piece about weddings in ski resorts and I was to produce a superlative picture to match.

'Spend whatever you need to,' said the deputy editor. 'Buy anything you like and hire whoever you want. Stay on and ski for a week if you want to.' (As if! I'd never been near a ski slope until that point.) 'Just make sure that you send back a bloody good picture,' he concluded. It goes without saying that the country wasn't in financial crisis at the time. And so Corinne, my long-suffering but loyal assistant, and I ordered a three-tiered wedding cake, champagne, confetti and an extravagant bouquet of dried bridal flowers—all carefully packed into trunks, along with an assortment of big white wedding dresses. I then went to a mountaineering shop and kitted us both out with Arctic survival gear.

The ensuing trip to Verbiers was one of my more enjoyable trips as a fashion editor. Unusually for a fashion shoot, no one had a personality disorder, and despite lots of standing around in temperatures of minus 17 degrees, there were lots of perks to the assignment, namely drinking copious amounts of *glühwein* to stay warm and watching members of the British army on cold weather manoeuvres nearby.

I look back fondly on that trip as I pull on the Sorel boots along with thick ski socks, thermal leggings, jeans, a black fake fur gilet and a knitted alpaca hat. The look—which is best described as 'gorilla-chic-meets-Scott-of-the-Antarctic'—is one that could potentially scare the French neighbours, but at least it's warm.

I head over to the Café du Commerce, the one café in the village that is open on a Monday. Arnaud and Basile are already installed on the beige vinyl banquettes, along with a couple of their old pals. They immediately start laughing when they see me, and it's not just because of what I'm wearing. I hear the phrase *c'est le bordel ici* and know immediately what they are talking about. I'm beginning to wonder if it's my use of the word *bordel*, which also means 'brothel' in French, but I've used the expression many times before to describe domestic chaos without inspiring such mirth. Eventually, it turns out that it's because I'm blaming Biff that everyone finds it so funny. Still, it makes me feel like the Dorothy Parker of the Poitou-Charentes.

'Listen!' I say, when they've all stopped laughing. 'Does anyone know where I can buy some wood?' There is silence for a minute and then a collective shaking of heads.

'It's not the right time of year,' says Basile.

'But don't worry, my little flea,' says Arnaud, squeezing my hand. 'Leave it with me and I will make some enquiries.'

Later that afternoon, he raps on my window

to tell me that it's not going to be easy. Not only am I asking at the wrong time of year—sensible people replenished their woodpile months ago—but there is also a general shortage this year. This is because of a sudden crackdown by the local authorities on *le marché noir*, or black market supply. Farmers who might previously have hacked down some trees on their land and sold it cash-in-hand, are now worried about being caught. And, thanks to the resulting shortage, Arnaud tells me, the price per *corde* or cubic metre has increased significantly. 'But don't worry,' he says, tapping the side of his nose, 'I have found you a source.'

He tells me that he can arrange for a *corde* to be delivered at midday on Saturday. Shortly before noon on the appointed day, he knocks on my door to check that I'm ready. Super-caffeinated as usual, he is hopping around with excitement as we throw open the garage doors and wait for the delivery. A short while later, Basile draws up in his van so that he, too, can share in the excitement.

After twenty minutes or so of standing around in the cold with no sign of the delivery, Arnaud looks at his watch and then makes a phone call. He tells me that they have been delayed and will now be arriving at 2.00 pm instead. We go back into our respective houses and reconvene at the appointed hour. Once again, I open the garage doors in readiness and we both pace around outside, Arnaud pulling on a cigarette. I notice one of my neighbours watching through her net curtains. The whole street seems excited about my wood delivery. But still there is no sign of it. My wood broker phones his secret suppliers again and is given the new estimated arrival time of 4.00 pm. But again, the delivery doesn't arrive.

Eventually, six hours later than arranged and under the cover of darkness, two furtive-looking men show up in a battered white transit van. Looking nervous, they throw open the rear doors. Even with an untrained eye, I can see that the cache of sodden logs inside won't amount to even half a cubic metre. Something tells me that I am about to be ripped off.

'I'm really not sure about this,' I say to Arnaud. 'The wood is soaking wet. And the logs are too big.'

He tells me that it doesn't matter, that the important thing is that it is 'seasoned'—left to dry out for a year or so after cutting—but I'm not convinced. Lighting a fire is not easy even with dry wood. Damp logs will not only generate a great deal of smoke but also gum up the chimney.

'I'm sorry,' I say, glad to have a reason to decline the delivery. 'I don't want this wood. It is too wet.'

Arnaud relays this message to the two men and an animated discussion follows. They try to dismiss my objections but I just shake my head. Arnaud says that it is not a problem as Félix, the artist who lives on the square, needs some wood, so they might be able to sell it to him. He makes another call and then nods at the two men. Then they all jump in the van and drive off.

A week later, I find a more expensive but legal supply of wood from a registered dealer. The wood, a mixture of oak and hornbeam, is expensive but it's dry and cut-to-size. Arnaud volunteers to help stock the mound of logs once it has been deposited in my garage.

It takes us two hours of hard, physical labour to ferry the wood to the back of the garage and stack it in a pile. Despite the cold, Arnaud is pink in the face and sweating profusely. He really should cut down on the caffeine and the cigarettes, I think to myself. When we've finished, we head over to the café in the half-light of the winter afternoon, with Biff trotting along beside us and I think how really very lucky I am to have such a kind and helpful neighbour.

Chapter 8

Valentine's Day

February arrives and with it an intriguing offer. Walking down rue St Benoit with Biff one lunchtime, I'm stopped by a lean, athletic looking man on a bike. He's in his early forties, with short, sandy hair and glasses. I've seen him before—he always looks cheerful and fashionably dressed—and he's nodded a friendly *'bonjour'* several times. He and his wife own one of the boutiques on the square.

He hops off his bike and holds out his hand with a big smile. He introduces himself as Pierre-Antoine before pointing to my bedroom window, which is still patched up with cardboard. 'I can fix that for you if you'd like,' he says.

'Oh, it's very kind but really not necessary,' I reply, as I don't want a strange man poking about in my bedroom—and especially not a married one.

'Really, it's no problem. I enjoy doing DIY,' he says. 'I could come this evening and take the measurements.'

'Um, no . . . I won't be there,' I lie, horrified, because my bedroom, like the rest of the house, looks like the aftermath of a freak weather event.

'Well, tomorrow evening then. Any time after 7.00 pm,' he persists. 'It won't take long. You must be losing quite a lot of heat through that window.'

I look up at the cardboard patch. It really is an eyesore and it will have to be fixed at some point. And so, on the spur of the moment, I accept his offer.

The following evening he arrives on my doorstep, beaming. I guide him through the *petit salon*, which looks as if it was recently pulverised by a twister, with a selection of my shoes and clothes strewn across the floor. I almost got round to picking them up earlier, but figured that Biff would only ferry them down from the bedroom again. Feeling embarrassed—there is something that doesn't feel right about this—I lead the way up to my bedroom with Biff scampering along behind us.

Pierre-Antoine spreads a piece of plastic on the floor by the window and unpacks some tools from a small canvas bag. He sets to work in an assured way, knocking out the remaining fragments of glass. He tells me that he loves working on old houses and has made lots of improvements to his own apartment above the shop. He uses the word 'I' rather than 'we' and makes no mention of his wife. Biff, meanwhile, has propped himself up with pillows on the bed and, like an eager chaperone, is watching our guest's every move with gimlet black eyes.

Pierre-Antoine is very methodical. After sweeping up the glass and plaster, he then measures the broken panel, writing down the dimensions in a little notebook. He tells me that he is going into Poitiers tomorrow morning—Monday is his day off—and will get the glass cut at Castorama. He will come at lunchtime to fit it.

'I'm really very grateful,' I say, mystified—and in truth, a little disquieted—by this random act of kindness.

'It's nothing,' he says with a radiant smile. 'Any time you need anything fixed, just let me know. I'm very good with my hands.'

'*Ah bon?*' I say, wondering if his wife knows about the time that he is spending in my bedroom. Before he leaves, I try to give him some money to buy the glass, but he waves it away.

'We can sort out payment another time,' he says.

'I wonder what kind of payment he has in mind?' says Travis, when I tell him, later.

'Oh, stop it. He's just being a good neighbour.'

'Yeah, right. He's already taken the fast-track route into your bedroom. He'll have his pyjamas under the pillow before you know it.'

'No way,' I say. And I mean it. Having proved that I have zero judgement when it comes to the male of the species, I am not prepared to put myself through the emotional

128

blender again. My plan is to live a quiet, simple life, finding happiness in ways that don't involve a man.

Pierre-Antoine returns at lunchtime the following day, carrying a tube of putty and a piece of bubble-wrapped glass.

'*Bonjour, Ka-renne!*' he cries with a disarming grin as he bends down to pat Biff. In my opinion, he looks quite dressed up for window fixing, in beige jeans, a slim-fitting paisley shirt and a brown leather jacket. Once again, I lead him up into my bedroom, where he unpacks the glass and squeezes the tube of putty. Nothing comes out.

'I'm afraid it's a little hard,' he says.

'That's a shame,' I say.

He tells me that he is busy for the next few nights but will come back on Friday evening with some new putty. 'That's if you are not doing anything?'

'No, I'll be here.'

'Then would you like to have dinner with me?'

My God, I think to myself. This man is utterly brazen. A *dragueur extraordinaire*. If he is going to cheat on his wife, he could at least target a woman in another village.

'I'm sorry. I'm very busy at the moment,' I say, trying to sound as stern as possible.

'*D'accord, c'est pas grave,*' (OK, it's no big deal), he says with another big smile.

On Friday evening he arrives with the right

129

kind of putty. I let him into my bedroom again and he fixes the glass in place, but still the business is not finished. The old wooden frame is disintegrating, so Pierre-Antoine has used little supports to hold the glass until the putty has set. He tells me that he can come over on Sunday morning to remove them.

'Sunday morning?' I say, surprised, for Sunday is Valentine's Day. 'Surely you want to spend the morning with your wife?'

Now it is Pierre-Antoine's turn to look surprised. 'What wife?' he says.

'The woman with dark hair who wears sunglasses on her head and is often with you.'

'That's not my wife. That's my sister, Héloïse.'

'Are you sure?'

'Yes. Absolutely sure. You've seen me talking to her because she owns the lingerie shop next door to mine.' He is, he insists, a *célibataire*—the horribly literal French word for a single person.

'Sorry about that,' I say, worried that I might have offended him. 'Sunday morning would be great.'

'Wow, straight guys are really devious,' says Travis, when I tell him. 'He's coming over on Valentine's Day in order to make doubly sure that you don't have a boyfriend.'

'Don't be silly. It's just that he works every other day apart from Monday.'

'Of course,' says Travis. 'And he's already

managed to stretch out fixing the window to three visits and counting. What else is he hoping to busy his hands with before he leaves?'

On Sunday morning, Pierre-Antoine arrives earlier than expected. I'm still in bed when he rings the bell, so I quickly throw on tracksuit bottoms, a sweater and the black gorilla gilet that has become my default winter outfit. I answer the door barefoot and looking quite scary. Unfazed, Pierre-Antoine greets me with another beaming smile. I lead him upstairs, where the bed is unmade and there are clothes strewn across the floor, but he appears not to notice.

'*Voilà!*' he says, when he has removed the supports from the window. 'Things should warm up in your bedroom now.'

'*Ah bon?*' I reply, and then, feeling guilty for having pigeon-holed him as a scheming adulterer, I offer him a coffee. As we sit awkwardly at the kitchen table, buffeted by the chilly breeze blowing through the windows and door, Pierre-Antoine eyes the gaps around the frames with concern.

'You could gain a couple of degrees in here just by filling those holes with insulation tape,' he says. 'I'm not joking.' Then, warming to his subject, he tells me that it is possible to have special double-glazing panels made to fit over old windows without ruining the appearance. 'I've got them in my apartment. Come over and have a look, if you like,' he says.

I feign interest in his insulating panels in order to keep the conversation on neutral ground. (Many French people, I've noticed, are obsessed by insulation, double-glazing and 'gaining degrees'.) But somehow Pierre-Antoine switches the subject to tennis. He asks if I play. I shake my head.

'I'm a member of a club,' he says. 'But it's all men. Unfortunately.' He gives me a coy smile, which I ignore. He tells me he likes very much 'the sport,' and lists kayaking, running, cycling and swimming as his main hobbies. I tell him I don't like any of those things.

'But I've seen you many times on your bike with your little dog,' he says.

'Ah, yes,' I reply, my cheeks reddening at being caught out. 'It's true. I sometimes cycle in the countryside. Now, what do I owe you for the glass?'

Pierre-Antoine is reluctant to accept any money but I insist. It's less than €20—a fraction of what I would have had to pay a builder to do the job. Finally, he gets up to leave, but not before assessing the heat-saving opportunities in the hallway.

'*Oh, la, la*, you are throwing money out of windows there,' he says pointing to the thin, ill-fitting door that leads to the garage. 'The heat from the radiator is going directly into the garage. You need to build another door behind this one. I could do that for you

132

if you like?'

I decline as this could mean him visiting my house for another decade. 'Listen!' he says, as I'm about to close the door. 'Would you like to go for a bike ride on Monday afternoon? I know some good routes. And you can bring your little dog.'

It seems churlish to refuse given that he has just fixed my window. And anyway, I might discover some new cycle tracks. 'OK,' I say. 'What time?'

As Pierre-Antoine leaves, Ruigi just happens to be coming out of his door further up the street. With a bit of luck, word will reach The Devil that I had a man in my house on Valentine's Day. I clip on Biff's lead to take him out for a walk, heading for a farm track a couple of kilometres from the village. If it wasn't for the biting cold, it could almost be spring: birds are tweeting and there is a weak sun in the wan blue sky. But, trudging along the grassy track, I can't help but feel sad as I think back to Valentine's Day last year. It was a Saturday, but by late afternoon I hadn't heard from Luis, so I walked over to the café to meet Delphine.

'I'm sure Luis will not disappoint you,' she said with a conviction that made my heart sing. 'I'm absolutely certain of it.'

And sure enough, as I was walking back down rue St Benoit in the semi-darkness, my phone rang.

'*Chérie*,' said a familiar growl of a voice. '*C'est moi, Luis.*' (As if I could possibly have mistaken him for anyone else.) I wanted to burst into tears of happiness that he had finally called.

'Where are you?' I demanded.

'*Chez moi,*' he replied. 'Listen, I am just about to take a shower and I will come over to your house at seven and we can have dinner together.'

'But where have you been all day?'

'*Chérie*, I had things to do. I will see you shortly.'

He arrived at my house at 7.30 pm—excellent timekeeping by his standards—and I was blown away by the effort that he had made. He looked and smelled gorgeous, his skin smooth and newly shaven. He'd also had a haircut—nothing dramatic, he looked like Luis, only better. Smartly dressed in a black shirt, jeans and a new tailored jacket in place of his usual bright colours and casual clothes, he looked like a rock star.

He kissed me passionately on the lips and handed me three roses—one red, one pink and one white—beautifully wrapped in cellophane and tied with red ribbon. Of all the flowers that I've received in my life, none has ever moved me as much as that simple bouquet. It was a beautiful gesture and much more in keeping with my tastes than a flashy bouquet of red roses. I felt a wave of pure, unadulterated love. He also gave me a bottle of scented oil and a CD of romantic music with a red heart on the front, called *Touchés En Plein Coeur*—a play on words meaning 'touched' or 'hit' in the heart, though 'stabbed in the heart' would have been more appropriate, given subsequent events.

I pulled him into the *petit salon,* where the fire was roaring and Biff was bouncing on and off the sofa, his joy mirroring mine. Displayed prominently on the fireplace was a mystery Valentine's card that had arrived in the morning post, probably from a former boyfriend. I had hoped it would provoke a reaction but annoyingly, Luis made no comment. When I brought it to his attention, he just said very simply, 'Put it in the bin *chérie,* please,' as if it were of no consequence. I did as I was told, half annoyed by his lack of jealousy and half amused by his calm self-assurance that there could be no rival for my love. Or more likely, given what I know now, he just didn't care.

I wonder if *la blonde* is being similarly feted with roses and romantic CDs today. I clip Biff back on his lead and we head home, where I discover that I'm out of dog biscuits and have nothing to give him for breakfast. There is only one thing for it: a trip to Intermarché. I look at my watch: 11.30 am. This is the most dangerous half-hour in the week, with a very high chance that The Devil will be in the supermarket before it closes at midday. I go upstairs and carry out a speedy makeover, twisting my hair up in a chignon and swapping my shaggy gilet and cold weather clothes for heels and my navy coat. If I bump into The Devil today, I want him to think that I'm en route to an interesting Valentine's assignation rather than staying home alone in trackie bottoms.

I make it to the supermarket with five minutes to spare. I get the dog biscuits and then, feeling emboldened, I make the mistake of heading to the dairy section to buy some yoghurt. That's when I see him, standing near the fish counter in a checked shirt and a new leather jacket. There is no sign of *la blonde*. But it pains me to see what he is looking at: smoked salmon. With a heavy heart, I march out of the supermarket with the sack of dog biscuits, grateful that he didn't see me. And then, on the spur of the moment, I stop off at the café. (I figure that Luis will be going straight home to *la blonde*.) Arnaud is sitting at a table inside and beckons me to join him.

'You are looking very nice today, my little flea. Are you going anywhere special?'

'No. I just um . . . felt like making an effort.'

Arnaud raises an eyebrow and orders me a coffee.

'How is your arm?' I ask.

He tells me that he is still signed off work but has been very busy all week, distributing

136

pamphlets on behalf of the socialist party. Apparently, his former boss is not taking it very well and has been threatening him. We've been chatting for about ten minutes when the door opens and in walks Luis with his bag of groceries. On his own. He orders a coffee and drinks it at the bar, looking like he is in no hurry to leave. Arnaud gives me a significant look.

'I know,' I say. 'I think I'd better be going.'

'I'll come with you,' says Arnaud, as I put some coins on the table to pay for the coffees. He stands up and puts his arm out as if to protect me from The Devil as we move towards the door.

'It's funny,' says Arnaud, as we walk home. 'You never see him with his girlfriend.'

'It's true,' I reply, deriving some solace from that.

Late the following afternoon, Pierre-Antoine arrives on his bike, wearing beige jeans and a grey zip-up fleece. Biff hops and jumps around in a state of extreme excitement as I get my bike out of the garage. I loop his lead over the handlebars and we set off at a surprising pace. Pierre-Antoine seems to think he is competing in the Tour de France and as we cycle along the curving uphill road, he makes no allowance for the fact that I'm struggling to keep a small, excitable terrier under control. After a couple of kilometres, we turn off the main road and onto a churned muddy path. I set Biff free while I concentrate on not ending up with my face in the sticky mud.

After a stressful half-hour of concentrating, pedalling and trying to respond to Pierre-Antoine's conversation—he keeps turning around and pointing things out, such as the river where he likes to go kayaking—the narrow path opens onto a flat landscape of red-orange earth. My cycling companion is relentlessly cheerful, talking about the benefits of regular exercise, being outdoors and appreciating nature. He and Travis should get together, I think, as we cycle along.

It's nearly dark when we arrive back in Villiers. Biff and I are both panting and covered in mud. Pierre-Antoine, who has hardly broken a sweat, asks if I would like to come up to his apartment for a drink but I decline, saying that I have work to do. He tells me that he is going to Paris tomorrow to do a course. 'We can meet up when I get back on Thursday,' he says, kissing me on the cheeks. 'I will give you a call. *À bientôt, Ka-renne.*'

On Thursday, he calls to invite me for a lunchtime coffee in his apartment. I decline, as I'm busy writing about jumpsuits. Later, as I'm walking around the square with Biff in the afternoon, he emerges from his shop to ask if I would like to have an aperitif with him that evening. He's very keen to show me his insulating panels.

I tell him I already have plans (I don't) and he immediately suggests tomorrow evening instead. I hesitate just long enough for it to be obvious I don't have anything planned and then feel obliged to accept his invitation.

'*Génial!*' (Brilliant!), he declares. 'See you tomorrow, any time after seven. *Bonne après-midi, Ka-renne.*'

Chapter 9

Dinner with Pierre-Antoine

Just as I'm about to go over to Pierre-Antoine's apartment, the doorbell rings. It's Arnaud, carrying a tray of food.

'I've made you some dinner, my little flea, as you looked like you needed cheering up,' he says, marching into the kitchen and unveiling roast guinea fowl with mashed potato and a slice of homemade lemon tart. This is very unexpected since, strictly speaking, it is my turn to cook for him. It's also an upping of the ante since Arnaud seems to have made quite an effort with tonight's menu.

'This is really very kind of you, Arnaud. But I'm just about to go out.'

'You're going out?' He looks taken aback.

'Yes, for an aperitif with Pierre-Antoine, the owner of the fashion boutique.'

'Oh,' says Arnaud. 'Well, don't worry. You can reheat the food tomorrow.'

'It's just a quick drink,' I say. 'I'm not staying out all night.'

'Well, have a good evening,' says Arnaud, heading for the door, a look of disappointment on his face.

I feel bad, as if I'm somehow betraying my fellow *célibataire* by going out when he is staying home with his cat. Actually, I envy him as I'd much rather be staying at home too.

Pierre-Antoine phones at 7.30 pm to check that I haven't forgotten tonight's invitation and to tell me that I can bring 'the little dog.' This is good news, as Biff has picked up on the fact that I am going out and is skipping around the *petit salon*, tossing my shoes into the air with excitement.

I throw on my passion-killing quilted coat that I bought specifically for dog walking, and head out into the shivery darkness. I've bought my host a good bottle of Bordeaux to thank him for fixing my window, but otherwise I haven't gone to any effort.

The air is filled with the scent of woodsmoke as I cross the square and ring the bell as Pierre-Antoine instructed. He comes down to let me in via the shop. It's the first time that I've been inside his boutique, which is full of asymmetrical clothing in crinkly fabrics, with frills, flaps and twiddly bits. Pierre-Antoine sells men's clothes, too, very

140

similar to those that he wears himself: namely, patterned shirts and jeans in a palette of sludgy neutrals. I notice that the mannequin in the window is wearing the very same brown paisley shirt and beige jeans that Pierre-Antoine wore on the day that he came to apply the putty to my windowpane.

He shows me through to a room at the back, where the extra stock is kept. The room is charming with wooden floorboards and French windows. There are various pieces of droopy clothing hanging in polythene bags on the walls, and a small table with a sewing machine positioned in front of a casement window.

'I had no idea your shop was so big,' I say.

'Ah yes, I'm enormous downstairs,' he replies in French, and I start to wonder if all these double entendres are deliberate. 'Follow me,' he says, opening the French doors and switching on an outside light.

I follow him out to a paved courtyard and a big barn opposite. 'This is my garage,' he says, pointing to a red sports car and an old BMW. He also points out his kayak, his skis and his collection of bicycles. It feels like a session of the kindergarten game, Show and Tell.

'We could go kayaking together when the weather gets warmer,' he says.

'Um . . . ' I say, shivering in the darkness.

It's a relief when we go back inside and climb the narrow wooden staircase to his apartment. He shows me into the sitting room, which has two windows overlooking the square. The decor is stylish but comfortable, with two battered leather armchairs, a big pot plant and a red Turkish rug over the wooden floor. There is a dining table in the middle of the room and a modern, open-plan kitchen to the left.

'This is very nice,' I say.

'Thank you. You can let your little dog free if you like,' he says, which immediately endears him to me. I let Biff loose and he runs into the kitchen to see what's cooking—nothing very much by the looks of it—while Pierre-Antoine opens a bottle of sparkling wine.

'I brought this for you,' I say, handing him the bottle of Bordeaux. 'A little thank-you for fixing my window.'

'It was no trouble to fix your window. I enjoyed doing it,' he says. 'But this is a very nice bottle of wine. I will keep it and one day we will drink it together.'

'Oh no,' I say. 'It's a present for you.'

My host places two glasses on the table and pours the sparkling wine, while I admire his old-fashioned fireplace. 'This must be so nice on a cold winter evening,' I say.

He shrugs. 'I only light it on very special occasions.'

'Oh, what a shame. I suppose it's a hassle to carry the logs upstairs?'

'It's because I have to think of my shop stock,' he says.

'You're worried that the clothes might catch fire?'

'No. I don't want them to smell of smoke. For the same reason, I don't cook anything with a strong smell.' He shakes his head, looking grave. 'I have to be careful. Garlic and onions are out of the question.'

'*Ah bon?*'

'Imagine if my clients were to walk into the shop and smell food cooking. This would not be professional. Not at all.' Pierre-Antoine shakes his head to emphasise the horror of this scenario. I shake my head too, for he has just given me a snapshot of his life as a *célibataire* living above the shop, forever consigned to eating bland food.

Still, at least his apartment is well insulated. He's gained at least three, possibly four degrees in here, he says, since he installed the detachable panels over his windows. He gives me a little demonstration of how they clip on over the old frames.

'*Merveilleuse!*' I say. Marvellous!

'I've got them in my bedroom, too,' he says, nodding at a closed door across the corridor. Fortunately, he does not suggest that we go in there. Instead, he sits down very close to me and pours the wine.

'So who looks after the shop while you're away?' I ask.

'My mother. Fortunately, she lives very close by,' he replies.

143

I ask about his training course in Paris and he tells me he has been learning to identify different types of customer. The easiest, he says, as he hands me a glass of wine, are the *'fidèles'*. They are polite, like to have a chat and trust the owner's judgement. 'They are the most likely to say "I need a jean or "I need a jumper to go with this skirt",' he explains.

I nod, marvelling at the idea that anyone shops in this way. Then there are the *'affairistes'* who sound as if they are up to serial naughtiness but in fact, Pierre-Antoine explains, they are looking for a bargain, not a love affair. The very worst kind of customer is the category known as the *'indépendante.'* *'Oh, la, la,'* he says, shaking his head at the thought of them.

It seems that they don't like to be helped, they often don't say hello and they can be very impolite. They know exactly what they want and they'll walk out of a shop within minutes if they don't see it. 'They are a shopkeeper's nightmare,' Pierre-Antoine concludes with a shudder.

I keep quiet about the fact that I am most definitely an *'indépendante.'*

'This wine is very nice,' I say.

'It's from my cousin's vineyard. Maybe we could go there one day.'

'Well, I'm very busy at the moment.'

He gets out his laptop to show me the notes from his training course. After a while, I allow myself to look tired and bored. I'm so over making an effort with men. I tell him I have to go and give the dog his dinner. Before I leave, he shows me pictures of his holiday apartment in La Rochelle.

'It's small, but close to the ocean, with great views. We will go there together in the summer,' he says.

Not likely, I think to myself. La Rochelle is a place I avoid as it has memories of my former French boyfriend and, on another occasion, a bad case of oyster poisoning.

'You will like it,' he insists. 'We can leave on Sunday morning—never Saturday, because I have to work—and come back late on Monday.'

This seems a little presumptuous given that it appears to be a studio apartment. He's obviously counting on us being on very close terms by then.

'Well, I must be going,' I say. Pierre-Antoine looks disappointed but tells me that next week, when he is less busy, he will take me to a restaurant in Poitiers that has live jazz music. I'm tempted to tell him that I'd rather spend the evening on the phone to France Telecom customer services—an experience I wouldn't wish on anyone—than listen to random blasts of loud saxophone. Instead, I say something non-committal and get up to go. Pierre-Antoine lets me back out through the shop and kisses me goodnight on both cheeks.

I walk back across the square exhausted by the dizzying array of plans he has made for me— visits to vineyards, kayaking, mini-breaks in La Rochelle and live jazz. It makes me even more determined to spend the next few months alone and behind closed doors.

The following morning Arnaud taps on the window. 'How did it go last night?' he asks. 'Did he try to seduce you?'

I laugh. 'No. He did not. But he showed me his sports car.'

'Pah!' says Arnaud. 'He has money so he thinks he can have anyone he wants.'

'Well, not me,' I say. 'I'm not impressed by money or cars.'

Arnaud looks sceptical. 'I'm just warning you, my little flea. Be careful.'

I spend the morning answering work-related emails and then, in the afternoon, allow myself a trip to Intermarché to buy some chocolate biscuits. Walking home, I see a thin blonde woman playfully creeping towards the pale green door of Luis's apartment with a bag of groceries.

'Excuse me,' I find myself saying in French. 'Are you the person I found in Luis's bedroom?'

'Yes, it's me,' she says, entirely devoid of guilt or embarrassment. 'Why?'

'There is something I would really like to know. That day that I found you with Luis, how long had you been seeing him?'

146

'Not long. Maybe a couple of weeks. But it was never serious with you. He told me.'

'Really?' I say, fighting the urge to tell her that Luis asked me to have a child with him.

She puts her shopping down. Then she narrows her sly, cat-like eyes and holds out her left hand to show me a gold ring.

'We're getting married,' she says. 'I told him at Christmas, either a ring or it's over.'

'Well done,' I say, feeling gutted, but taking some solace in the fact that The Devil didn't surrender the ring willingly. Triumphant, *la blonde* starts to walk away, swinging her hips in her too-tight jeans, and tossing her long blonde hair. I'm doubly upset, knowing how fiercely The Lion values his space and privacy, to see that she has keys to his apartment. That hurts way more than the gold ring. Biff sits patiently at my feet, looking up at me with doleful eyes. But *la blonde* is not done yet. She hesitates before turning the key in the lock and looks over at me again, her face twisted into a scornful expression.

'I knew all about you,' she says. 'Luis told me everything.'

'Really?' I think back to the scene in the bedroom when she declared that she had 'no idea' that Luis had a girlfriend. I knew at the time that she was lying.

'Yes. The whole time he was with you, he was seeing someone else.'

'Is that so?' I say, trying to sound casual.

'Who?'

'A married woman called Anna who lives in a nearby village. And a woman in Poitiers.'

'Really?' I say, feeling like she has punched me in the solar plexus. 'That would have been difficult, as he works very long hours and he spent most nights and weekends with me.'

'Yes, I know he works long hours,' she says, with another nasty smile. 'But he has a long break at lunchtime, don't forget.'

It's true. When they were living next door to me the Portuguese builders did sometimes come home at lunchtime for a couple of hours, although not very often. But there might be some truth in what she says. Luis was, when I think about it, always quite secretive, and he could quite easily have been seeing someone else while pretending to work late or at weekends.

In a daze, I walk past the café, where Arnaud waves at me from a table outside.

'Are you OK, my little flea?' he asks, putting his arm around my shoulders.

'No. I just bumped into Luis's girlfriend.'

'Sabine? The girl with the long face?' he asks.

'Yes. Luis is going to marry her,' I say, thinking that it is typical of Arnaud to have found out her name.

Arnaud starts to laugh—a genuine, deep belly laugh, which makes me want to hug him. 'He is not going to marry her,' he says. 'No

148

way! It won't be long before he throws her aside like an empty beer can. Everyone says that they are always fighting.'

'Well, they don't seem to be fighting today,' I say.

This information has cast everything in a horrible new light The Devil had many opportunities to cheat on me. I recall all the weekends when he dropped off the radar. While I thought he was working hard in Cognac or Niort—and was busy preparing meals for his return—it now seems that he was fornicating his way around the village. I was feeding him up ready for the next one. This discovery is even worse than finding *la blonde* in his bedroom. Emotionally, Luis left me feeling like the victim of a hit and run; now I feel like the car has reversed back over me.

Still, it's odd, because The Devil was conspicuously lacking in a girlfriend for most of the time that he lived next door to me. (Of this I can be sure, since we slept on different sides of the same thin wall for over a year.) After he charmed his way into my walled courtyard, his popularity with women seems to have soared—to the extent that he went from having no girlfriend to having three of us overnight (and quite possibly in the same night). What, I wonder, did I do to turn him into the Valentino of Villiers?

Upset, I call Delphine and tell her what I have discovered.

'That is certainly not great news. But are you sure? Who told you this?'

I tell her about the conversation with his girlfriend.

'How do you know she is telling the truth?'

'She told me the name of one of the women and said he went there in his lunch hour.'

'Hmm. I think you should be careful what you believe. This new girlfriend probably feels very threatened by you. She might be telling you this in order to keep you away.'

'I already was keeping away.'

'My impression is that for Luis, you were a four-course gourmet meal,' says Delphine. 'But sometimes a man cannot resist a quick snack. That is what this girl was to him—just a snack between meals. And she probably offered herself to him on a plate. That is why she is so insecure, because she knows he would prefer to go back to his four-course dinner.'

I manage a weak laugh at this. It makes me feel marginally better to think of myself as a gourmet dinner as opposed to a takeaway burger, but if *la blonde* is telling the truth, Luis was gorging on greasy snacks all around the village. The pursuit of happiness has just been dealt a major blow.

Chapter 10

Magda

'I am gorgeous and *amazing*,' I say to myself, as I walk Biff under a pumice-coloured sky towards the end of February. 'I *will* be happy again.'

The dark days of winter will soon be over. Already, the ground feels firmer, the air fresher, while the strengthening sun has burned away the smell of damp and mouldy leaves. Farmers are out in their tractors sowing their crops, and in the mornings, I see my neighbours tending their vegetable patches or allotments by the river. One evening in March, there is a breakthrough moment when I'm out walking the dog and I realise it is past 6.00 pm and still light.

If only there could be a similar lightening of my mood. The mantra with which Travis insists I should start each day does not seem to be working. I tell myself I am gorgeous and amazing but I don't believe it. What I really am is a loser in love—a phrase Travis has banned me from using. I'm also depressed. Despite the lighter mornings, I struggle to get up, no matter how much sleep I've had. If it weren't for Biff sitting patiently at the side of my bed, his kind black eyes staring directly at

151

me, I probably wouldn't bother getting up at all.

I can't even be bothered to brush my hair before I take him out for the first walk of the day. Instead, I bundle him into the car and drive to a lonely farm track so that I don't have to see or converse with anyone in the village. And when people ring my doorbell unexpectedly—which is surprisingly often—I just don't answer. As for the phone, I never pick it up when it rings—it is starting to feel like an enemy—and often I don't check my messages for days.

I feel as if I am plodding through life with lead platforms on my feet, each step requiring huge and painful effort. I can't concentrate long enough to do any work, struggling to stay in front of my computer for even half an hour. It's a good thing that life in the French countryside costs a fraction of my old lifestyle in London. Sometimes, in the afternoon, I crawl under the duvet exhausted from doing nothing and seek solace in an hour or two of sleep, before waking up sluggish and miserable to face the long evening ahead. Then I sedate myself with a couple of glasses of wine before a sleepless night spent wondering why my life has not turned out the way I hoped.

The house is a perfect reflection of my mind. There are ashes piled up in the wood burner and three or four days of unwashed dishes in the kitchen sink. 'Sorry about the mess,' is my default greeting to visitors on the days when I do answer the door. There are niggling problems at every turn, including a dripping tap in the kitchen and a blocked bathroom sink. To deal with any of this— even just to call the plumber—feels like a Herculean task. The mere thought of it makes me want to go back to bed. No matter how bad I feel, I still manage to get my act together to walk and feed Biff. But that's about it. I am exhausted, physically and emotionally. I am tired of life.

Travis takes to dropping by unannounced, usually en route to Castorama to buy DIY supplies. (He has finally decided on and bought his kitchen units and is now desperately searching for a builder to install them.) He tells me that I have to get a grip, that I must keep putting one foot in front of the other and one day I will skip again. 'You have so much going for you,' my cheerleader-in-chief tells me on a daily basis, but all I can see is loss and failure.

Arnaud, by comparison, is determined to put his *célibataire* days behind him. One afternoon in March, I spot him enjoying a cigarette and a glass of strawberry-flavoured water (his second favourite beverage after coffee) with a tall, slender woman, recently arrived from Guadeloupe. Arnaud introduces her as Yvette, a former masseuse who has just taken over the lease on the tiny fashion boutique next to the café. It went into liquidation under its previous owner, so this is a brave move. She flashes me a big smile and tells me she is very excited about her new venture. Arnaud, it seems, has been very helpful in introducing her to all the right people in the village.

In the weeks that follow, they become a permanent fixture on the café *terrasse,* shivering or smoking furiously in the weak spring sunshine. I'm not surprised that Yvette has stationed herself there: two people would be a tight squeeze in her boutique, which is not much bigger than a jewellery box. And although she is stocking some nice pieces— there are some brightly coloured handbags that have already caught Delphine's eye— Yvette does not appear to be inundated with customers.

One Monday morning, I'm sitting in the Café du Commerce staring out at the sudden squall of rain falling on the deserted square and waiting for Arnaud to arrive. He's late, so I figure he must have another meeting with the *médecin du travail,* or work doctor, hoping to be signed off again.

Sitting at an adjacent table is a girl with long, dark hair and crystalline green eyes. Her skin is perfectly brown, like a pecan nut. I've spotted her a few times, swinging her curvy hips around the village, nearly always in high heels and jeans so tight that she looks like she has been dipped into them. She is Portuguese, very pretty and quite mysterious. Unlike the other Portuguese women in Villiers—there are at least half a dozen of them whose husbands work for Supodal—she appears to have arrived here alone. I've spotted her on the *terrasse* of the café several times, occasionally talking to Basile, who seems to be besotted with her, and sometimes with other men that I haven't seen before.

This morning, her ample chest looks as if it's been vacuum-packed into a scarlet, plunge-neck sweater and her hair is twisted into a neat chignon. Speaking in her mother tongue, she appears to be relaying some major catastrophe to a slender woman with dark hair and big brown eyes. Eventually, her companion stands up, squeezes her hand with a look of sympathy and departs.

I watch as the mysterious Portuguese girl twiddles with her black crystal cocktail ring, seemingly lost in anxious thoughts. We are alone in the café and it seems rude not to talk.

'It's cold today,' I say, in French.

'Yes,' she replies, also in French. 'Are you English?'

'Yes. How do you know?'

'Aha!' she says teasingly, a smile as white as a ski slope illuminating her beautiful brown face. 'I lived in London,' she says, suddenly switching to English. 'For five years. I was workin' in one of the big hotels there.'

'You speak English really well,' I say.

'And Spanish. I spik four languages in total.'

'How long have you been in Villiers?' I ask, intrigued.

'Two years. I came 'ere to live with my aunt.' She pulls a face. 'But she is a beech.' (It takes me a moment to realise that she means 'bitch'.)

'Was that the woman you were just talking to?'

'No, that is Cristina, my neighbour. My aunt iz blonde.'

'So what made you move to a small village in France?'

'It's a long story,' she says. 'And you?'

'Also a long story.'

'But you are 'ere alone?'

'Yes.'

'Me too. Maybe we can take a coffee together some time?'

'That would be very nice,' I say.

'*Lees-en*. I dunno your name.'

'Karen. And you?'

'Magda,' she says, getting up from the table with another radiant smile. 'Nice to meet you, *Ka-renne*.' And with that she is gone, explaining that she has an interview for a cleaning job.

I leave shortly afterwards, and as I'm crossing the square I see Pierre-Antoine coming towards me. *Merde.* Over the past few months, I've been dodging him with the same

156

diligence that I've been dodging housework and journalism. But he keeps taking me by surprise—tapping me on the shoulder while I'm queuing in the *boulangerie*, for example, or ambushing me in the post office or as I'm crossing the square. Always it is with a friendly smile and an invitation to come over for a coffee, an aperitif or dinner. Turning him down has become embarrassing.

'*Bonjour, Ka-renne!*' he cries when he sees me. 'How are you? How is your little dog?'

I stop and kiss him hello. He asks what I've been up to (not a lot) and invites me to have dinner with him on Saturday evening. After a quick mental calculation, I accept. Saturday is five days away, which gives me plenty of time to think of an excuse to cancel. Chatting to Travis later, he tells me I should go.

'You can't sit at home feeling miserable forever. You've got to get out there,' he says. 'And the guy is French which means that he's probably a good cook.'

'Not necessarily,' I reply, thinking of the two sisters in Puysoleil.

But on Saturday evening I fight the urge to stay in with Biff and a good book and instead, get ready to go out. I make a bit of an effort—in other words, I wear a dress and brush my hair. It's now light at 7.30 pm—the clocks went forward last weekend—but still extremely cold as I walk across the square and ring Pierre-Antoine's doorbell. While waiting, I turn

157

around and see Luis standing outside the café alone, pulling moodily on a cigarette. He is looking directly at me. *Perfect.* It was worth dragging myself into some decent clothes just for this. When Pierre-Antoine opens the door, conscious that Luis is watching, I greet him with enthusiasm and a flurry of kisses.

'Come in, come in,' he says, and I make my way between the rails of frilled clothing, and follow him up the narrow stairs to his apartment. I am surprised to see that there is a fire crackling in the grate. Pierre-Antoine told me that he only lit it for special occasions.

'Oof, I've really worked hard today,' he says, taking a bottle of Vouvray out of the fridge. 'I haven't stopped.'

'You had a lot of customers then?' I say, sitting down at the dining table.

'*Bah oui,*' he says, as he pops the cork on the sparkling wine.

Unlike Yvette's boutique, which is struggling to attract custom, Pierre-Antoine has a very loyal clientele. Many of his customers are the well-to-do friends of his mother who, I recently discovered, is very wealthy. Her house, a former horse farm on the outskirts of the village, surrounded by high stone walls, is easily the most desirable in the area.

'You can let your dog free,' says Pierre-Antoine, pouring the Vouvray. 'Would he like some water?'

'Yes please,' I say, touched, as I was last time, by his hospitality towards Biff. But I wonder what we are having for dinner, as apart from a faint aroma of vanilla, there is no evidence of any cooking.

'So what have you been up to?' I ask.

'Well, I went to Paris for the day on Thursday to buy some new stock,' he says. 'Would you like to see the pictures?'

'Why not?' I say and immediately regret it. We pore over photographs of his summer purchases for well over an hour, which is only mildly interesting to me, as looking at clothes was what I once did for a living. I'm also conscious that I could be depriving him of valuable time in the kitchen.

Then, just as he is about to close down his computer, Pierre-Antoine asks if I would like to see the photographs of his recent holiday in Tunisia. We spend another hour looking at those, by which time Biff has fallen asleep at my feet and we've finished the Vouvray. We've also made good progress through a bottle of Pouilly-Fumé. There is still no sign of any food. But I'm pretty sure that the invitation was for dinner.

'Are you hungry?' my host eventually asks. He tells me that he has made a *torteau fromager*, a semi-spherical cheesecake made from goat's cheese, with a thin black crust. But what, I wonder, are we having for the main course? Pierre-Antoine gets up and goes into the kitchen—I assume to make something speedy and delicious from scratch, such as a risotto. But instead he asks if I like oysters. Oh dear.

'I like oysters, but they don't like me,' I say, repeating the joke that I've used many times since moving to France.

'Ah,' says Pierre-Antoine, opening the fridge. 'This could be a problem. Let's see what else I've got. I have a little bit of ham and I've got some nuts. Oh, and some bread.'

And so, while Pierre-Antoine tucks into a giant pile of oysters, savouring each and every one, I nibble the nuts and try to eke out the bread and ham. I console myself that it's just the starter, but gradually it dawns on me that this is also the main course. I remember what Pierre-Antoine said about avoiding cooking smells. Still, at least there is the *torteau fromager* to look forward to.

As he shunts the slippery bivalves down his throat, Pierre-Antoine makes plans for the months ahead. He does this with the confidence of a man who is rarely refused. In May, there is Roland Garros (as the French Open tennis tournament is known in France); in June we are going on a mini-break to La Rochelle; and in July I am invited to accompany Pierre-Antoine and his friends on a camping trip to Bordeaux. There will also be barbecues to attend, along with a visit to his cousin's vineyard and dinner at his favourite restaurant in Poitiers.

It is past midnight when he finally pulls the *torteau fromager* out of the oven and tells me to help myself, while he goes to the bathroom. Ravenous, I cut myself a huge slice and take a sneaky forkful only to find that he has put salt in it instead of sugar. I quickly feed most of the chunk on my plate to Biff, who is lying patiently under the table. When Pierre-Antoine returns, he eats his slice without commenting, which makes me wonder if he planned to make a savoury version.

I'm still not sure if I'm on a date or not. The oysters, the Vouvray and the crackling fire would certainly suggest so, as would the soft music. I wonder if Pierre-Antoine will make some sort of move after eating all those oysters. At the very least, I figure that I will probably have to fight off an unwanted lunge at the door. He is, after all, a Frenchman. But to my relief I am dispatched into the moonlight with the obligatory two kisses and a cheery *'À bientôt.'*

The following day, after taking Biff out for a short walk, I stay in bed until noon recovering from last night's huge intake of wine. When Travis calls, I adopt a cheery voice and tell him that I have been out for a jog, cleaned the house and had hot water and lemon for breakfast. He sounds sceptical, and rightly so. As I sit in bed surrounded by empty coffee cups and croissant crumbs, with clothes and books scattered on the floor, I am grateful that he cannot see the true snapshot of my life.

In the afternoon, with the aid of two Nurofen and a large bottle of water, I get my bike out for the first time this year. I cycle to a country track and Biff runs along behind me for nearly an hour. Spring has officially begun and the countryside looks fresh and sparkling. The glossy green shoots of new crops are visible, while crocuses, snowdrops and dandelions have popped up in the hedgerows, along with a small purple flower whose name I don't know. There is a bracing wind as I cycle along, but the soft sunlight throws a flattering haze over the green fields and dusty blue sky.

We cycle through hamlets where the pungent smell of ammonia and animal hangs heavily in the air, then we emerge on the other side to the faint but cleansing aroma of sliced apples, cucumber and freshly popped peas. Soon, the air will be scented with lilacs and honeysuckle, which will eventually give way to jasmine and my favourite lime blossom. Everything is starting over. Yet none of this makes me feel better. Luis's betrayal has left my soul in a dark, hermetically sealed space, where no light can get in. I cycle along surrounded by beauty, but in my head everything is black and ugly.

Not long after I arrive home, Arnaud knocks on my door. He's wearing jeans— the first time that I've seen him in casual clothing—and even more surprisingly, a necklace of wooden beads on a leather thong.

'Listen, my little flea, I have some news for you,' he says, looking very serious. 'Last night the gendarmes were called because Luis and his girlfriend, Sabine, they had a big argument.'

'Really?' I say, barely able to conceal my delight. (It's not karmically correct I know, but I can't help it.)

'Yes. *Oh, la, la.* The neighbours they were all disturbed by the shouting and screaming. Apparently, he was trying to throw her out of his flat.'

'What time was this?'

'The police were called at about eight o'clock,' he replies.

I do a quick calculation: that's about half an hour after Luis saw me going into Pierre-Antoine's building. Again, I know I shouldn't, but mentally, I'm running a lap of victory.

'So how did it go with the other one?' asks Arnaud.

'The other one?'

'The owner of the boutique. Didn't you say you were having dinner with him last night?'

'Oh, he's just a friend. I'm not interested in anything more and neither is he.'

'Pah!' says Arnaud.

'He seems like a nice guy,' I say. 'But I can't believe that a man with all those assets and a red sports car has never been married.'

'It's because no one was ever good enough,' says Arnaud, putting his finger under his nose and throwing his head back, to indicate that Pierre-Antoine is 'très snob'. He goes on to tell me that Pierre-Antoine is also a *dragueur* of the first degree. 'He has women everywhere. Not just in this village but all the villages around. He is only after one thing,' he says, archly.

'Are you sure?' I say, feeling a little miffed that he isn't after it from me. 'Who exactly?'

'There's the woman at the end of our street, for a start,' says Arnaud.

It's true that I've seen Pierre-Antoine visiting her, but it seems unlikely, as our neighbour is a lesbian and has a very butch girlfriend with spiky black hair and tattoos.

'So have you seen Yvette recently?' I ask.

My neighbour rolls his eyes towards heaven. 'Yes,' he says. 'I'm exhausted.'

'Oh?'

'She sent me a text at 5.00 am this morning,' he says, lowering his voice. 'Just as I'd fallen asleep, because you know that I suffer from insomnia.'

I nod. Arnaud has told me before that he reads political books and magazines until at least 4.00 am, most nights. His insomnia must be really bad if that doesn't send him to sleep.

'She asked me to go over to her apartment and make love to her.'

My eyes widen. This all seems a little

164

unlikely—not least because Yvette is in her early thirties and looks like a model, while Arnaud is in his fifties and only comes up to her shoulders. From what I've seen, Yvette regards Arnaud in the same way as I do: as a kindly uncle.

'What did you reply?' I ask, doing my best to look serious.

'I told her that I wasn't interested.'

'You *did*?'

'Yes. I'm looking for a genuine relationship and I think she's just after sex.'

I bend down to pat Biff for fear that I might start laughing. 'Are you sure you're not tempted? She's very attractive.'

He shakes his head. 'If it's not sex, I think she might be after me for who I know,' he says.

Again, I do my best to stop my lips curling. It's true that Arnaud has taken Yvette to a couple of socialist meetings in nearby villages and he is also very friendly with the mayor of Villiers. But I'm quite sure that most Frenchmen in the village would have stripped naked faster than you could say 'Speedos' if Yvette had propositioned them.

'Anyway, my flea, shall we have coffee together tomorrow?'

'That would be nice,' I say. 'And thanks for the information about Luis and Sabine.'

'Just call me Agent Arnaud,' he says, with a raucous laugh. 'I'll see you tomorrow.'

165

Chapter 11

Watercress

The following morning, I find Arnaud sitting in the Café du Commerce alone, wearing a pair of headphones, which he removes when he sees me. I almost don't recognise him, as he's sporting another new look: pale cut-off trousers and a blue checked shirt, with open-toe sandals. Encouraged perhaps by the first hint of spring sunshine, he appears to have swapped 'grandad chic' for 'surfer chic'.

'Aren't you a bit cold?' I ask, looking at his exposed feet.

'It's spring, my little flea. Time for change,' he says.

'What are you listening to?' I ask, pointing at the headphones, fearful that he is going to say Lady Gaga or a hard-core rap band to go with his cool new image.

His answer surprises me. 'I'm learning English.'

'You *are*?'

'Yes. I've been doing an audio course for a couple of weeks now. I practise at home in the afternoons, and sometimes at night when I can't sleep.'

'Wow,' I say. 'Why are you doing all that?'

'I would like to read your new book when it

comes out.'

Oh dear. Perhaps I shouldn't have mentioned the book that I've written about my love affair with Luis.

'Well, it won't be out until August,' I say. 'So you've got some time.'

While we are sitting in the window chatting, Magda walks past looking very serious. When she sees me, she waves and marches purposefully into the café.

'*Lees-en*, *chérie*. I need to ask a favour. Can you take me to Poitiers this afternoon?'

'Does it have to be this afternoon?'

'Yes, *chérie*. I 'ave to go to the clinic.' She fixes me with an intense look, her eyes like green tourmalines.

I'm not sure which clinic she means, but it doesn't seem to be an emergency so I explain that unfortunately, I have to wait in for an oil delivery.

'But any other time, I'd be happy to take you.'

'OK, *chérie*. Don't worry. I will ask someone else.'

'What's up with her?' says Arnaud, as she leaves. 'She looks very unhappy.'

A couple of days later, I'm waiting for Delphine in the local Bookshop, when Magda struts out from the Internet section at the back. She is wearing tight white jeans with a coriander-coloured top that drops in a deep 'V' at the collarbone, while her feet are encased in gold wedge sandals, revealing coral-painted toes. She has two small children in tow, both plump and with pierced ears.

'Magda!'

''Allo, *chérie*,' she says, sounding glum.

'Are you looking after someone's children?'

'*Non, chérie*. These are my girls, Chanelle and Kyla.'

'You have two children?'

'Three, *chérie*,' she says, laughing at my surprised expression. 'I have another one at home, Janinha, but she eez sick.'

'I hope it's nothing serious?'

'She has been having treatment for a tumour of the brain.'

Oh, my God! I suddenly feel terrible for not taking Magda to Poitiers a few days ago. I didn't realise she had a sick child. I didn't even realise she had children. She told me she was alone.

'Is that why you needed to go to the hospital?'

'*Non, chérie*. I 'ad to go there because I'm pregnant.'

This is surprising news. I thought Magda was a *célibataire*.

'Congratulations,' I say.

'Thanks,' she replies. But she doesn't look too pleased about it. '*Lees-en*, I need to ask another favour. Can you take me to Poitiers later this week?'

I nod, then write down my phone number

and tell her to call when she needs a lift.

'*Merci, Ka-renne*,' she says, clutching it to her chest as she leaves. 'You are very kind.'

Delphine arrives, carrying a big Union Jack tote bag in which she ferries around her students' essays.

'I'm sorry I'm late. I just saw Arnaud,' she says. 'My goodness, he looks so different. Has he dyed his hair?'

'Oh, that's what it is,' I say, for I knew that there was something different about him other than his clothes. 'What do you think of his new surfer-dude look?'

Delphine purses her lips in mock exasperation. 'What is that old goat up to? He is dressing like one of my students. Maybe he is trying to attract a younger girlfriend?'

'Well, apparently Yvette who owns the boutique on the square is after him.'

Delphine looks at me over the top of her glasses. 'Hmm. According to whom? Arnaud?'

I laugh. 'So how was your morning?'

Delphine has been teaching at the agricultural college in Clussay and I know that her (all male) students can be hard work. I really admire her energy. Often she is in her *mairie* by 7.00 am, dealing with the mad dogs and other problems of her *commune* before driving 30 kilometres to teach 'the mad ones' as she calls a particularly difficult class.

'At the moment, I 'ave many problems with farmers,' says Delphine. 'One is accusing

169

another of putting some big stones on the other's field during the night.' She rolls her eyes. 'These farmers, they can be very difficult. The trick is not to be intimidated by them. One of them, he came to see me and he was very much on his high horses [sic]. "Madame," he said, "I can be very nasty".'

'What did you say?'

'I leaned very close to him in my high shoes and said, "Me too, Monsieur."' She grins. 'Now he is always very nice when he sees me.'

As Delphine returns to Puysoleil to deal with recalcitrant farmers, I go home to write about the return of the kitten heel.

*   *   *

By the end of the first week in April, the countryside is quivering with life. When I walk Biff around the *plan d'eau* in the morning, the air crackles with the amorous croakings of the frogs. (It's nice to know that some living creatures are having fun.) And when we walk in the countryside in the evening, *le colza,* or rapeseed, is as high as my collarbone. It stretches like a canvas of cartoon yellow across the horizon. Many people dislike its stale smell, but it doesn't bother me as it means that summer is on the way.

No matter how bad I'm feeling, the sight of Biff bunny hopping through a field of tall blades of grass never fails to bring a smile to my face. All I can see is a black head and ears bobbing up and down, as if he is doing the breaststroke in a sea of vivid green. Meanwhile, the grassy tracks that we walk along are decorated with dandelions, bluebells and snowdrops; and on some days the sun glitters like 200 carats in a flawless blue sky. The village looks equally joyful, with lavish displays of lilac wisteria blooming on old stone walls, and pale pink tulips popping up in the window boxes outside the *mairie*. Late in the evening, when I take Biff for his bedtime walk, it's surprising to find that the temperature outside is the same as it is within, and that the air smells of clean laundry.

In contrast to all this burgeoning life and beauty, my little walled garden is a graveyard. This year, I haven't bothered with my annual trip to Jardiland to buy flowers and plants; nor have I removed the moribund selection of dried-out twigs left over from last summer. In place of blue hydrangeas, red-purple roses and sweet-smelling jasmine, there is a profusion of dead plants and overgrown weeds. Thick moss covers the ground and the pièce de résistance is the discarded Christmas tree that has dried out to a brittle shade of bronze, while waiting to go to the tip. Arnaud has very kindly volunteered to help clear the courtyard, so one morning I go to the café to find out when I might be able to avail myself of his services.

I spot him sitting at a table in the weak

sunshine with Basile. They are both wearing Wellington boots.

'Bonjour, ma petite puce!' he yells, waving his arms at me.

'Why are you dressed like that?' I ask.

Arnaud taps the side of his nose to convey secrecy and tells me that they are going on a little expedition to collect . . . watercress.

'You are going to collect watercress?' I repeat, my eyes as big as sunflowers. In common with the actress Liz Hurley—who swears by watercress soup for losing weight—I love *cresson*.

Arnaud tells me that he knows a secret source—a grotto where the water is as clear as Evian. There follows an animated discussion of the many things you can do with watercress— salad with goat's cheese, beetroot and walnuts is another of my favourites—and suddenly people at other tables are also extolling its virtues.

In the late afternoon, I return from a bike ride with Biff to find that a plastic bag has been left on my doorstep. It is filled with a tangle of wild watercress which, unlike the pre-packaged variety, is a dense, chlorophyll green. It also tastes different, with an intense, peppery flavour that warms the mouth and throat like medicine. I'm a little nervous about eating stuff that's been plucked from the wild, but a few hours later I'm not foaming at the mouth or anything so I figure that Arnaud

172

knew what he was doing. I spend the evening converting the contents of the carrier bag into watercress soup, having Googled Liz Hurley's recipe. (It couldn't be easier: you boil a chopped onion and a couple of potatoes in some chicken stock, add a few bunches of cress at the last moment—so as not to destroy the vitamin C—and then run it through the blender.)

The following morning, I knock on Arnaud's door to thank him and give him a big jar of my beautiful pale green soup, along with a homemade shepherd's pie (his favourite English dish). He looks delighted and tells me that he will be going to pick more cress soon. I'm surprised that he hasn't already plucked the grotto bare because each time I bump into him that day, he is on his way to deliver a carrier bag of watercress to someone. Everyone from the baker to the beautician, it seems, shares my passion for the green foliage. I'm convinced that the entire village will soon be buzzing with good health thanks to the sudden intake of vitamin C and iodine in place of the usual caffeine and nicotine. Soon, complete strangers are approaching Arnaud in the café to ask when the next watercress run is going to take place. My neighbour's popularity in the village has ratcheted up another notch. Even the baker's mother-in-law—a feisty, raven-haired Spanish lady who has so far remained aloof to Arnaud's overtures—

suddenly smiles when he approaches.

A few days later, Arnaud asks if I'd like to accompany him to the grotto. I've pulled on my boots before he's even finished the sentence. That afternoon, we drive the 15 kilometres to the little village of Payré, not far from Puysoleil. We park the car by the roadside and follow a gravel path into a damp green wood that smells of moss and ferns. Even though the sun is shining somewhere above the forest, the ground is wet and the bushes and trees appear to be creaking with moisture. We follow the path for about half a kilometre with Biff racing on ahead. I hear the sound of running water first, and then I see it: at the end of the path, partially sheltered by trees, is a glistening green carpet that seems to float on a pool of clear water.

'Voilà!' shouts Arnaud, throwing open his arms proudly. I stop for a second to take in the perfection of the scene: the soothing tinkle of the water coming from the nearby rock face, birds singing, and the pale blue butterflies— yes blue!—fluttering in front of my eyes. There are white ones too, dancing around the dandelions and buttercups in the wild grass nearby. The grotto is the quintessence of clean, green purity. Given all the talk of our polluted planet, it is reassuring to know that a place like this exists.

Arnaud gives me a speedy lesson in the art of watercress collection. It's important to pick here at the source he says, pointing to the small cave from where the water is flowing, as further downstream, animal droppings may have polluted the water. He tells me to pick cress where the water is moving rather than stagnant. He also instructs me to avoid at all costs a pointy, oval leaf, as it is likely to be water hemlock—a poisonous plant that grows alongside watercress.

Standing ankle-deep in the icy, meandering water, we fill several carrier bags with cress, while Biff splashes around nearby. I pray that he doesn't *faire pipi* in the pristine water, but as it turns out, it is not Biff that I should have worried about. Without warning, Arnaud suddenly wades out of the water and when I turn around I'm forced to avert my eyes. Like a true Frenchman, he sees no shame in urinating in public and hasn't bothered to hide discreetly behind a tree, or even turn his back.

Picking watercress is back-breaking work, perched uncomfortably on pebbles in the cold water. Back home, I wash the harvest thoroughly and trim off any roots. I put most of it in the fridge ready to make another batch of soup and I then prepare a salad for dinner. It is the most enormous buzz, eating the peppery leaves within hours of picking them. As I climb into bed that night, I realise that Arnaud has given me a gift as good as diamonds—and possibly almost as rare. It's

175

impossible to think of that tranquil green grotto and not feel a little flash of happiness.

The following morning it is the village *foire*—the big market that takes place twice a month. Still on a high from all the vitamin-packed greenery that I've consumed, I set out early hoping to get to the goat's cheese lady before she sells out of her pouf-shaped *chèvres*. The scent of stressed animal hangs heavily in the air. As we approach the livestock section Biff plonks his bottom on the ground and refuses to budge, staring at the wire cages in rapt fascination. I have to look away. The sight of these poor birds crammed beak by jowl and moving as one mass is profoundly distressing.

I wince at the sign on one cage: '*Coqs à rôtir*,' (Cocks to roast). Those doomed creatures—still looking proud and haughty despite the indignity of their situation—have no idea how close they are to The End. I drag Biff onwards, past the *pintades*, or guinea fowl—my favourites, as they look so chic with their grey and white spotty feathers. He comes to another abrupt halt in front of some fluffy lemon chicks—innocent and adorable with their pale pink beaks. Suddenly, I see Magda coming towards me, strutting past a table of roasted eels, with her own little brood waddling along behind her. As usual, she looks like she has been suctioned into her pale blue jeans.

It's the first time that I've seen her since I bumped into her in the bookshop and she asked for a lift to Poitiers. She introduces me to Janinha, an enormous, sullen looking child in grey marl leggings, with a big white bandage around her head. From behind her glasses, she fixes me with dark, knowing eyes and a hostile look. This must be her sick daughter.

'Do you still need that lift to Poitiers?' I ask Magda, after the usual greetings.

'Ah, *non, chérie*. I already went.'

'You did?'

'Yes. Cristina, my neighbour, she took me.'

'How are you feeling?' I ask.

She gives me a sideways look as if she is not sure what I'm talking about.

'Are you suffering from morning sickness?'

'Ah, *non, chérie*. I'm not pregnant any more.'

Oh dear. 'You mean you've lost the baby?'

She nods and looks away.

'I'm really sorry to hear that, Magda,' I say.

I don't ask any more questions and she doesn't offer any more information.

'Maybe we can take a coffee together soon?'

She nods. *'Lee-sen, chérie.* Can I hask [sic] a favour? I have no money to feed *les enfants*. Can you possibly lend me €10 until next week?'

I get out my wallet and give her €20. She throws her arms around me and there are tears in her eyes. 'Thank you, *Ka-renne*. Thank you so much.'

Feeling sad, I watch the four of them walk towards a stand selling jellybean-coloured jewellery. I feel bad for Magda, whatever the story.

Chapter 12

Ticket to Ride

May arrives and the wheat is pushing up in the fields around Villiers. So, too, are the leafy green stalks of the sunflowers. The village is encircled by a landscape of gold and many shades of green. Blades of glass glisten in the soft sunlight and there is beauty at every turn. The mornings are bright but cold, the afternoons as hot as high summer, before the day slowly segues into stars and silence. As I walk Biff round the village in the blueberry-coloured light of early evening, jasmine and lilac jump out from neighbours' gardens, seducing my nose with their beguiling scent.

One morning, I'm sitting outside the café with Arnaud and Basile, when Magda arrives.

'*Bonjour, tout le monde,*' she says with a big smile.

'*Oh, la, la.* It's the beautiful Portuguese lady,' says Basile, suddenly sitting up straight.

Magda laughs a loud raucous laugh, and gives him a playful push. I've noticed that

Basile has the same look about him when he sees Magda, as Biff does when I take a roast chicken out of the oven.

'*Chérie*,' she says in a wheedling voice. 'I need to ask a favour. Can you take me to Poitiers to buy a bus ticket to Portugal?'

'Yes, but wouldn't it be easier to buy it over the Internet?'

'Non, *chérie*. I 'ave to pay in cash. Oh, and I 'ave the €20 that I owe you,' she says, handing me the money.

Eager to embrace a distraction from work—this one masquerading as a good deed—I arrange to meet Magda at the café at 4.00 pm. When I arrive, she is standing in the sunshine, smoking. She is always nicely turned out, her face scrubbed bare, hair in a neat chignon and clothes perfectly pressed, but this afternoon I almost don't recognise her. She is wearing red lipstick and her hair is loose and curled. Her breasts have been scooped into a tight, white broderie anglaise top—a lime green satin bra visible underneath—and her jeans are so tight that I fear she won't be able to sit down. She looks as if she is out to bag a Premier League footballer rather than a bus ticket to Portugal.

'You look very . . . dressed up,' I say, as she pours herself into the passenger seat.

She gives me a wink and a playful smile. 'Thank you, *chérie*. *De temps en temps*, I like to make an effort.'

As we drive to Poitiers in the sunshine, I ask

179

about Janinha.

'She 'as 'ad an operation to remove the tumour and she might need some more chemotherapy. We 'ave to wait and see.'

'You must be very worried,' I say.

'I am, *chérie*, but I know God eez gonna keep 'er safe.' She joins her hands together and looks up to heaven, bracelets jangling.

I can't help but admire Magda. She is a single mother with three children, one of them seriously ill, yet she shows no sign of self-pity.

'So is that why you came to France, for the medical treatment?' I ask. (It's not unheard of for British people to decamp to France for the superior health care, so why not the Portuguese?)

'*Non, chérie*. I was 'ere with my 'uzband.'

'The father of your children?'

'Yes, *chérie*, 'e iz a bastard. He threaten to kill me.'

'Oh, my God! What happened?'

'We were in Paris and I told 'im I was leaving 'im. He take everything. The girls and me, we had no clothes, no money, nothin'. We couldn't go back to Portugal, so we come 'ere to Villiers to live with my aunt.'

'But what did you live on?'

'The *mairie* found me a house. And before Janinha got sick, I 'ad a job, working as a waitress in a restaurant in Buisson.'

'Buisson? That's over 10 kilometres away.

180

How did you get there without a car?'

She smiles and pulls a face. 'I know, *chérie*, tell me about it! Some days I took the bus and some days Cristina, my neighbour, she give me a lift. And sometimes I walked.'

'You walked to Buisson?' I say, in disbelief.

'Yeah, *chérie*. I worked there for over a year and 'ad to walk many times. Once in the snow.'

'Not in your high heels, I hope?'

She fixes me with her dazzling eyes, then throws her head back and laughs her raucous, masculine laugh. 'Are you fuckin' crazy or what?' she says.

When we arrive in Poitiers, Magda instructs me to go to the underground car park on rue Carnot. As we emerge into sunlight, she lights a cigarette. 'The travel agent, 'e is down 'ere,' she says, and I follow her into a narrow side street, her black patent heels clip-clopping on the pavement. Heads turn in her wake. We make an unlikely trio: Magda dressed for a nightclub, me in scruffy jeans and flip-flops, with a little black dog panting along in excitement at this unexpected excursion.

'So why are you going to Portugal?' I ask.

'I 'ave to sign some documents, *chérie*.'

'Who will look after the girls while you're away?'

'My aunt.'

'But I thought you said she was a bitch?'

'She is. But she is family, an' she is nice to my *filles*. OK, we are 'ere.' She takes a final

181

drag on her cigarette, grinds the butt into the pavement with her heel and pushes open the door.

The ticket clerk is with a customer as we enter the office, but indicates for us to take a seat. It's not long before he summons Magda to his desk. She smiles and slowly swings her hips towards him, easing her curvy body into the seat opposite. Legs crossed, scarlet nails splayed on the counter, she leans forward so that he can see enough of the smooth brown gorge between her breasts to make beads of sweat pop out on his brow. He blinks behind his glasses and says, 'What can I do for you, *Mademoiselle*?'

'I'd like a return ticket to Portugal, please,' she says, making it sound like an indecent proposal.

What follows is the most flirtatious, sexually charged purchase of a bus ticket that I've ever witnessed. For nearly fifteen minutes, I watch open-mouthed as Magda tosses her hair, crosses and uncrosses her legs, smiles, giggles and laughs her deep, throaty laugh. You'd think that it was Johnny Depp sitting before us rather than a short, fat man with a dwindling supply of hair. I am amazed. So, too, is the clerk, who is sweating so much that I fear he might evaporate. I doubt he has *ever* had a woman flirting with him like this before. Magda jiggles her bracelets (among other things) and leans forward a little more, to encourage him.

'Are you under twenty-six?' he asks, looking directly at her cleavage. The charmer! Magda is beautiful but she is very clearly in her thirties. She rewards him with a coquettish tilt of the head and then laughs.

'Why you hask me that?' she says.

'You could qualify for a discount,' he says. 'Or perhaps you're a student?'

Magda shakes her head with a slow smile but now I see what she is up to. This man is *desperate* to get her the best deal possible. He would sell his mother to a Columbian drug cartel in order to get Magda a discount on her bus ticket to Portugal.

I watch, exhausted by the exuberant display of gallantry (him) and brazen coquetry (her). It's a relief when Magda produces a white envelope containing several crisp €50 notes and hands them over. Finally, all the flirting and foreplay culminate in the issue of a ticket. Flirtatious farewells are said and, job done, Magda struts back out onto the street.

'OK, *chérie*, now we take a coffee,' she says, so that it sounds like an order.

Biff and I follow her to a table outside a café on Rue Carnot. She plonks herself down on a wicker seat, lights a cigarette and throws her hair back.

'Magda,' I say. 'That man was practically slobbering over you.'

She laughs. 'I know. But *lees-en*. I don' need

no man, *chérie*. I'm a *femme toute seule* (a woman alone) and I am 'appy. I don' need no man for nothin'.'

'Apart from a ticket to Portugal.'

She laughs again and the waiter appears to take our orders. On seeing Magda, he develops the same flustered look as the travel agent.

'So why are you really going to Portugal?' I ask.

'You don't believe what I'm tellin' you?' she frowns.

'But how can you afford to go to Portugal? You told me you had no money.'

Her face breaks into an involuntary grin. 'OK, *chérie*, it's true. I 'ave a boyfriend in Portugal. He pay for my bus ticket.'

'You have a boyfriend?' I say. So much for her being a woman alone.

'But I spik the truth when I say I go there to sign some documents.'

'So your boyfriend, was he the father of the baby?' I ask.

She nods, looks away and lights another cigarette. I worry that I might have upset her. But after a few drags she narrows her eyes and looks directly at me. 'So what about you?'

'I really am a *femme toute seule*,' I say. 'Ever since I split up with Luis.'

'Luis?' she says. 'You were the girlfriend of Luis, *le Portugais*?'

'Yes,' I say, thinking that she is being

184

disingenuous. As a member of the Portuguese community in a small French village, she would have known that I was going out with one of her compatriots. 'Do you know him?'

'Yes, of course I know 'im,' she says. 'Everyone knows Luis.'

'Please don't tell me you've slept with him, too?'

She laughs. *'Non, chérie,* I don't like the men like Luis.'

Privately, I think they'd make an excellent match. They even share the same mannerisms—the raucous laugh and knowing wink, the larger-than-life personality and liberal use of the word *'chérie.'*

'Non, chérie. I like the men who iz very quiet and borin',' she continues. 'My boyfriend Roberto, 'e iz not good-lookin'. He is wearin' all the time the suit and the glasses.' She holds her hands to her heart and smiles, as if the thought of his suit and glasses was enough to give her palpitations.

I ask how she met him and she tells me that they met on the Internet earlier this year and that he came to Villiers to visit her.

'What does he do?'

'He does the marketin' on the telephone. You know, I'm-a gonna tell you somethin' *chérie.'* She beckons me closer and lowers her voice as the waiter arrives with our coffees. 'The first time I saw Roberto, I think to myself, "I don't know what this man iz gonna be like

185

in bed. I think, most probably 'e iz gonna be crap." An' you know what?'

'What?'

'I was right. He was fuckin' terrible.' She throws her head back and laughs again. 'But I think to myself, "I gonna teach 'im." The first time I sleep with him, he come three times in less than an hour. Afterwards, he cannot speak. He say, "My God, I never 'ad sex like that before . . . where did you learn to do those *trucs*?"'

I laugh, half tempted to ask what those *trucs* might be. The waiter hovers, his eyes fixed on Magda. I look at my watch. It's past 6.00 pm. 'Listen,' I say. 'Would you like a glass of wine?'

She shakes her head. '*Non, chérie*. I never drink the alcohol.'

'Never?'

She shakes her head. 'I take the pills for depression. I mustn't take the alcohol.'

'Oh,' I say, surprised. Magda strikes me as one of the least depressed people I've ever met. But then I think of the sick child, the lost baby and the fact that she is a single mother struggling to cope alone in a foreign country. It all makes sense. I order two more coffees. But the mood has changed and Magda has become quite sombre.

'*Lees-en, chérie*,' she says. 'I 'ave done some terrible things in my life, may God forgive me.' She bites her lower lip as if trying not to cry, then fixes me with those luminous green eyes.

186

'Do you 'ave any idea what it's like to 'ave three young children and no money to feed them?'

I take her hand and squeeze it. 'Magda, I think I can guess what you are going to tell me. I don't have children and so I've never been in that position. But I'm quite sure that I would do whatever it took to feed them. No one has the right to judge you unless they've been in that situation.'

She stares into the middle distance, wipes away a tear and then turns to face me. 'Thank you, *chérie*. You are a very good friend to me.'

We sit in silence for a few minutes and drink the second round of coffees. Magda seems very pensive. Then she tells me that we must go, as her aunt is picking up the children from school.'

'Come on then,' I say, after we've paid the waiter. 'Let's go.' As we cross the road to the car park, I turn around and see him staring in Magda's wake.

'So is that why the other Portuguese women don't speak to you?' I ask as we drive across the Pont Neuf, back towards Villiers, a warm breeze in our hair.

She nods. 'They are not spikin with me because they think I am a poot.'

Poot? This throws me for a second and then I realise it is the abbreviation of *putain*, the French word for whore.

'But I don't give a fuck what they think,'

187

she says, tossing her hair back. 'They say the bad things about everyone.' She gives me a sideways glance. 'You wanna know what they say about you, *chérie*?'

'Go on.'

'Nah, *chérie*. I think you're gonna be hupset.'

'Tell me!' I say, turning to look at her.

'They think you are a poot, too,' she says.

'That's nice. Why do they think that?'

'They say you are fuckin' with the man who owns the dress shop.'

'Really?'

'And that you are also fuckin' with your neighbour.'

'Arnaud?' I say, surprised. 'Why do they say that?'

'Because you are always takin' the coffee with 'im. And 'e is on his own. And you are on your own. Everyone, they see you all the time together.' She waves her arms around. 'This is how the Portuguese think.'

'Do you really think I am sleeping with Arnaud?'

She gives me another sideways glance. '*Non, chérie*. Me, I think you're still in love with Luis.'

I laugh. 'No way,' I say, pulling the sun visor down and squinting in the strong evening sun, which is like a searchlight being flashed in my eyes. 'I'd have to be mad to be in love with Luis after everything that has happened.'

188

Now it is Magda's turn to laugh. 'Yeah, *chérie*. But that's the point. You *are* mad.'

When we reach Villiers, Magda directs me to her road, a keyhole-shaped cul-de-sac on the outskirts of the village. The houses are characterless, concrete blocks, the colour of Band Aids.

'*Merci, chérie,*' says Magda as I pull up in front of her house. I watch as she totters up the path and opens the door. Three chubby children run out to hug her, delighted that their mother is home, and I feel a pang of envy. Magda might not have any money, but the thing she has in abundance—a far more rare commodity—is love.

As I pull up outside Maison Coquelicot, I see Yvette driving away from Arnaud's house.

'*Bonjour, ma belle,*' he says, smiling over at me. '*Ça va?*'

'Is Yvette still chasing you for your body?' I ask.

He shakes his head and looks suddenly very serious. 'She came to ask for advice,' he says. 'She hasn't sold a single thing for three days and her morale is very low. She's not sure if it is worth carrying on with the business.'

'Oh dear.'

'The problem is that no one here has any money. And if they do, they go to the big stores in Poitiers,' says Arnaud, referring to the big hypermarkets that circle the city.

I shake my head, feeling sad for Yvette and

her little shop. It's another reminder of just how difficult it is to run a business in rural France.

'Wait a minute, little flea, I have something for you,' says Arnaud, running back into the house. He reappears, his arms weighed down with another pile of political magazines.

'Great! More bedtime reading,' I say, while wondering if this is actually a clever ruse by my neighbour to ensure that he never has to go to the recycling bins.

I have only been home a few minutes when the doorbell rings. It's Pierre-Antoine. Ever since the night of champagne and oysters, he has been bombarding me with invitations—for coffee, dinner, dog walks—both by phone and in person. But armed with the knowledge that he is a *dragueur extraordinaire*, I've doubled my efforts to avoid him. Unfortunately, it's not easy in a small village.

'*Salut, Ka-renne!*' he says, propping his bike against my wall and looking as cheerful as ever. 'Listen. Are you free on Saturday? I have two tickets for a Spanish-themed evening in Vaux.'

I assume he means the following Saturday, and say yes, as right now I can't think of an excuse that I haven't already used a dozen times.

'Great. I'll pick you up tomorrow at 7.30 pm,' he says

'You mean *tomorrow*?' I say, taken by

surprise.

'Yes,' he says. 'See you then.' And before I can say anything else, he jumps on his bike and cycles away.

The following morning I meet Delphine in the market.

'Did you get my messages?' she asks.

'Um . . . sorry, no. I haven't been very good at checking messages recently.'

'I was wondering what you are doing this evening?'

'Nothing,' I reply. 'I've been invited to a Spanish evening in Vaux but I'm planning on getting out of it.'

'Oh,' says Delphine. 'That is exactly what I was going to invite you to.'

It turns out that Delphine knows the mayor of Vaux and has agreed to help serve the tapas. Her friend Joelle, recently divorced and visiting from Paris for the weekend, will also be there.

'Well, maybe I'll come along after all,' I say. A night of cheery salsa music has got to be more conducive to happiness than staying home alone.

And so when Pierre-Antoine pulls up outside my house at 7.30 pm with the roof on his red sports car down, I'm ready and waiting in a ruffled green dress and high heels.

'*Bonsoir, Ka-renne*!' he says, kissing me on the cheeks as I get into the car, which is surprisingly low on the ground. It's also

191

quite chilly with the roof down, but suddenly I don't care. For as we are driving out of the village, past the café on the corner and the apartment with pale green shutters, Pierre-Antoine is forced to slow down. Crossing the road in front of us with a bag of groceries, is none other than The Devil. He does a double take when he sees Pierre-Antoine and the red sports car, and for a fraction of a second looks me directly in the eye. Then he looks away. If I had to describe the expression on his face, I would say angry and humiliated—exactly how I felt when I found him with the French girl.

I turn to Pierre-Antoine with a big smile. 'I'm looking forward to this evening,' I say.

As we speed past the blonde fields of wheat en route to Vaux, I think how nice it is to be picked up and driven for the evening. As always, we keep the conversation neutral and DIY-based, chatting about some work that Pierre-Antoine has been doing to his mother's house. He has yet to ask me any personal questions and I haven't asked any, either. It's as if we have an unspoken agreement.

Inside the *salle des fêtes*, a Spanish flag has been hung above the small stage and posters of matadors with enviably taut buttocks have been put up at strategic points around the room. People are milling by the bar. Delphine comes over to greet us, looking more Spanish than French this evening, in a red gypsy skirt and black cardigan, a scarlet rose in her black

192

hair. I introduce her to Pierre-Antoine and she introduces us to Joelle, a petite amber-blonde with a bob, glasses and a ready smile. I notice that she is wearing professional dancers' shoes.

We mill around for well over an hour before sitting down for the meal. (According to Delphine, it is a common ploy to delay the meal in order to get people to spend more at the bar.) I'm glad that she and Joelle are there, as Pierre-Antoine and I have exhausted all DIY-related topics.

Eventually, we head towards one of the trestle tables arranged around the dance floor. Joelle sits opposite Pierre-Antoine and immediately engages him in a jolly conversation. Looking around, I suddenly have a premonition of what life might be like in a retirement home. Our table is the youngest by several decades. As Pierre-Antoine fills our glasses with the fruit punch (or 'poonch', as he pronounces it) that has been left on our table, Delphine arrives with bowls of olives and cherry tomatoes, a dish of spicy prawns and a plate of Spanish omelette cut into squares.

While we nibble, we are treated to a tango display by four couples. In each pairing, the female dancer is tall and lean, while her partner is barrel-shaped and barely reaches her collarbone. I try not to giggle. Joelle, I notice, has mastered the art of dancing in her seat, moving her head and shoulders

193

suggestively, and clicking her fingers in time with the music. When the display is over, a man with a microphone announces that it's time for some salsa and invites everyone onto the dance floor. Joelle jumps up, reaching her hands across the table for Pierre-Antoine.

Honestly, it's a good job that I'm not interested in him romantically, as I'd feel like I'd just been mugged.

'Joelle just really loves dancing,' says Delphine, as if reading my mind.

'I can see that,' I say, noticing that Pierre-Antoine is not a bad dancer.

'So how do you know Pierre-Antoine?' Delphine asks. 'He seems a very nice fellow.'

'He fixed my bedroom window a few months back,' I say.

When the music finishes, they return to the table, cheeks flushed and smiling. We are then treated to a flamenco display (by the same four couples, who've now swapped partners). When it's time for the next round of audience participation, Pierre-Antoine turns to me. I'm half pleased and half dreading the idea of dancing with him. But as we move around the dance floor, his hands around my waist, I notice that he has agile hips and a surprisingly good sense of rhythm. We spend the rest of the night dancing together and at one point, I realise that I've pretty much forgotten about The Devil. Joelle, meanwhile, has found herself another partner from among the professionals.

It's gone midnight when we leave. A full moon lights up the countryside on the way home and we are treated to an amazing display of animal acrobatics. First, a rabbit leaps cleanly across the narrow road in front of us, as if performing the long jump. Birds swoop down in front of the car, gliding out of the way at the last moment and a deer leaps across a hedgerow with breathtaking elegance. The countryside is buzzing with life tonight. I wonder what will happen when we arrive back in Villiers? If I count the bike ride, this is our fourth date—although actually, I'm still not sure if we have been on dates or not. But if Pierre-Antoine is going to make a move, it will almost certainly be tonight, especially after all that hip-against-hip action on the dance floor.

In my head, I work out polite ways to turn him down. But as he pulls up outside my house, he keeps the engine running. I wait for him to suggest coffee or a digestif, but instead, he leans over . . . and plants a chaste kiss on both cheeks.

'*Bonne nuit, Ka-renne,*' he says, beaming in the moonlight.

'*Bonne nuit,*' I reply, as I get out of the car, half relieved and half insulted that the biggest *dragueur* in the village has not tried to *drague* me.

The next morning, Arnaud taps on my

195

window. 'So,' he says, with a meaningful look. 'Did anything happen last night?'

I laugh. 'No, it did not. Pierre-Antoine is just a friend.'

'Well, I have news for you,' he says. 'Luis and *la blonde* had another big fight last night.'

'Really?' I say. There is definitely a pattern emerging here.

*   *   *

The final weekend in May arrives, a long weekend, as Monday is June 1st, a bank holiday in France. On Friday afternoon, I start to panic when I realise that I have no plans. Travis is leaving tomorrow morning to visit an ex-boyfriend in Biarritz and Delphine's son and daughter are visiting her. Other friends are away in the UK, so I'm pretty much on my own.

Late on Friday afternoon, Arnaud knocks on my door unexpectedly with a medley of cooked meats and some cold potatoes—his return volley after I made him Delia Smith's Moroccan chicken with couscous a few nights ago.

'Listen,' he says. 'I have to tell you something and you are not going to like it.'

I immediately feel sick and shaky. 'What?'

'Luis's girlfriend is pregnant.'

I freeze. 'Are you sure?'

'She told the woman in the newsagent's this

morning.' Arnaud takes my hands in his. 'I'm sorry, little flea.'

This would be bad news at the best of times, like bleach poured into an open wound, but on the eve of a long weekend, doubly so. I'm staring down the barrel of three empty days with nothing to do but mull over this cruel piece of news. Luis's girlfriend has been given the thing that I so desperately wanted; and she will now own a part of him forever. I'm ashamed to say, that I feel nothing but envy that she is carrying The Devil's child.

I spend a couple of hours surfing the web and making some urgent phone calls. By 8.00 pm, I've booked myself on a ruinously expensive spa break in Spain. Sarah and Steve will look after Biff. I leave tomorrow.

It's close to midnight and I'm throwing clothes into a bag when the phone rings. I don't answer. It's probably Travis, to lecture me on the folly of spending so much money on a spa holiday when he could achieve similar results by handcuffing me to the treadmill in his spare room for a week and throwing me the occasional crispbread. But when I check my messages, I receive a shock. The gruff voice is joltingly familiar.

Speaking in Portuguese and running down a staircase, Luis has dialled my number by mistake and left a message for his colleague, José.

It's odd because my recorded message, in

French and then in English, should have made it clear that he was calling me. I'm not sure what to make of this. I'm just very relieved that I'm leaving tomorrow and will have a week away from the village to get my head together.

Chapter 13

Cucumber Juice

The flight to Malaga from Stansted is full of good-looking people travelling in packs, most of them on the pull and planning to massively intoxicate themselves in the coming days. I know this because of the posse of loud, plummy-voiced schoolgirls who, within minutes of squeezing their bottle tans, tight jeans and jaunty cowboy hats into the seats behind me, have hooked up with a gang of twenty-something males in checked shirts and baggy shorts, sitting across the aisle. For them, the party has already started: they laugh, shout and flirt their way through the flight. Me, I sit quietly among them sipping mineral water and contemplating a week of raw vegetables. I can guess who will have the better time.

Disembarking the plane in Malaga is like stepping into a warm bath, while the setting sun casts everything in a rosy pink light. As instructed, I head for the café opposite the arrivals gate, where a representative from Total Detox—an upmarket outfit that runs small, very exclusive yoga breaks in privately-owned villas around Europe—is supposed to meet me. I scan the café for someone suitably fit and luminous, but it's mostly people tucking into burgers. I wait. And I wait some more. Then I see a man rushing into the hall with a mobile phone clutched to his ear and a sign saying, 'SIGNORA WOLLER,' handwritten in red letters.

'I think that might be me,' I say. The driver, who is in his early twenties and dressed like an advertising executive in sharply tailored trousers and a deep purple shirt, looks sceptical. I'm guessing that, in my old jeans and flip-flops, I don't fit the usual profile of the Total Detox client. After verifying that I am indeed Mrs Woller—or something close to it—my visit to Spain gets off to an exhilarating start. He drives along the curving autoroute at 140 kilometres an hour, talking very animatedly into a hand-held mobile phone. So far, so normal; after all, I live in France, a country known for its audacious driving, where cars drive close enough on the motorway to pluck the 'GB' sticker from your bumper. But my Spanish driver takes it to a new level. Frequently, he throws the hand that isn't holding the phone into the air to emphasise a point, which means he is driving around the curving autoroute entirely hands-free.

'Excuse me,' I say, but he doesn't hear me. Not only is he fully engaged in his conversation, but there is a football match playing loudly on the radio, and the commentator is shrieking as if he were on a high velocity theme park ride.

'EXCUSE ME!' I yell again as we sweep towards the setting sun. I tap him on the shoulder and, having got his attention, make calming motions with my hands to get him to slow down. He frowns and hits the accelerator. I sit back and resign myself to my fate. On the plus side, if I die in the back of this cab tonight, at least I will never have my heart broken again.

The villa is just over 100 kilometres from the airport, so I calculate that at this speed we should be there in roughly a quarter of an hour.

The light fades quickly and it's dark by the time the cab speeds into the grounds of the villa, through an impressive arched entrance. The front door is open and all is silent within, although outside, the warm night air is alive with the sound of crickets. Then I hear the click-clack of high heels on terracotta tiles and a tall blonde woman appears. My first thought is that I am in the wrong place, as she is dressed for a cocktail party in high heels and a short, floral dress by a very fashionable Italian label. In an American accent, she introduces herself as Catriona Mace, the owner of Total

Detox.

She looks me up and down as if carrying out a full visual appraisal. I have a sneaking suspicion that she is also assessing my net worth. I can tell that she doesn't like what she sees. Neither do I, when I look in the mirror. Over the past six months, I've been relying on vast amounts of caffeine to jolt myself awake in the morning, a shovelful of chocolate to keep awake in the afternoon, and then a couple of glasses of wine to celebrate the end of the working day, which very often hasn't involved any work at all. Apart from the need to get away from my village, I've justified the huge expenditure on this spa visit on the grounds that if my car broke down, I wouldn't think twice about spending money to fix it. Right now, I feel that *I* have broken down— I'm chemically and emotionally unbalanced— and need to be patched up. Failing that, I'll settle for a few kilos of weight loss and glowing skin.

I realise that not everyone can run away from a bad situation like I just have. I also see the awful irony in paying a small fortune not to eat for a week, when so many people in the world are starving. But despite the guilt, despite Catriona Mace's disapproving looks, and despite the fact it will take a year to pay off the credit card bill for this jaunt, I am very happy to be here—and not just to escape the scenario unfolding in my small village. Having spoken to friends in the beauty world, I know that Catriona Mace, a Californian by birth, brings the fastest results possible in one week. And after three hours of yoga a day, I hope to leave here exuding such Zen calm that I can face The Devil and the thought of his dark-eyed offspring—for it is certain to have his eyes and hair—with equanimity.

Catriona tells me that I am the last to arrive and that everyone else is in bed. Do I want to do the 'check-in' now or wait until tomorrow morning?

'I might as well do it now,' I say.

A chiselled twenty-something called Derek appears, armed with a tape measure and a clipboard. I follow him into a side room. The humiliating half-hour that follows includes a weigh-in and extensive logging of body measurements. On a positive note, it's been a while since anyone showed such interest in my inner thighs.

'What's your main objective for this week?' asks Derek, all dazzling smile and breezy manner.

'To lose weight,' I say. I don't add that I've come all this way to avoid my former boyfriend and his pregnant girlfriend.

'How fit are you?'

'Pretty fit. I do a lot of walking and cycling. And I've got a lot of stamina.'

'Good. We'll put you in Group A for hiking. And have you ever done any yoga?'

'Lots,' I reply, dropping the name of a world-famous guru. (In fact, it's over six years since I last went to his lunchtime class, and even then it was only to have a bit of a lie-down after a morning of guerilla warfare among the staff at the health and beauty magazine.)

'Great stuff,' says Derek, looking impressed. 'I'll put you in Group A for that too.'

Finally, Derek leads me to my room, which is accessed across a large, rectangular courtyard with a fountain in the middle. Dinner is waiting on a table. I never thought I'd be so overjoyed to see a raw salad. I do a quick check that it doesn't contain any cucumber, the one salad ingredient that I detest, but fortunately it doesn't. While I'm eating my way through the great mound of leaves and chopped vegetables, a schedule is pushed under my door. At 7.00 am tomorrow morning, I must report to the lounge for the early morning hike with the A's.

I switch on my phone to set the alarm and it starts to buzz with missed calls. Six of them are from the same person and just the sight of his name has an effect like walking into an electric fence. Luis has been trying to contact me.

It's only taken him eight months—which gives some clues as to how much he cared—and he hasn't left any message, but he appears pretty keen to talk to me now. The calls started shortly after I went to bed last night in France and finished at 6.00 am this morning, just before I got up to drive to the airport. How weird that he should intrude on my life at the moment when I'm most trying to escape him. Not for the first time, it feels to me that he can hack into my thoughts. I'm surprised, intrigued and, shameful though it is to admit it, thrilled by this unexpected development. Luis is with Sabine, Sabine is pregnant, but Luis, for whatever reason, is thinking of me. At last, I've had the pleasure of rejecting him—albeit unwittingly, by not answering my phone.

The next morning, I wake to startling sunshine. Cheered by last night's discovery, I head to the villa's all-white lounge, where several women in expensive fitness kit and sparkly FitFlops are sitting on overstuffed sofas discussing their private chefs. I feel like I'm crashing a posh cocktail party, where the only drink on offer looks and smells like a milkshake made from grass cuttings.

My fellow guests, I note, are all over fifty, which makes me worry that the hikes won't be rigorous enough. I haven't come here for a gentle stroll.

'Morning,' I say cheerfully, but only one person responds. I help myself to a large glass of grass cuttings. 'What does this taste like?' I ask the room in general.

'What do you think? You're not here for the cuisine,' says a brusque Swiss-German woman, whom I later discover owns a well-known health food brand. Feeling well and truly put in my place, I retreat to an armchair on the outskirts of the group with my juice.

Catriona appears, dressed in a purple Lanvin cocktail dress and silver high heels. I figure she won't be leading from the front on the hike. At her side are three instructors in taupe shorts and apple green polo shirts, who look like male models. (Later, I discover that two of them *are* male models and have been booked for a catalogue shoot at the end of the week.)

'Morning, ladies. Has everyone had their cucumber juice?'

Cucumber juice? I put the glass down faster than if she'd told me it contained polonium.

'Yes. There is one whole cucumber and two sticks of celery in each glass,' says Catriona, looking at me as if I'm already trying her patience. 'It's very alkaline and very cleansing. It helps to balance all the acid in the body. You'll be drinking it four times a day.'

My stomach lurches as I imagine piles of this vile vegetable curled up in the kitchen.

'The Group A's are waiting for you outside,' says Catriona, looking at me.

'Oh right, better get going then.'

'You've still got time to drink the juice,' she says, sternly.

I take a glug and it's as repellent as it looks—warm, sludgy and tasting of greenhouse. I hold my nose, throw my head back and hurl it down in three horrible hits.

Outside, I'm shocked to find six super-toned women limbering up as if for the Olympics. In their thirties and glowing with health, it's difficult to see how they can improve on what they've already got. To book into a boot camp spa when you are already that slim and toned, is a bit like signing up for a quit-smoking course when you don't actually smoke.

We set off at a cracking pace. Determined not to be outdone I position myself near the front, but we're barely out of the gates before I've dropped to the back. Armed with a bottle of water each and a bag of nuts and seeds, we head along a dusty, orange-coloured road, past some ramshackle houses, across a stream and up a mountain. We march in an upward direction for two hours in blistering heat, during which I'm obliged to make increasingly stilted small talk with Derek, who has been posted at the rear to sweep up the stragglers.

As I drag myself up the narrow path, past scrubby bushes and boulders, I wish very much that I'd erred on the side of understatement when asked about my fitness levels. Pretty fit? Lots of stamina? What *was* I thinking of? Fortunately, Derek is too polite to mention it. Meanwhile, the others have long disappeared and about twenty minutes or so later, I start to hear voices behind us. The Group B's, who are supposed to be walking at a much slower pace, have caught up. I'm mortified as several of them march past. On the other hand, at least I'll get a break from Derek's valiant attempts at conversation. I'd much prefer to pant my way up the mountain in solitude.

'This is bloody hard work, isn't it?' says a fiftysomething B, falling into stride beside me. I recognise her as one of the women I overheard discussing their private chefs this morning. But, dressed in a foreign legion style hat with flaps at the back and sides, and her beige combat trousers tucked into thick socks, she looks much less intimidating now.

'I'm Vivienne, by the way,' she says, with a hint of an Australian accent. 'I could see you struggling with the slime juice this morning.'

'Slime juice? That's a really good description of it,' I say. 'I don't love cucumbers.'

'Me neither,' says Vivienne, gasping for breath as we turn a corner and see the A's marching back down from the summit.

'How far is it?' Vivienne calls out. 'Are there cocktails waiting for us at the top?' But the A's march past with barely a smile. It seems that they've given up their sense of humour along with the sugar and fat (for I can't imagine such vices ever passing their lips).

Vivienne tells me that the last time she did this detox, not only did she lose three kilos, but it also led to a much healthier lifestyle.

'After the first visit, I bought a juicer for all

my homes,' she says.

'How many homes have you got?' I ask, stunned by the implied boast.

'That's a good question,' she says and starts to count on her fingers, one of which sports a diamond that could buy several more houses. 'The duplex in Monte Carlo, the villa in St Trop, the apartment on Park Avenue, our house in Chelsea, a place in Palm Beach and we've just bought an estate in Scotland for the shooting. Oh, and I almost forgot, the house in the Hamptons. And the villa in Barbados, though we hardly use that.'

'That's a lot of juicers,' I say, trying not to smile.

An hour or so later, we limp back into the villa's grounds, barely able to speak. In that time, I've learnt that Vivienne, originally from Australia, is married to the owner of a private hedge fund based in London. We've bonded over our mutual dislike of cucumbers and I've been won over by her dry sense of humour. Back at base, we are rewarded with another glass of cucumber juice. Then Vivienne and I part company, for as I point out, I am Group A for yoga and she is a B. I make my way across the parched, scrubby lawn in front of the villa towards the yoga hall, a cool space with colourful Moorish tiling on the walls. My fellow A's have changed into up-to-the-minute yoga kit and, while waiting for class to start, are stretching out their limbs as though they were made of elastane.

I'm so exhausted that all I can do is lie quietly in the pose of the corpse, while my head thumps from caffeine withdrawal. The yoga teacher—an angel in stretchy lilac pants and a white vest top—comes over to ask if I'm OK and then, to my relief, leaves me alone for the rest of the class. Afterwards, she suggests in the kindest way possible way that I might be better off with the B's. I couldn't agree more.

For lunch, tables for two have been set up around the courtyard, all but one of them in the shade. This turns out to be my allotted table. I've already told Catriona that bright sunshine gives me a headache, but nonetheless I've been thrown on the mercy of the brutal Spanish sun. Worse, my lunch companion is the snarky owner of the health food brand. Citing a potential migraine as the excuse, I ask one of the male models if I might move into the shade, thinking that they will make a space for me at one of the other tables. Instead, Catriona instructs him to set up a table for one in the covered walkway that surrounds the courtyard. Vivienne, of course, has the best spot in the house—under a cream canopy near the arched entrance to the pool.

'What are you doing there on your own?' she calls over, signalling for one of the male models to set up an extra place. 'Come and sit with us.'

After a jolly lunch of soup and salad with

209

Vivienne and her friend Geraldine, who owns a chain of wine bars, we gather in the white lounge for a talk. The theme is written in large letters on a white board: 'HYDRATION'.

'I'd like to begin by asking how much water you drink in a day,' says Catriona, looking at me. 'Let's start with you.'

'Um . . . about a litre,' I say, immediately regretting it.

'A *litre*?' A look of angst flashes across her beautifully made-up face.

'Yes, but I also drink a lot of green tea. And I have a large glass of carrot juice every day,' I add, embellishing the truth more than a little in order not to cause her too much distress. But such is her horror, I might just as well have confessed to drinking a bucket of gin for breakfast instead.

'OK, what is green tea full of?' she asks, scanning the room.

'Caffeine,' says my Swiss nemesis, looking very smug.

'Correct. Thank you, Elsa,' says Catriona, turning again to me. 'Green tea will dehydrate you and carrot juice is full of sugar, causing your blood sugar levels to soar and crash.'

Vivienne winks at me from the opposite sofa, as if to say, 'That's telling you!'

While I am reeling at the idea that carrot juice could be dangerous, Elsa earns gold stars for drinking three litres of water a day. The talk then turns to alcohol.

'Who here likes a drink?' Catriona asks, looking at me.

'Do bears defecate in the woods?' says Vivienne, and I struggle not to laugh.

'Anyone here like a glass of champagne?' Catriona persists and for a foolish second I forget where I am and think she is going to offer us one. Instead, she proceeds to slander one of France's finest exports, rattling off its toxic qualities: 'Acidic . . . fermented . . . yeast . . . packed with sulphites.' It's like hearing someone say bad things about one of your best friends.

'Is white wine a better choice?' someone asks.

Catriona grimaces. 'White wine is *much* worse,' she says, before launching into a spiel about its higher acidity and sugar content.

'So what *is* the least harmful drink?' asks Geraldine.

The answer is surprising. 'Gin,' says Catriona.

'Great news,' says Vivienne. 'That's my favourite drink.'

In the early evening, after a protein shake dinner, Vivienne, Geraldine and I huff and puff our way up another hill together. The more time I spend in Vivienne's company, the more I warm to her upbeat personality and the fact she nearly always says what she thinks. I also like the fact that Catriona seems a little scared of her. On day two, after the detox queen puts me back into solitary confinement for lunch, Vivienne—who thinks that Catriona is playing a game of divide and conquer—requests, in a way that brooks no argument, that a permanent place be created for me on her table.

By day three, our group has expanded to include a lovely Irish woman and her property developer husband (one of just two men on the retreat), and the courtyard rings to the laughter from our table. In the evenings, while the A's are doing additional exercise sessions by the pool, the B's crowd into the small room set aside for computer use, and the laughter and conversation continues until bedtime. The B's might not be the fastest or the most flexible, but they are definitely the most fun. Meanwhile, my caffeine withdrawal headache has disappeared and I'm surprised to find that I'm having a good time.

On day four, we are accused of forming a clique. But Vivienne, bless her, is a formidable ally. She tells me that I remind her of her daughter—who, like me, was born on July 17th. I've always struck up friendships with older women, perhaps because I never had a close relationship with my own mother (something that Luis and I had in common). Vivienne willingly adopts the role, even checking me in for my flight home.

'Give me your passport and booking reference,' she commands and I hand them over happily.

One evening when everyone has gone to bed, I Google Vivienne and her husband and discover that they are well-known art collectors and philanthropists. In one photograph, taken at a charity dinner in New York, I hardly recognise my spa buddy. Dressed in diamonds and a purple gown, with a curtain of shimmering blonde hair, Vivienne the beautiful socialite looks very different from my outspoken spa buddy in her cut-off trousers and strange hat.

Catriona, meanwhile, 'forgets' to book me in for the daily massage. If I get a slot at all, it is the slot that no one else wants, or else my appointments clash with each other. As a beauty journalist, I've been incredibly spoilt over the years, visiting many of the world's top spas on what is euphemistically referred to as a 'facility trip' (otherwise known as a freebie). In return, I was expected to provide a glowing write-up—an arrangement that I never felt at ease with, as it seemed a little grubby and dishonest. If you've received a freebie worth several thousand pounds, you might for example, forget to mention the over-enthusiastic masseuse in the Italian spa who nearly dislocated your shoulder; or the therapist at a French thalasso centre who wrapped you tightly in cling film and self-heating seaweed and then failed to return— as once happened to me. (Someone did eventually hear my cries for help but it took a while.) It's almost a relief to experience a spa as a normal paying customer rather than a journalistic freeloader. But, after years of being treated like a princess, it's galling to find that I am the lowest priority.

One of the highlights of my day is Catriona's after-lunch talk, which always has comic potential. One afternoon, I walk into the white salon, where the word 'CHAKRAS' is written on the white board. Despite having worked on a health and beauty magazine, I'm still not sure what they are. (Something to do with energy centres, I later discover.)

To keep them balanced, Catriona tell us that we should only ever wear hats made of natural fibres—in either white or purple—while red is the colour to wear in the pelvic region.

'I remember that you told us that last year,' says Vivienne, looking very pleased with herself. 'And I only ever wear red knickers now.'

I can't tell if she is being facetious or not. Either way, it's a struggle not to laugh.

There is one talk, however, which I take very seriously indeed. I rush into the lounge late, since the talk clashed with my reflexology session, to find, 'EFFECT OF FOOD ON YOUR MOOD' written on the white board. Catriona is explaining that depressed people have 'no energy, no motivation, no initiative'.

She's basically describing the last six months of my life.

'They can't get out of bed and they often feel completely alone in their misery,' she continues, looking directly at me. 'But the thing to remember when you feel depressed is that almost everyone recovers.'

Certain foods, she tells us, can help alleviate depression, while others—alcohol, caffeine, and sugar—contribute to it. This is hardly 'newsflash' material, but it starts to really make sense as Catriona explains how my three favourite vices deplete levels of magnesium—a mineral necessary for the calm functioning of the nervous system and brain, as well as a good night's sleep. Foods that are rich in magnesium include almonds, pumpkin seeds, sesame seeds and walnuts, as well as leafy green vegetables, all of which feature in our daily rations. Maybe this is why I feel so calm and happy here.

Catriona then writes 'SEROTONIN' on the board. She explains that conventional anti-depressants work by increasing serotonin levels in the brain—and in some cases medication is necessary, as levels are so depleted that you cannot hope to get them up to normal levels by any other means. But it seems that there is plenty that you can do to boost serotonin naturally. Exercise, fresh air and daylight can help, she says, while certain foods contain an amino acid called tryptophan, which is necessary for making serotonin. These include turkey, chicken, eggs, pheasant, oily fish (such as salmon, sardines and tuna) walnut oil, bananas, pulses, beans and avocados. As Catriona reels off a list of happiness-boosting foods and talks about the importance of being in bed by midnight, I start to warm to her. In fact, I wonder if she has put together this talk especially for me. Is it that obvious I wonder, that I have been living in a black space? Either way, by the end of the session I have a new respect for the detox guru and want to jump up and hug her by way of a thank-you.

On the final day, I discover that I've lost three kilos and many centimetres from various parts of my body. Catriona dispatches Vivienne and Geraldine to the airport in a black Mercedes ahead of me, and tells me that, along with the Swiss-German health-nut, I must wait for another car (actually a bumpy minibus) that shows up a little later.

I catch up with Vivienne at the British Airways check-in desk, where she warns me never, *ever* to put my diamonds through the X-ray machine. Apparently, a friend of hers once lost a multi-million pound Cartier necklace that way in Miami. It didn't emerge on the other side. I nod and try to look concerned, while thinking, 'Frankly, Vivienne, losing my diamonds is one thing I *don't* have to worry about. Losing my marbles seems far more likely.'

The visit to the Spanish spa has been

life affirming. I'm leaner, looser and fitter. I've learned to love Catriona and bonded with unlikely strangers. Never could I have imagined that losing three kilos could be so much fun. I will probably never see Vivienne or Geraldine again, but thanks to them I managed to keep smiling as I glugged countless litres of cucumber juice and hiked up hills and through orange groves.

I'm determined to make changes when I get back to France. And not just with my diet: I'm going to clean up my emotional life, too. Luis, I realise, has become an addiction. Ever since the break-up, I've been experiencing a high just at the sight—or sound—of him. (I checked my phone several times to see if he called again while I was at the spa, but he didn't.) I have no idea what situation awaits me in the village, but I'm confident that I'll be better able to cope, now that my chakras are balanced and my serotonin levels boosted by several kilos of nuts and pumpkin seeds.

I refuse the gin and tonic on the flight back to London and in the days that follow, I manage to ignore the Bakewell tarts giving me come-hither signals in Pret A Manger. Instead, I go to Whole Foods and buy a giant tub of coconut oil—the healthiest fat to cook with, according to Catriona—along with several kilos of almonds and an assortment of seeds. This takes me comfortably over the Ryanair luggage allowance for the flight back to France. As a result, I'm forced to stuff the pockets of my Barbour with nuts at the check-in desk, like a giant squirrel, and wear a dress and two extra cardigans over my jeans. This means that I arrive at Poitiers airport looking ten kilos heavier than when I left.

Travis is waiting for me outside. I'd been hoping that he'd say something like, 'Wow! You look amazing.' Instead, as I waddle through the arrivals gate in several layers of clothing, he looks at me strangely and asks (again) how much the trip cost. He shakes his head in disbelief.

'Karen Wheeler, you are quite mad,' he says.

'Maybe,' I say, jumping into his convertible. 'But I feel great.' We head out of the airport with the roof down, listening to Lady Gaga (again) and singing along to *Just Dance*.

'You'll be pleased to know, Travis, that I feel like a new person,' I say, as we speed down the N10 in the sunshine. 'I did quite a lot of thinking while I was away and I can see now that Luis did not deserve me. It's time to draw a line under the past.' (How much easier it is to say this, when there are signs that the other person might want you back.)

'*Halle-fucking-lujah*! It's only taken you nearly a year to come to that conclusion.'

'Eight months, actually. Can you turn the music up?'

Travis suggests going to Ruffec, a

picturesque town about 40 kilometres from his village, for an early evening drink. He's heard that it is 'really rocking' in the evening, although in rural France that means two or three people standing at the bar. But I don't have to pick Biff up from Sarah and Steve's until tomorrow, so I agree.

'It's almost summer. The party has to be somewhere,' I say.

But when we get to Ruffec, the only place open is a kebab bar. We drive back to Sommières-du-Clain, a little village near where Travis lives, just in time to have a drink at the café before it closes. 'You know what?' he says, as we sit in the spring sunshine. 'I've come to the conclusion that you can't go looking for the party. In rural France, you have to *be* the party.'

'I'll drink to that,' I say, clinking my glass of Evian against his bottle of beer. 'To the party!'

Chapter 14

Cherry Picking

A Saturday afternoon in early June: it's burningly hot and almost everyone in the village has taken refuge behind closed shutters, but Biff needs a walk so I reach for my floppy sun hat and head towards the square. It's deserted, but the door to Pierre-Antoine's boutique is open and I can see him inside, unpicking the hem of a pair of trousers at his wooden desk. He beckons me in, kisses my cheeks and points to the beige pants in front of him.

'I always need to be doing things with my hands,' he says. 'I told my client that I would take up three pairs of trousers by this evening.' He shakes his head to convey the madness of it. '*Ouf*, I've really worked hard today, that's for sure.'

I try not to smile. Pierre-Antoine makes owning a boutique—one that opens at 10.00 am and closes for two hours at lunchtime—seem like harder work than a twenty-four-hour shift in Accident and Emergency. He stands up and indicates for me to follow him. He leads me to a room at the back of the shop, looking out over the sunny courtyard and the barn that houses his red sports car and extensive collection of sporting equipment. He sits down at a Singer sewing machine and, with his back to me, says, 'There are two questions that I want to ask you, *Ka-renne*.'

This is it, I think—the moment when his intentions will finally become clear.

'OK. I'm listening.'

He turns and looks me directly in the eye while snapping a thread off the trouser hems.

'The first question is, do you know a

220

journalist who can write about my cousin's vineyard?'

I try not to look surprised. He has mentioned this vineyard before, but this surely can't be the reason why he has bombarded me with invitations for dinner, drinks and bike rides over the past six months?

'Unfortunately, I don't know any wine writers,' I say.

'Could it not make an interesting story for you?'

'Well, no. I write about fashion.'

'I see.'

Silence hangs in the air, as heavy as the languid afternoon heat, while he lines up the trousers under the needle of the sewing machine. He hits the pedal hard and attacks the hem in short, aggressive blasts, while Biff and I stand and watch.

'So, what's the second question?' I ask in a pause between bursts of machining.

'*Un moment,*' he commands. He finishes the trousers and then signals for me to follow him back through the shop. Although I'm not attracted to Pierre-Antoine I am a little miffed, given his reputation as a ladies' man, that he hasn't made any kind of move on me. As I follow him into a small storeroom I wonder if he is going to push me against the viscose-mix dresses and press his lips to mine? But, no. Instead, he opens a cupboard, reaches inside and pulls out . . . a red Henry Hoover.

221

My mouth falls open in astonishment. Even Biff's eyes widen. There are no words.

'Do you know where I can get some bags for this?' he asks.

'That's what you wanted to ask me?'

'Yes. It's not possible to buy them in France.'

'I see.'

'And it was made in the UK. So I thought you might be able to help.'

'Well, I can certainly try next time I'm in London,' I say. 'But now I must walk Biff.'

'Wait a moment,' he commands. 'I'll get the instruction manual and you can write down the model number.'

'Good idea,' I say, trying to look enthusiastic as he rifles in his desk for the manual, then copies the details onto a yellow Post-It sticker.

'*Voilà,*' he says, handing it to me. 'See you soon, *Ka-renne.*'

I am surprised and a little humiliated. According to Arnaud, Pierre-Antoine is the biggest *dragueur* in the village, but all he wants from me is vacuum cleaner bags. As I step back out into a wall of heat, I glance over at the café on the corner to see if The Devil is there. But the *terrasse* is deserted. He is probably in a darkened room, sheltering from the sun with his pregnant girlfriend. Arnaud has not volunteered any further news on that front and I have not asked. Nor have I seen Luis or Sabine since returning from my spa

222

trip.

The following afternoon, I'm watching a World Cup football match on TV when Pierre-Antoine taps on the open window to ask if I'd like some cherries. His mother has got so many in her garden that she doesn't know what to do with them. He tells me to bring my bike to his shop when I'm ready, so that we can cycle the short distance to her house and pick some.

I say I'll be over as soon as the match is finished. Then I get ready in a yellow and white checked dress and sandals decorated with daisies. It's a little dressed-up for cherry picking, I know, but the effort is all for his mother, who is formidable. I've met her a few times in the boutique and every time she looks at me, it's as if she is sizing me up as daughter-in-law material.

Outside, it's hot enough to flay sunflowers. Wheeling my bike over to the boutique with Biff bobbing along beside me, I notice that my tyre is flat. When I explain this to Pierre-Antoine, he tells me to come round to the rear of the shop, where he will pump it up. I hold the bike steady while he crouches down by my knees and connects the pump. I can't help but notice that he looks very manly and capable as he thrusts air into the tyre.

'How hard do you want it?' he asks.

'Quite hard,' I say, prodding the firm tyre and trying not to smile.

We cycle down the hill and along the river

towards the lane where his mother lives, with Biff running alongside my bike. As we reach the big wooden gates of the old farmhouse, I can hear music playing. It's very tinny, as if it is coming from a transistor radio. I imagine that his mother is in the garden sunbathing, but a much stranger spectacle waits on the other side of the high stone wall.

The cherry tree is magnificent, dominating the clipped green lawn that stretches from the house down towards a vegetable patch and wild meadows beyond. Its branches are sagging under the weight of ripe purple-black cherries. But it's not the cherries that I notice first. It's the transistor radio, silver handbag and mirrors that are also dangling from the branches. Equally disconcerting is the scarecrow guarding the tree, which is dressed in plush pink chenille. Closer inspection reveals that it's an upturned broom, wearing a dressing gown.

Pierre-Antoine explains that the point of all these props is to scare away the birds, but this little scene is like something out of a Hitchcock movie and could frighten quite a few humans, too. Even Biff looks a little freaked by it.

Pierre-Antoine closes the gates so that we are completely hidden from the outside world and then goes into the house. I sit under the tree with Biff and admire the garden, which is stunning, striking just the right balance between wild and cultivated. I resist the urge to tuck into the cherries in case *maman* is watching from the window. Pierre-Antoine eventually reappears with two plastic buckets.

'Where is your mother?' I ask, as he hands me one.

'She's gone away for the weekend.'

'Oh,' I say, feeling like I've just been freed from a tight-fitting jacket. I won't have to be my most ingratiating self after all. For some reason, her absence makes the innocent act of cherry picking seem a little illicit.

'You can release the dog from his lead,' says Pierre-Antoine. As Biff sniffs his way around the lawn, his little tail bobbing with joy, I sink my teeth into the first of many of those fat black orbs, dying my fingers and lips with the purple juice. Only last week I wrote a feature entitled, *The Return Of The Cherry-Stained Lip*, and described a three-step procedure for achieving it, involving gloss and a lip pencil called Very Cherry by Laura Mercier. Much easier to bite into the real thing, I realise.

Pierre-Antoine and I work in silence. He perches on an old wooden ladder, while I pick from the lower branches and Biff lies panting in the shade of the tree. A silence that is neither comfortable nor uncomfortable hangs in the heavy air. The French word for it is '*troublant*', which means 'disturbing', usually in an amorous sense. It must be the heat, but I find myself imagining what it would be like if Pierre-Antoine tried to seduce me under the cherry tree. I think I'd like him a lot more if he at least tried. Hidden as we are by the high walls, in this stunning garden and on a hot day, it would be the perfect setting for a seasoned *dragueur* to make his move.

I look at the pink-white hollyhocks thrusting up against the old stone walls and my thoughts turn unprompted to Luis, who would have seized the moment as soon as the gates were closed. In fact, I doubt if he'd have been interested in plucking cherries at all.

But I am barking up the wrong tree with Pierre-Antoine. He makes no amorous moves whatsoever. Instead, when the buckets are full, he climbs down from his ladder and shows me his vegetable patch.

'There are lots of potatoes, some carrots and *oh, la, la,* so many tomatoes,' he says, shaking his head in wonder. As we walk back to the garden, scented molecules of lime blossom and jasmine drift over on the warm evening air, while crickets sing in the nearby meadow. This could all be so erotic. But it isn't. Behind his friendly smile, Pierre-Antoine is as cold as a cave.

He goes back into the house to lock up and I wait by the bikes, noticing that my tyre has deflated again. We walk slowly back to the village in the melancholy light of a summer evening. When we arrive back at Maison Coquelicot, I'm surprised that Pierre-Antoine

226

hands me both buckets.

'Don't you want some yourself?' I say.

'No, we picked these for you,' he says. 'You can freeze them if you want, but if you do, it's best to do it with the stalks still attached and the stones still in them.'

'That's very kind of you,' I say. 'Are you in a hurry?'

'Not especially,' he says with a shrug.

'Then would you like to come in for an aperitif?'

'It's not obligatory,' he replies, which is not the most enthusiastic response I've ever had to a drinks invitation, but he follows me into the cool interior of the house.

'What would you like?'

'What have you got?' he asks.

I open the kitchen cupboard and run through the possibilities. He points to the (unopened) bottle of port that Luis once brought me back from Portugal. Pierre-Antoine then asks if he can watch the football, so I turn on the television and while he focuses his attention on Argentina versus Mexico, I go into the kitchen to grill a burger and boil up some basmati rice for Biff's dinner. This, I think to myself, is probably what married life is like—drinking your aperitifs in separate rooms, one of you glued to the telly. Despite this, I find myself asking him if he would like to stay for dinner.

'Nothing special,' I say. 'Just pasta with

some fresh tomatoes and basil.'

'Why not?' he replies.

It doesn't take long to chop up some tomatoes and fry them with garlic and olive oil. I lay the table in the courtyard, lighting some candles and opening a bottle of wine and, since my guest is still watching the football, I go upstairs to check my emails.

'Are we going to eat soon?' he calls, just as I switch on my computer.

'It's ready,' I say, feeling like I've morphed into a long-suffering wife. 'I was waiting for you.'

'I can't stay late. I'm visiting my sister tomorrow morning,' he says, as I lead the way into the candlelit courtyard.

'Where does your sister live?' I ask, imagining he is going to say Bordeaux or somewhere at least an hour's drive away.

'Poitiers. But I'd like to be up and ready to leave by 8.00 am.'

I try not to laugh. Poitiers is less than half an hour away from our village. Had I been harbouring any misplaced ardour for Pierre-Antoine, this surely would have killed it faster than a bullet felling a wild boar. I can't help but compare him with Luis, who would stay up laughing and talking well beyond midnight even if he had to be up a couple of hours later to go to a job 200 kilometres away.

Over dinner, Pierre-Antoine tells me again that he hardly ever cooks at home. He can't be frying onions or making stews, he says, as he has his clothes and his shop to think about. But I'm not really listening. I'm ashamed to say that I'm thinking about Luis and the summer evening that I invited him into my courtyard for the first time. I remember the energy—like an electrical storm in a confined space, the humid night air was practically fizzing with it. Pierre-Antoine, by contrast, is like a fire extinguisher, quelling any potential spark of attraction with just a few words.

At one point, as the conversation is thinning, I tell him about the cocktail party that I'm planning to hold at La Grande Galerie, an art gallery in a nearby town, to launch my book next month.

'What night of the week is it?' he asks.

'It's a Thursday—early evening, from 7.00 until 9.00 pm.'

Immediately, he shakes his head and looks grave, as if I were about to suggest an all night rave and a tequila-drinking contest, or some other debauchery.

'It's not possible for me to come,' he says, explaining that on weekdays he has to go to bed early for work so that he can be 'on form' the next day.

This is one squirt of the fire extinguisher too many.

'You're selling clothes, for God's sake,' I want to shout. *'You don't start work until 10.00 am and you live above the shop.'*

229

Again, my thoughts are pulled, as if by a rip current, towards Luis. I think of him getting up at dawn to work twelve-hour shifts and never once complaining that he was tired. On the contrary, as I now know, he had enough energy for two women.

When Pierre-Antoine has left for his early night, I think how he and Luis represent two extremes. There must be something in the middle, I tell myself—a *normal* man.

Later that night there is a storm, creating dramatic flashes of white light outside my bedroom window, and a downpour of rain that finally sweeps aside the thick, humid air that has been smothering the village for days. A couple of days later, I go up to Paris for a beauty launch, leaving Biff with Arnaud, who has kindly offered to look after him for the day. In rural France, a man walking a small dog might just as well be strutting around the village with a handbag and high heels, so unmacho is it considered. But Arnaud seemed very excited this morning when I handed him my house keys.

Now here I am, perched on a cardboard chair, in a room specially constructed for today's event. Everything in the room is made out of paper, including the faux fireplace and coffee table. The marketing director of a luxury beauty company is unveiling a series of eco-initiatives, designed to establish it as a 'planet friendly' brand. These include refillable

230

bottles and a plan to make the head office, um . . . a paper-free zone. I fidget on my paper chair in the paper room, wondering if they've really thought this through.

'The problem with luxury is that it usually means more of everything, while being eco-friendly means less,' she concludes. I couldn't agree more, which is why I'm a little taken aback when, at the end of the presentation, I'm given a bag containing several kilos of glossy, laminated press releases. I stagger back to Montparnasse station under their weight, stopping at the Pierre Hermé patisserie on the Left Bank, to buy Arnaud one of the famous pastry chef's limited edition vanilla cakes to thank him for looking after Biff. I wanted to pay my neighbour—he's been off work for so long that I figured he could use the money—but he wouldn't hear of it.

Biff gives me a slightly contemptuous look when I arrive home. Arnaud knocks on the door almost immediately and tells me that Biff made one sad little bark after I left, but other than that was fine and he's had five walks.

'Thank you so much,' I say, handing Arnaud the cake that I've bought him.

He looks embarrassed and tells me that I shouldn't have. I ask if he'd like to have lunch with me tomorrow, but he tells me that he has arranged to go into Poitiers with Yvette. She needs some legal advice as she has finally decided to close down her boutique.

'That's really sad news,' I say.

Arnaud shrugs. 'That's life,' he says. 'No one around here has any money.

*　　　*　　　*

The following afternoon, Arnaud returns from Poitiers in exceptionally high spirits despite the horrendous heat.

'*Tout bio,*' (all organic), he declares, handing me a large paper bag filled with vegetables.

'These must have been expensive, Arnaud,' I say.

'About €10,' he shrugs. 'I bought them from a farmer on the way back from Poitiers.'

'Here, let me give you the money.'

'It's a present,' he says, waving the note away. He tells me that he just bumped into Delphine in the square and he'd like to make dinner for us both tonight.

'That's very nice of you,' I say, feeling embarrassed.

'*Nickel,*' he replies. Perfect! He tells me that he will prepare the food next door—'nothing fancy, just a chef's salad'—and bring it round to mine.

'Well, it's a bit of a mess in here,' I say, looking around at the untidy kitchen. 'But I suppose we could eat in the courtyard.'

I tell Arnaud that I'm planning to ask Magda to help me with the cleaning.

'The Portuguese girl?'

'Yes.'

'Well, I wouldn't leave her in the house alone. And be sure to hide your valuables.'

'Why do you say that?'

He shrugs. 'Just be careful.'

But my mind is made up. No matter how hard I try to keep on top of the cleaning—which isn't *very* hard, I admit—Biff and I are living in slum conditions. He seems more than happy with the arrangement but there is no doubt that if he were a human *enfant*, he would have been put into foster care by now. Between all the dog walking, grooming—Biff swims or rolls in something unpleasant most days—and trying to scratch a living as a freelance journalist, the daily battle against dirt is one that I can't win alone. Magda is the obvious choice, since she needs money and I need help. And if she's not interested, she might be able to recommend someone who is, since several of the Portuguese WAGS (Wives And Girlfriends) have part-time cleaning jobs. The only problem is that I haven't seen her in a while. Like an exotic bird, Magda seems to have flown the village.

While Arnaud prepares dinner next door, I lay the table and light some candles in an attempt to make the courtyard—still a flower-free zone—a little more appealing.

Delphine arrives looking bemused. 'My goodness, what is Arnaud up to? He was jumping around like a crazy thing when I saw him this afternoon.'

I laugh. 'It's true. I'm not sure what Arnaud got up to in Poitiers today but he did return in a highly excitable state.'

The man himself comes marching through the kitchen and into the courtyard with two dishes covered in tinfoil and a baguette tucked under his arm. '*Voilà*, ladies! Dinner is served,' he cries, unveiling the salad, which is an artistic arrangement of grated carrot, tuna, green beans, red peppers and slices of hard-boiled egg, arranged in concentric circles around a mound of shredded lettuce. He then removes the foil from the second platter to reveal a lavish selection of cheeses and *pâtés*.

'This is really very generous of you, Arnaud,' I say, wondering how he can afford such a spread when he is not working.

'Help yourselves!' he cries with a twirl of his wrist, on which there is another new bracelet. As we eat, Arnaud asks Delphine what is happening with the café in Puysoleil, where (predictably) the two sisters have handed in their notice.

'Nothing as yet,' she replies. 'But eventually we will have to look for new tenants.'

For the next hour, Arnaud tells a series of anecdotes about his life in Puysoleil, speaking very quickly and using a lot of local dialect and slang, which makes it hard for me to follow. I can tell from the way that Delphine

234

is laughing, that the stories are highly entertaining.

'Arnaud says that when he lived in Puysoleil, there were six couples on the *lotissement*, or housing plot, and four of the wives were having affairs,' she says. 'Two of them with him.'

'He was having affairs with two women in the same cul-de-sac?' I say, as my neighbour sits back in his chair looking very pleased with himself.

'Yes,' says Delphine. 'One of them was the wife of the butcher. The other one, Mme Mabillon, is very surprising. She is very correct and married to a local businessman.'

'Mme Mabillon? Wasn't that the woman that I met at the bar opening?' I say, thinking back to the woman in the tan trousers and navy blazer who was so snooty about Arnaud.

'Yes,' says Delphine. 'That was her. He says that he and the butcher's wife used to drive around in a small van doing the deliveries and that is when they had their liaisons. Apparently, some elderly people were very helpful and let them use their barns for this business. And sometimes they would stop at Arnaud's mother's house to do the deed, and she would make them a coffee afterwards.'

'That was very accommodating of her,' I say.

When Arnaud goes next door to fetch dessert, Delphine lowers her voice and says, 'Apparently, he was a very good lover. That is what everyone in the village said, anyway. But

235

my goodness, what an old rogue.'

Arnaud returns with a *fraisier* or strawberry gateau, and the conversation turns to Puysoleil's annual Celtic music festival, which takes place this Saturday. Before the evening is over, it is decided that we will go along together.

*   *   *

On Saturday evening, I collect Arnaud from the *terrasse* of the café, where I find him drinking strawberry-flavoured water and attempting to *drague* every female who enters his orbit, by cracking jokes and making facetious comments.

'You look very nice, *ma puce*,' he says, taking both my hands in his—just at the moment that The Devil comes out of the *tabac* next door, opening a packet of cigarettes. It's the first time that I've seen him since he bombarded my phone with calls. Dressed in a turquoise top and jeans, he looks startled when he sees me with Arnaud.

'Let's go,' I say to my neighbour, eager to get away.

'OK, *ma puce*, let's go and DANCE!' he cries, loud enough for everyone to hear.

As we drive towards Puysoleil, past beautifully lit fields of wheat and barley, Arnaud asks if I have any plans to go to Paris again and reiterates his willingness to look after Biff.

'Well actually,' I say, 'I was wondering if you could look after him this Thursday? But it will be two dogs, as his friend Milou is coming to stay.'

'No problem,' says Arnaud. 'No problem at all.'

We park the car in the designated field and walk down towards the river, where a stage has been erected for the musicians, and long trestle tables set out for the communal meal. I'm wearing a paisley print maxi dress and Biff looks smart with a *tricolore* ribbon tied around his neck. But our neighbour, dressed in cropped trousers and a new T-shirt by the trendy surfer brand, Quiksilver, upstages us both. I suppose I should be grateful that he isn't smoking pot and calling everyone 'dude'.

Heads swivel in his direction as we head to the bar. This is probably the first time that his former friends and neighbours have seen him since his makeover. One man gives him a thumbs-up sign as we wait for our Cokes, while another slaps him on the back and says, 'Bravo, old chap. What a change! You've certainly turned things around for yourself.' I'm not sure if he is referring to his new look or the fact that he is no longer an alcoholic. Either way, Arnaud seems mighty pleased.

Biff, meanwhile, is having a marvellous time, running around like the Pied Piper of Puysoleil with a string of small children in hot pursuit. I can see that he's running at a fraction of his normal speed in order to give them a chance to catch up. Every now and then, he turns around to see where they are and then slows down even further. He seems to have quite an audience. At one point, a man comes up to me and says, 'He's very funny, your dog—the best entertainment here.'

I look over at Biff who is tossing a stick into the air for his own amusement and giving little barks of excitement, and feel really proud of him. He's such a happy little dog, bringing joy wherever he goes.

Delphine, as mayor, gets up on the stage to give her usual welcome speech, thanking the musicians and the people who've organised the festival. Then, after introducing the first band, she joins us for the al fresco meal of steak and chips, followed by apple tart. As the violins and the melancholy voice of a barefoot Irish singer fill the night air, my thoughts drift to last year's festival when I sat in almost the same spot with Luis. It feels like another life ago.

Later in the evening, Arnaud tries to get me up to dance. 'Maybe later,' I say. Undeterred, he heads towards the dance floor alone, where he performs a strange but energetic jig, hopping from leg to leg and twirling his arms in the air.

'Look at the old goat,' says Delphine. 'He's really enjoying himself.'

'Yes. And he looks like he might have pulled,' I say, for Arnaud is soon dancing with a neat looking woman in her fifties. They're an unlikely combination—she is dressed as if for a wedding in a polka dot dress, Arnaud for a Bondi Beach bar—but as I watch my neighbour twirling his new friend around the grassy dance floor, I'm happy that his scattergun flirting appears finally to have paid off. Biff, I notice, has also made some new friends and is running around with a pack of (much bigger) dogs. I'm proud to see that despite being the smallest, he appears to be the leader.

'It's almost time to light the pyre,' says Delphine, who can never relax until the fire, expertly built by Bruno and Rémi, has burnt down to a circle of glowing embers. The bar and the dance area in front of the stage are really crowded now, thanks to a second wave of younger people arriving after dinner. I'm not sure where they have come from—the Celtic festival attracts people from all over France—but the girls are dressed in long skirts, with bare midriffs, while the males have long hair and are wearing pyjama-style trousers. I've recently written a feature on this summer's must-have 'traveller pants' and although I'm sure that they don't know it, many of them have nailed the trend.

To clapping and cheering, the pyre is eventually lit and orange flames climb into

239

the purple-blue sky in an almost vertical roar. (This is a relief for Delphine, who quietly panicked one year when gusts of wind pushed the flames perilously close to nearby trees.) Bongo drums take over from the violins and a rhythmic tribal dance starts up around the fire. The fact that the pyre hasn't been cordoned off, feels like a glorious defiance of 'health and safety' and I'm proud of Delphine for presiding over such an effortlessly bohemian event.

The dancing and the drumming eventually reach a crescendo and Arnaud returns to the table, his face flushed. I ask him if he minds if we leave soon.

'Don't worry about me, my little flea,' he winks. 'I'm pretty sure I've got a ticket home.' He nods towards the woman in the polka dot dress.

'Your new friend lives in Villiers?'

'Yes,' he says with a wink.

'Well, good luck.' I say goodnight to Delphine and then make my way through the opaque darkness to the field where the car is parked. Not for the first time in the French countryside, I wish I'd brought a torch.

Back in rue St Benoit, I'm letting Biff out from behind the passenger seat when I see (and hear) Sabine coming towards me, hunched over in the darkness and propped up by a female friend. Hysterical and openly sobbing, she is the very definition of wretchedness. I almost feel sorry for her. What, I wonder, is she doing in rue St Benoit? My intuition tells me that she is looking for Luis. If so, it's interesting that she thinks she might find him here. I slip into Maison Coquelicot avoiding eye contact and marvelling at the destruction that The Devil seems to leave in his wake.

The next morning, walking back from Intermarché, I notice that one of the panels in Luis's bedroom window is broken. As I'm passing by the café, Arnaud calls me over.

'You made it back from Puysoleil then?' I say.

'Yes, no problem,' he says, motioning for me to sit down.

'The lady you were dancing with looked very nice,' I say, but Arnaud pulls a face as if to suggest that he is not interested.

'Listen, I have some news for you,' he says. 'Luis and Sabine had a really big fight last night. The gendarmes were called. Things were thrown and a window was broken.'

'I saw. But they should be careful. If Sabine is pregnant, this is no way to carry on.'

'Sabine is no longer pregnant,' says Arnaud.

'Since when?'

'I don't know. Maybe a couple of weeks ago.' Arnaud shrugs. 'Apparently, she told the woman who works in the *tabac* that she'd ended it.'

'But surely this is not what Luis would have

241

wanted?' I say.

'I don't know,' says Arnaud. 'But I told you Luis doesn't love her. Do you want a coffee, my flea?'

I hesitate for a moment, tempted by the smell of roasted coffee beans. Then, with a huge amount of willpower, I drag myself away from the café and its seductive offerings and head back to Maison Coquelicot, where a fridge full of cucumbers awaits. I wonder how much of this story is true and whether Sabine really was pregnant? I've learnt not to trust the village gossip. But is it just a coincidence, I wonder, that Luis always fights with her within hours of seeing me with another man?

*   *   *

On Monday afternoon, Steve and Sarah drop off Milou for a week-long stay while they return to the UK. Steve looks understandably nervous.

'The thing is,' he says, as he brings in Milou's doughnut bed, 'the last time we gave you a dog to look after, you didn't give him back.'

'Sorry about that. I promise I won't do it again,' I say, while secretly thinking how great it would be to have a little friend for Biff, especially one who is fluffy and white and roughly the same size. Together, they would make a nicely co-ordinating set. But helping yourself to a friend's dog is the sort of stunt you can only pull off once. Biff, meanwhile, is delighted to have Milou staying with us, pulling her around the *petit salon* by her lead as if to show her who's in charge.

In the days that follow, another heatwave descends on the village. It's so hot that I adopt the French habit of leaving the shutters just a few centimetres ajar to block out the heat, while letting in some light. It turns the *petit salon* into a haven. But even in the relative cool, the dogs lie around listless for most of the day. More often than not, I wait until early evening and walk them around the local lake, where invariably they slip into the stagnant water for a swim. Two dogs, I've discovered, are twice as messy as one. When I find a piece of pondweed and some leaves tucked down the side of the leather sofa, I decide that the house needs an intensive clean. And since I haven't yet managed to speak to Magda, I have no choice but to do it myself.

I put on some loud music and reacquaint myself with the vacuum cleaner. I start in the hallway, where I notice something that stops me in my tracks. My Terramundi pot no longer has notes sticking out of the top. I pick it up and am shocked to find that it is only two-thirds full. The last time I looked, there was only room for a few more pound coins. I distinctly remember thinking that it was almost time to break it open, and feeling sad that there was no possibility of the wish that I'd posted inside it coming true. How weird. Perhaps I only imagined that it was full? But no, that's not possible . . . There have been several storms lately and the air has been very heavy and humid. Maybe atmospheric pressure has somehow forced the money, most of it in £10 and £20 notes, down inside the pot. Yes, that must be it.

I decide to stick with this theory because the alternative—that someone has plucked the notes out from the wide slot at the top—is just too horrible to contemplate.

Chapter 15

Money Pot

The following Saturday, Delphine and I take the train to Paris for the day, to celebrate her divorce settlement. (Her former husband has finally agreed a figure for her share of their house.) And since I'm always looking for an excuse to vacate the village at weekends when The Devil looms largest, I need little persuasion to join her for lunch in Paris.

Early on Saturday morning, I walk Biff and Milou over to the café and hand them to Arnaud, along with my spare set of keys. As he takes the dogs and kisses me on the cheeks, an old boy driving a pea soup-coloured 2CV toots his horn at him and makes a strange congratulatory gesture with his arm.

'He'll be boasting around all over the village with those dogs,' says Delphine, when I tell her how thrilled Arnaud was to have custody of Biff and Milou for the day.

On arrival in Paris, we head to St Germain and Les Deux Magots—or 'The Maggots' as Delphine and I affectionately call it— for a late breakfast. After ordering, we sit back and admire the waiters. Tall and slim in their immaculate, long white aprons, they turn waiting tables into high theatre, moving around with grace and precision. Our other favourite pastime is a game called 'Left Bank Man,' which involves spotting a certain type of elderly Parisian male who sits at cafés alone, pretending to read *Le Monde* while secretly checking out the women. Wealthy, with greying hair and the slightly crumpled air of the intellectual, he is easily identifiable by his pale, unstructured jacket and round tortoiseshell glasses.

'Left Bank Man is thin on the ground today,' I say, scanning the rows of empty chairs.

'It's July,' says Delphine. 'He is on the Île de Ré.'

I don't blame him. I love the glamour of Paris in the winter but I can see why the French vacate the city en masse during the

245

summer, when the metro smells like a cowshed and the streets a ferment of stale sweat, nicotine and melting dog *crotins*. At the first sign of a heatwave, I, too, would be on the next train out. Still, it's nice to be in Paris for the day.

Delphine and I spend a few hours ambling around the shops on Boulevard St Germain, before heading to lunch at Le Procope. The oldest restaurant in Paris, this was once frequented by leading figures of the French Revolution, including Rousseau and Voltaire. It is not so much a restaurant as a townhouse, decorated in plush Belle Époque style and divided into many small dining rooms and secretive enclaves—although nowadays, those sitting in the cosy scarlet nooks are more likely to be planning an illicit affair than revolution.

I manage, with not very much effort, to resist the veal's head 'cooked as it was in 1686'. Instead, after the sparkly blue *cocktail du jour* (blue curaçao with champagne), we have Le Procope's signature dish, 'drunken' *coq au vin*, served with great elegance from a copper saucepan, by a waiter with a handlebar moustache. It's delicious but if I'm honest, not the best choice for a tropical day in Paris. I make a mental note to return in winter and to skip breakfast beforehand.

After lunch, we cross the river to the Marais, stopping in Thé Mariage Frères to stock up on exotic teas, including my favourite

Buddha Blue (a green tea with little blue flowers in it). We take respite from the heat among the potted palms of the tea salon at the back, served by waiters in cream colonial-style suits. Then it's back to the concrete carbuncle of Montparnasse for the train home, where I realise I've forgotten to buy Arnaud a gift for looking after the dogs.

'Don't worry,' says Delphine. 'You can take him out to lunch instead. I'm sure he'd like that more.'

We drive home in beatific light, our journey paved with jolly sunflowers and the gold of the wheat and barley fields. Villiers is quiet, as it always is after the 7.30 pm watershed. I'm expecting Arnaud to jump out and greet us when he hears Delphine's car pulling up outside, but he doesn't. Inside the house, Milou and Biff are lying on the leather sofa like yin and yang, looking exhausted. Their fur is damp, which means that Arnaud must have taken them out recently and let them swim in the river. In the kitchen, there is a pan of rice on the stove, which is still warm. I'm touched to see that my neighbour has added a stock cube and seasoning.

'Good old Uncle Arnaud!' I say to Biff and Milou. 'There aren't many doggies lucky enough to have their dinner cooked by a professional chef.'

Arnaud doesn't answer when I knock on his door to thank him. I can hear his cat mewling in the kitchen but otherwise his house is silent. I bang on the door again, in case he is upstairs with his headphones on, listening to his English language CDs. Still no reply. It's odd as he asked me twice what time I'd be home and gave the impression that he'd be waiting for me. I hope he's OK. I go back home and call his mobile but it's switched off. A little while later, he calls. 'Is everything OK?' he asks, his tone somehow implying that it might not be.

'Yes, everything is great. I hope the dogs behaved themselves?'

'*Si, si,*' he replies. 'I took them out four or five times and then I made them dinner.'

'Thank you so much. Would you like to go to lunch at the campsite in Clussay tomorrow—my treat, to thank you for looking after them?'

'No, no, it's not necessary,' he says. 'And anyway, I'm in Poitiers right now and I won't be back until Tuesday.'

Arnaud sounds cagey, so I don't press for more information. He's probably at one of his political meetings.

'Well, have a good weekend,' I say, thinking how lucky I am to have him for a neighbour. 'And thanks again.'

The following morning, the dogs wake me up early by scratching at the bedroom door. 'OK, OK,' I say, feeling quite bullied by them. I throw on some clothes and drag myself downstairs, the dogs running laps of excitement around my ankles. As I unhook their leads from the coat pegs in the hall, the money pot on the table catches my eye. Although I've tried to push it to the back of my mind, it still bothers me that I can no longer see the £20 notes through the slot. I pick it up and am shocked to find that it is even lighter and emptier than last time. It is just over half full now. 'Atmospheric pressure' cannot possibly explain this.

As I walk the dogs around the square, I mull over the possibilities. The money pot was stuffed with notes to the very top. Now it is not, which means that someone has stolen from it. The slot is wide enough to pluck the notes out with a pair of tweezers. But that would take time. The thief would have needed to be in the house alone and undisturbed to do it. I feel sick as I consider the most likely explanation. Surely it cannot be possible?

Back home, I take the pot into the courtyard and drop it on the ground several times before it breaks, spilling notes and one pound coins into a dull little pile. I can see immediately that there is less money than there should be. In notes alone, I've deposited at least £800 over the years—and that's a very conservative estimate—but when I add everything up, there is less than £300.

I feel shocked and I feel angry that the thief thought (erroneously) that I'd be too stupid—or too awash with money—to notice the disappearance of nearly half the contents. As I pick up the broken pieces, I see the little piece of paper on which I wrote the wish five years ago. Feeling sad and angry, I throw it in the bin along with the broken pieces of pottery. The money feels tainted now and I'm too shocked to decide what to do with it, so I throw it into a plastic bag and shove it in a desk drawer.

My first thought is to call Delphine, but since the matter involves a mutual friend, I'm too embarrassed to discuss my suspicions with her. Instead, I phone Travis and ask his advice. He laughs out loud when I tell him that my first thought was to blame atmospheric pressure.

'For an intelligent woman, you sometimes say the daftest things,' he says. 'If Arnaud is the only person who has had uninterrupted access to your house, then he has to be the prime suspect, not atmospheric pressure or whatever you call it. Honestly, what kind of physics did they teach at your school?'

'But how could he steal money from a friend?' I say. 'Why would he risk my friendship? Everyone says that it is largely thanks to me that his reputation is rehabilitated in the village. It can't possibly be him.'

'Maybe he needed the money. And he probably thought you wouldn't notice.'

'But what's he going to do with British money?'

'Ooh, let me see . . . change it into euros in the post office? It *is* possible to change money in Villiers, you know.'

'I just find it so hard to believe that he did this.'

'Well, the alternative explanation is that he left your front door open and someone came in with a pair of tweezers or, more likely, a knife, and helped themselves,' says Travis.

'Yes, maybe that's it,' I say, although even I can see that the idea of an opportunist thief taking some money rather than running off with the entire pot, is unlikely.

Later, I find myself Googling: 'How can you tell if someone is guilty of stealing from you?' It transpires that there are two key signs of culpability: firstly, the thief will try to avoid their victim; and secondly, they will have difficulty making eye contact. The most obvious thing to do is to call the gendarmes, but I doubt very much that they will take a raid on a piggy bank seriously. Plus I've broken the pot and the pieces are now covered in my fingerprints. The thief was probably too smart to leave any.

*   *   *

It's Tuesday afternoon when I next see Arnaud. He does not greet me as he normally

251

would, but instead crouches down and addresses Biff.

'Ça va, Arnaud?'

'Si, si,' he says and looks away. 'Was everything OK when you got back on Saturday?'

'With the dogs, yes. But unfortunately, I have a problem that I can't talk about now.'

'Nothing serious, I hope?'

'Yes, quite serious. Possibly a matter for the police.'

Normally, this would be the cue for Arnaud to ask lots of questions, to invite me for a coffee and a chat. But all he can manage today is a mildly interested, 'Oh?'

I think back to the organic vegetables that he bought me—probably with my own money—the lavish spread to which he treated Delphine and me, and his enthusiastic offer to look after Biff while I went to Paris. All those acts of kindness take on a horrible new significance now.

I think of how he warned me not to leave Magda in the house alone. Why? Was he worried that she would get to the money first?

I spend the new few days mulling over the possible scenarios. When I next see Arnaud sitting outside the café alone, I ask if he might be free to come to my house that afternoon, as I need some advice.

'Of course,' he says, looking nonchalant. 'Is it about the problem you already mentioned?'

'Yes,' I say. 'It is.'

When he arrives, he sits on the sofa opposite me. Mercifully, he spares me the brash laughter today. I thank him for coming and then, with a surprising calmness, launch into the speech that I've rehearsed in my head.

'Arnaud, you're a man of the world and you've had a lot of experience of life. I'd like to ask your advice about a matter that has been bothering me very much,' I say. He nods. 'The thing is that someone has stolen money from me. Someone I considered a friend.' I look him directly in the eye and pause for effect.

'How good a friend?' he asks.

'A good friend.'

I'm surprised that he hasn't asked the obvious. My very first reaction if someone told me that money was missing and I'd just had access to their house, would be, 'I hope you don't think it was me.' Instead, my neighbour asks, 'Are you sure?'

'Yes, I'm absolutely sure. The money has gone.'

'Was the money stolen from your house?' he asks.

'It doesn't really matter. The point is that it was stolen and it's a lot of money. I think this friend thought that I wouldn't notice.'

'What are you going to do about it?'

'I'm thinking of going to the gendarmes. But first, I'd like to give this person the possibility to amend the situation.'

'Ah bon?'

'Yes. I'd like to say to them, "I know you've done this and I'd like to give you the opportunity to give it back . . . "' I look him directly in the eye but he does not shrink from my gaze. 'And if you return the money, I won't take any further action. Instead, I'll consider the matter closed."' I pause and scrutinise Arnaud's face for signs of guilt. 'What do you think?' I ask.

He merely shrugs and looks away. 'I don't know. It's up to you,' he says.

If he has taken the money, he's showing a remarkable sang-froid. If he hasn't, he's showing very little outrage or concern that I might think he is the culprit. He has surprisingly little to say on the matter—no comment such as 'How awful', or 'How could a friend do this?' Or even, 'Who do you think might have done this?' And he offers no opinion at all as to what I should do, which is most unlike him.

We sit in silence for a few moments and then I say, 'I think I will give this person until the end of the week to return the money to my post box; and if they don't, I'll call the gendarmes.' He shrugs again, seemingly disinterested. There is nothing more to say.

Each morning, I check my post box to see if the culprit's conscience has got the better of him, but by the end of the week the money has not been returned. Arnaud, meanwhile, has become very elusive. When I do bump into him, he is subdued and it is Biff that he greets, not me.

'Well, you did say he was a socialist. And I guess that's what you call socialism in action,' says Travis when I tell him.

'Er, not quite. I thought the point of socialism was that you took from the rich to help the poor. I'm not exactly rich.'

'You are by some people's standards,' says Travis. 'Let's hope the thief feels that it was worth it.'

'Yes,' I say. 'I hope so.' I try to think benign thoughts like, 'Perhaps the thief really needed the money,' but my faith in human nature has been rocked. This is almost as big a betrayal as Luis's infidelity. I just can't believe that someone I counted as a friend could steal from me while thinking that I'd be too stupid to notice.

Of course, I will never know for sure if my neighbour took the money or not, but I'm grateful that, in the weeks that follow, I see very little of him. He is never at home and rarely in the café. The word is that he has a new *copine* and has virtually moved in with her.

Then one morning I notice Arnaud walking towards me, arm in arm with his new lady friend. I recognise her as the woman that he was dancing with at the Celtic festival. He looks away when he sees me.

*   *   *

Returning from a shopping trip to Poitiers one afternoon, I spot Magda sitting outside the café. She gives me a cheery wave. I stop the car and beckon her over.

'*Ça va, chérie?*' she says, her brown arm leaning on the car, in the classic pose of hooker negotiating with kerb-crawler. Dressed in jeans, with a fitted black shirt and an armful of jangly gold bracelets, she certainly looks the part (and I mean that as a compliment, since 'streetwalker chic' or tight jeans and tarty shoes, is a look that is very in vogue at the moment).

'Listen,' I say. 'I need someone to help me with the cleaning. Do you know anyone who might be interested?'

Her face breaks into a radiant smile. '*Moi, chérie,*' she says, pointing with both hands at her chest, which is barely contained by the shirt. She looks so thoroughly delighted at the prospect of cleaning my muddy floors that I am touched.

'It will be three hours a week,' I say. 'Possibly more.'

She nods, doesn't even ask what I'll be paying. 'When do you want me to come, *chérie?*'

'What about this Saturday?'

'OK, *chérie*. At 9.00 am?'

'Perfect.' She blows me a kiss as she drives away.

*   *   *

Magda arrives to clean for the first time wearing a white vest top, white leggings and a scarlet thong. I can only think that she is trying to balance her chakras, but every time she bends over, her vest top rises and a small triangle of red satin is visible above the leggings. I make her a coffee and she sets to work with a worrying amount of noise. I don't mind the sound of the vacuum cleaner banging into things, or cushions being beaten—it can only mean that she is doing a thorough job—but the violent clanging of dishes in the sink is a little disconcerting. And whenever her mobile phone rings, which is often, she answers it with lots of energetic shouting and gesticulating, which sends Biff running upstairs to take refuge under the bed.

Magda speaks an endearing form of franglais—mostly English, peppered with a few French words. She is particularly fond of the word *trucs*, or 'things'.

'Look, I do all the *trucs*,' she says, pointing underneath the kitchen cabinets, keen to let me know that she is not cutting corners. By the end of her visit, several dishes are badly chipped, including Biff's bowl, and my nerves are a little jangled, but order has been restored

257

and the bathroom is sparkling like a princess-cut diamond.

'*Regarde!* I make everything spink and span,' declares the world's most glamorous cleaning lady.

'Yes, very spick and span,' I agree. 'But next time, don't worry about doing the washing-up as I quite enjoy doing that myself,' I lie.

As I hand over payment, she looks at me with real gratitude in her green eyes and hugs me. 'Thank you, *Ka-renne*. Now I can go and buy food for *les enfants*.'

'No, Magda,' I say. 'Thank *you*.'

A couple of days later, I see Magda outside the café looking glum.

'Everything OK?' I ask

'Nah, *chérie*. I 'ave no money to buy food. Tonight, l have only the breakfast cereal to give *les filles* when they come home from school.'

'But what about the €30 I paid you earlier in the week?'

'It's gone, *chérie*.'

I'm alarmed that things are so desperate, but I'm also surprised, as I know Magda is receiving support from the French social system. Rather than just give her money, which could set a dangerous precedent, I rack my brain for ways in which she could earn it.

'Would you be free to come over and do some ironing for me?' I say.

Her face lights up. 'What about now *chérie*?'

258

'Perfect. Let's go.'

She grins. 'Thank you, *Ka-renne*.'

Back home, I carry the wicker basket containing several months' worth of ironing down to the kitchen. Magda zips through the pile in just over an hour. Impressed by her speed and honesty—she could easily have drawn the job out for longer—I pay her for two hours. Before she goes, I make her a coffee and over a chat in the courtyard, she suggests that we should go dancing together in Poitiers one night. Frankly, the idea strikes me as terrifying. Perhaps sensing my reluctance, she tells me there is going to be a *bal populaire* or disco in Villiers on July 14th (Bastille Day) in the public park. She will be there from about 10.00 pm to watch the firework display and tells me that I should come along too. In the end I don't, as I fall asleep. This turns out to be a blessing, because the following day Magda tells me that Luis was there with Sabine. She watches my face for a reaction.

'Ah bon?' I say, surprised at how much this hurts.

'And your neighbour, he was there too,' she continues, before informing me that Arnaud is planning to leave Villiers to go and live in the Gers with his new lady friend.

'How do you know?' I ask.

'Basile, he tell me. And Arnaud, yesterday he was talkin' about you with his new *copine* in the café, *chérie.*'

'Really?'

'She hask him about you. He say that all the time you are tellin' 'im you want to sleep with him, but 'e is not interested. He say that is why you are no longer spikin with him.'

'You overheard Arnaud telling his girlfriend that I'm pestering him for sex?' I say.

'Yeah, *chérie.*'

I start to laugh. But if what Magda is saying is true, I have to admire his audacity.

Chapter 16

Firestorm

The autoroute curves around sharply and, as if out of nowhere, the Millau Viaduct—the twelfth highest bridge in the world—looms into view, draped in a diaphanous mist. I've been staying with friends in Provence for the past week, and driving in fierce heat and sunshine since this morning. Unfortunately, I missed the turn-off for Millau earlier, thereby adding over 150 kilometres to my journey. Lost in thought, I continued driving west along the foot of France. It was only when I saw a sign for Spain—I'd been hoping for one for Paris—that I realised I'd gone wrong.

It's just turned 8.00 pm and I'm finally approaching the bridge, which slots almost unobtrusively into the dramatic landscape of the Massif Central. I've crossed the viaduct, which was built by the British architect Sir Norman Foster, several times before and I'm always struck by how fragile it looks—36,000 tons of roadway seemingly suspended by fine cables from the clouds.

I decide to stop for a break at the services just before the bridge. Walking Biff around the car park, it's a shock, after the heat of Provence, to discover how cold and misty it is here. But the restaurant is impressive—a sweeping, modern space with views of the viaduct, and food that looks surprisingly edible (Later, I discover that it was created by a Michelin-starred chef.) I buy a Niçoise salad and a Diet Coke (for the purposes of staying awake) and sit by the window in the mostly empty restaurant, with Biff curled up at my feet. I've had a wonderful week with my friends, but there is nothing like dining *toute seule* in a service station on a Saturday night to make you feel lonely. I can't even call Travis, as my phone is dead. I've got a six-hour drive ahead of me and the light is already fading. It's unlikely I will make it back to Villiers tonight. Instead, I will drive for as long as possible and then check into a cheap motel.

And so, in the dying light of a July evening, I cross the viaduct that is, in my opinion, the most impressive structure in France after the Eiffel Tower. Unlike most bridges, where the urge is to look down, the Millau Viaduct draws your eye upwards towards the sail-like cables and masts. I just wish I had someone beside me to share the view.

Eventually, I turn off the autoroute and onto a road that seems to go on forever, twisting and winding for several hours from one somnambulant village to another. It's the sort of driving that requires a lot of concentration. But, as darkness falls, I decide that I can't face another night alone in a soulless motel room. I want to get back to my village, sleep for a few hours in my own bed and go to the local café tomorrow morning, where at least I'll be among familiar faces. And so I push on through the changing landscape towards Rodez, then Figeac, gripping the wheel like a robot, eyes dry and unblinking as they focus on the dark road ahead. Finally, I reach Martel and pick up the motorway towards Limoges.

It's nearly 4.00 am when I arrive back in Villiers. I'm so tired that my legs wobble when I get out of the car. I walk Biff around the dark square and then fall into bed exhausted but happy to be home. The following morning, I leave my mobile to charge while I'm in the shower. It being Sunday, when the entire village seems to gravitate towards the *terrasse* of the café, I make the usual effort to look like I haven't made an effort at all (or 'no make-up make-up' as it's known in the beauty world). Then I head towards the café and the addiction that I have tried—and failed—to kick.

Even though it's mid-July, there is a chill in the air, so I take a seat inside and switch on my phone. It flashes up a missed call and my heart stops when I see whom it is: The Devil. There is no message. I check the time and see that he called while I was sitting in the Millau service station feeling lonely and, if I'm honest, thinking about him. Had my phone been working last night, I wouldn't have trusted myself not to take his call. And just as I am thinking this, the door of the café opens and my heart stops for a second time, for there he is standing before me, dressed in black jeans and a black T-shirt. What's the occasion, I wonder? He only wears black when trying to impress.

A familiar look of resignation flashes across his face when he sees me checking my phone. I put it away and open the French memoir that I am currently reading (written by an expat male journalist who's had more success at finding love in France than I have). I hold the book in front of my face to block The Devil from my view. He drinks his coffee standing at the end of the bar and then slips away. *And oh, the irony!* After he's gone, I notice the title of the book that I was holding up for him to see: *Je t'aime à la Folie*—a play on words meaning, 'I love you to the point of madness'.

* * *

On Monday morning Magda arrives to do the ironing, wearing new leather boots. 'Those are nice,' I say, wondering how she can afford them.

'My boyfriend, 'e bought them for me,' she says, looking embarrassed. She opens the fridge to put in a carton of juice. '*Lee-sen*, why you 'ave so many of these *trucs*?' she says, pointing at the pile of cucumbers liquifying on a shelf. I shrug. The cucumbers—which caused the checkout boy in the supermarket to smirk when I bought them over two weeks ago— represent another good intention gone wrong.

'Next time I come, I'm gonna clean this out for you,' says Magda. 'It's a fuckin' mess.'

When Magda has finished the ironing, I offer to run her home for fear that she will dislocate a knee or worse, walking back to her cul-de-sac in those high-heeled boots. As we drive past the Café du Commerce, I see Pierre-Antoine sitting outside. Magda waves at him and he waves back.

'You know him?' I say.

'Yes, I clean the house of his sister, Héloïse. She's very nice.'

'So has Pierre-Antoine tried to flirt with you?' I ask, intrigued.

'Nah, *chérie*. His sister, she say 'e 'as never 'ad a girlfriend. Ever.'

'Really?' This completely contradicts what Arnaud told me about Pierre-Antoine being the biggest *dragueur* in the village. But his sister, if anyone, should know.

'He looks to me like he is scared of women,' says Magda.

'Possibly. Or maybe he is just not interested in them,' I say. Either way, it makes me feel better to know that I'm not the only female in the village that Pierre-Antoine hasn't tried to seduce. But really it's irrelevant, as all he wants from me is friendship and vice versa. He's kind and friendly and he knows a lot about insulation. He has a good heart. Slowly, I'm learning to appreciate people for the ways in which they enhance your life, rather than counting the ways that they don't.

*   *   *

The first weekend in August arrives and the temperature on the pharmacy clock rises by several degrees. I stay at home reading, doing the laundry and occasionally venturing out to walk Biff under the blazing sun. On Sunday, I go to a barbecue in Sarah and Steve's hamlet. It's a jolly mix of French and English, sharing their pork sausages and potato salads at long trestle tables in an open-sided barn. Although I smile and chat to the people on my table, my mind is elsewhere.

In the late afternoon, Biff and I climb into

the car, which is as hot as a magma chamber, and drive home. The usual Sunday silence has descended on the village and, not for the first time, I wonder what my neighbours do behind their closed shutters.

I pull the bedroom curtains against the glare of the sun, switch on my laptop and start to write. I'm lost in a world of metallic fashion, advising readers how to adopt the trend without looking like an oven-ready chicken—actually impossible—when Biff starts to bark. I lean out of the window to see what has disturbed him and there, standing in rue St Benoit and looking directly up at my bedroom, is The Devil. My heart lurches. What is he doing here?

I don't get to find out because the moment that he sees me, he turns and walks away looking embarrassed, as if he wasn't expecting to find me at home. It's just gone 7.00 pm. Shaken, I call Magda who invites me over for a coffee.

She answers the door in denim shorts and a yellow halter-neck top and indicates for me to follow her through to the kitchen, where she is preparing dinner for *les enfants*. It's the first time I've been inside her house, which is comfortable, clean—not a mark on the white-tiled floors—and cheerfully decorated. I notice that there is a flat screen TV and an expensive laptop in the sitting room. Sliding glass doors lead to a rectangular garden, where children are playing noisily on a trampoline. I follow Magda through to an orange-painted kitchen, dominated by a huge American-style fridge.

'So Luis, 'e probably wants you back,' she says, boiling water for the coffee. 'He was 'ere yesterday.' She points to the house next door where Cristina, whose husband also works for Supodal, lives. 'He was drinking beers in the garden with 'is friends from work. Sabine, she wasn't with him.'

'Did he speak to you?' I ask, for I know that most of the Portuguese give Magda the cold shoulder.

'Yeah, *chérie*. Luis, he is always very nice to me. I was wearing my bikini and playing in the paddling pool with *les enfants,* and Luis, 'e come to the fence to spik to me.'

I can imagine the scene: Luis would have been drawn to Magda in her bikini in the same way that Biff would be attracted to a juicy lamb joint.

'Luis, 'e say to me, "Ah Magda, why you no 'ave a Portuguese boyfriend?"'

'But you do have a Portuguese boyfriend.'

'I know, *chérie*, but it's best if the Portuguese think I am a *femme toute seule.*'

She opens the fridge and I'm happy to see that, despite her frequent lament that she has nothing to feed the children, it is packed with food—albeit the highly processed variety. She takes out a box of spring rolls from Lidl, marked *Promotion XXL*. They are as big as bread rolls and glossy with grease and hydrogenated fat. I wince as she drops them into a saucepan of popping oil.

'So how is Janinha doing?' I ask, as the kitchen fills with the smell of deep fat frying.

'Good, *chérie*. She is still having the treatment at the 'ospital. But the doctor, 'e is telling me all the time that my girls are overweight.' She hits her forehead with the flat of her hand. '*Ça casse ma tête*,' she says (literally: that breaks my head).

I watch as she puts two baguettes and an enormous slab of Brie on the table, along with a jumbo bottle of full-sugar cola. I almost wish that Catriona Mace were here to deal with this. There is not a vegetable in sight, but it doesn't seem my place to say anything. Amid much shouting in Portuguese, Magda's three tubby offspring and their two friends (Cristina's children) are called in for a feast of artery-furring food. Magda then indicates for me to follow her outside to the patio, where she kicks off her flip-flops, lights a cigarette and puts her feet up on the chair opposite, her long brown legs stretched out before her. I notice that her toenails are painted a vivid pink.

'*Lee-sen*, *chérie*, I need to ask a favour,' she says, taking a deep drag on the cigarette. 'My mother, she is coming to look after the children and on Friday, I'm going to Portugal.'

'Again?'

'*Oui, chérie.* Can you give me a lift to the station?'

I nod. In the kitchen, I can hear Janinha yelling. A fight has broken out. Magda rushes in and shouts at the children in Portuguese until order is restored. I get up to leave.

'Where you goin', *chérie?*' she demands.

'I've got to give Biff his dinner,' I say. 'See you Friday.'

I drive home marvelling at Magda's ability to cope with chaos and a sick child, while keeping her house dazzlingly clean and her toenails painted pink. Despite all her problems, she still has enough energy to jump on a bus for a romantic assignation in Portugal—the reason, I suspect, that she is going back to her motherland.

* * *

In the days that follow, I feel restless. It's clear to me that something in my life has to change. I find myself almost envying Arnaud who, if the local gossip is to be believed, is about to run away to the Gers with his new love. On Friday afternoon, I drive Magda to the bus station as promised.

'Have a good time, *chérie*,' I say, as she scoops herself out of the car.

'I will,' she says, with a cheeky wink. 'Thank you, *chérie.*'

I smile as she totters into the station, an

irrepressible life-force with her pull-along suitcase and quilted pink vanity case.

On Saturday afternoon, Delphine phones to see if I would like to have a drink with her in the café on the corner. I cross the square, relieved to see that there is no sign of The Devil, but it's not long before he crops up—in conversation, at least.

'I hope you don't mind me mentioning it, but I saw Luis this morning,' says Delphine, after we've each ordered a Perrier *fraise* (Perrier with a dash of strawberry syrup).

'You did?'

'Yes. I was sitting with my cousin on the bench opposite the Crédit Agricole and he walked past, on his way to the cash machine, looking very pleased with himself. He bowed when he saw me and said *"Bonjour"* very nicely.' She does an impersonation of Luis executing a gentlemanly bow from the waist. 'It was almost as if he was saying: "Now go and tell *Ka-renne* that you have seen me and that I am looking very 'andsome."'

I manage a laugh. Luis was always very charming towards Delphine.

'I also bumped into Arnaud this morning,' says Delphine. 'What is going on with him? He is behaving like a teenager, rushing off to live in the Gers with a woman he has known for less than two months. He also asked me why you were avoiding him?'

'He's being a little disingenuous,' I say.

'The truth is that Arnaud is avoiding me. And anyway, I hardly ever see him these days. He's always over at his girlfriend's apartment.'

The conversation then turns to the medal that Delphine is soon to be awarded by the district council for twenty years of service to the community. The ceremony will take place in August and I have offered to help prepare the canapés and cocktails for the drinks reception afterwards. Delphine, as always, has been trying to think of ways to get Barack Obama to come to Puysoleil.

'Well, that might be difficult. But you could always invite Sarkozy,' I say.

'I thought about it,' says Delphine. 'But the problem is that he might come.'

I laugh. 'Do you really think so?'

'Oh yes. He will do anything to win some votes in the rural communities. But I would be very unpopular if I invited him to Puysoleil.'

*   *   *

The following morning, I get up early to walk Biff before the sun is too intense, meandering along a cool, grassy track for over an hour. Then I go through the usual Sunday ritual of washing my hair and applying fake tan, before heading over to Intermarché to buy more cucumbers in an attempt to get my healthy lifestyle back on track. While I'm there, I bump into Yvette.

271

'I'm sorry to hear about your shop,' I say.

'*C'est la vie,*' she shrugs. 'Listen, do you want to go for a coffee? I'd like to talk to you about our good friend Arnaud.'

The offer is irresistible. 'Why not?' I reply, as my heart speeds up at the thought of entering the Sunday morning danger zone. But to hell with it: my hair is bouncy and shiny, my skin is golden and I'm wearing red knickers (with purple satin bow ties). The Devil can't harm me today.

Laughing and chatting, we cross the road in front of his apartment and sit down under a parasol at the corner café. Within minutes, The Devil appears—just as I knew he would—and sits at the table behind us. Alone. My antennae tell me that he is feeling vulnerable today. *Advantage me, already.*

I ask Yvette about her plans for the future now that her shop is closed and she tells me that she's applied for a job as a cashier in Lidl. It's a shame, as she had a good eye for fashion and it pains me to think of her wearing Lidl's unlovely uniform.

'So have you heard the news about our good friend Arnaud?' she asks.

'Yes. He's certainly leaving town in a hurry.'

'It seems to me that he's ashamed of something,' says Yvette.

'I've noticed that, too,' I say, hesitating before deciding not to go into further detail.

'He also has a very overactive imagination,'

272

says Yvette. 'I hear that he's been telling people that I tried to seduce him.'

'Yes, I'm afraid that's true. He told me that you sent him texts asking him to sleep with you.'

Yvette starts to laugh. 'In his dreams maybe.'

'Don't worry about it. He's been saying the same about me.'

'Oh, and look, there he is!' says Yvette with a fixed smile, as Arnaud walks into the café.

He looks sheepish and actually a little worried when he sees the two of us together and he doesn't come over to say hello.

I carry on chatting to Yvette, whispering, laughing, flicking my recently highlighted hair around, and looking very animated. I might be smiling, but deep down I know that I'm throwing negative energy around the *terrasse*, hoping to provoke a reaction, to create something of a firestorm. The person I want to get at is not Arnaud; it's the brooding presence behind us, who I'm quite sure is taking in every detail. I want him to see that he is absolutely insignificant to me, and I want to cause him pain. And yet . . . as I get up to pay for the coffees and see him sitting there alone, I have a very strong, inexplicable urge to talk to him. It feels as if I've punished him enough, ignoring his calls and following Arnaud's advice to act as if he were dead. It hasn't worked. Sitting there in his orange T-shirt, sleeves rolled up to the elbows to reveal his strong brown arms, he's never looked more alive.

I cannot and will not take him back, but for the first time, it occurs to me that maybe I should call a truce on this ridiculous game of cat and mouse that we've been playing for nearly a year. I could tell him that I've written a book about him and that he is even featured, in a small illustration, on the front cover—something I know that he'd love. He did, after all, bring me a lot of happiness in our two summers together. Perhaps it's the heat affecting my brain, but I even toy with the idea of inviting him over to Maison Coquelicot later this afternoon to pick up a copy of *Toute Allure* (subtitle: *Falling In Love In Rural France.*) Heart thumping, I exit the café determined to act on my instincts and talk to him. But when I turn to look at The Devil, he stares into the middle distance, proud and defiant, and does not meet my eye. The opportunity has gone. Later, I will look back on this as the moment that I could have changed everything. Instead, I walk home, satisfied that I made an impact on the *terrasse* this morning and certain that, by showing him what he can no longer have, I will have made him want me more.

I think about The Devil all day, wondering if he will come to my house again as he did last Sunday. But he doesn't. In the late afternoon, I take Biff on a walk that meanders between sunflower fields before climbing upwards on a narrow path that overlooks a river and a lush green field of sheep with their lambs. It's one of my favourite walks, but not today. As I move leadenly under the August sun, I feel agitated, restless. I can't stop thinking about The Devil. At one point, I look at the heat haze shimmering over the fields and experience a feeling of deep despair, as if a hole is about to open in the parched earth before me. I wonder again what went through Luis's head when he sat so close to me in the café this morning. Is he, I wonder, thinking of me now? As I walk home, I hear sirens slicing through the silence of the Sunday afternoon.

I spend a sleepless night tossing and turning, the air in my room pressing down on me like a hostile force. Why, I wonder, did Luis not show up this evening? Deep down, I was certain that he would. Lying in the darkness, I experience a moment of clarity. I cannot carry on living like this, in the same village as The Devil.

The following morning, I go to the French estate agent on the square and instruct them to sell my house as quickly as possible. As I sign the contract agreeing to sell, I request a *For Sale* board outside. How quickly can they put one up? To be doubly sure, I call a British estate agency called Leggetts—the name seems very apposite—and instruct them, too. Once again, I emphasise the need for a board. It's for one person only: Luis. I want him to know that I am leaving.

A charming *Anglaise* arrives within half an hour to collect a set of keys and tells me that they might have someone interested already. But it's almost irrelevant. Whether the house sells or not, I'll be gone by the spring.

Pleased that I've taken decisive action, I pack a small suitcase and, as pre-arranged, drop Biff off at Sarah and Steve's. The following day, I take the TGV up to Paris with Delphine.

'Are you OK?' she asks, over lunch in Les Deux Magots. Possibly she has noticed my strange mood and that even jokes about Left Bank Man can't make me laugh today.

I tell Delphine that I put my house on the market yesterday and that I'm leaving Villiers.

'Are you sure this is what you want?' she says.

'Yes. I decided on Sunday. I can't carry on living in the same village as Luis.'

'But Luis won't be in the village forever,' says Delphine. 'I'm sure of it.'

'I know,' I say, as tears start to roll down my cheeks. 'I think the same thing. But he's here at the moment, which means that I must go.'

Later that afternoon, I say goodbye to Delphine, who is staying overnight in Paris with a friend. Then I head to the Eurostar terminal to go to London to publicise the book that I've written about falling in love with The

Devil.

As the train pulls out of the Gare du Nord, I wonder if he will feel a pang of regret when he sees the *For Sale* sign. Whatever happens, I tell myself that he will never forget me, just as I will never forget him. I'm panicked by what I've done—I have no idea where I will go—but proud that I've taken my future into my own hands. What an arrogant assumption. I've no idea what a curve ball life is about to throw me.

Chapter 17

Crash

The following day, I'm walking along Kensington High Street in the sunshine, on my way to meet a friend for lunch, when a seemingly innocuous email comes through on my phone. It's from Stephanie, an expat I know in France but haven't seen for a while. *Umbrella, ella, ella* is the subject line, referencing the pop song by Rihanna. At first, I think the email is just a reminder about an umbrella that I left at her house over a year ago. But then I see the cryptic message at the end: 'If you need anything, let me know. I've just seen the *Nouvelle République* today and I'm worried for you. *Bisous*, Steph.'

There is a link to a local newspaper and an article entitled: *'Éjecté de sa voiture en pleine ligne droite'*—something about being thrown from a car in a straight line. Unfortunately, my phone won't download the link, but why would Steph think this is anything to do with me? Feeling sick and shaky, I head back to the Internet café in my hotel lobby. And there, surrounded by a coach party of excitable Italian tourists, I click on the link to the *Nouvelle République* and an image so shocking that it slams down on my world like a meteorite. It is a picture of a mangled white Clio, its doors and registration plate missing and its windscreen entirely blown out. I don't need to read the text to know whom the car belongs to.

The article explains how on Sunday 8th August, three days ago, the driver lost control of the car while travelling on a straight road out of Villiers in the direction of Confolens. 'The two Portuguese men in the car, including the driver, Luis Duarte, thirty-two, were taken to the CHU de Poitiers, Hôpital de la Milétrie,' it says, and are 'grievously injured'. The car overturned several times and the driver wasn't wearing a seat belt.

My first reaction is denial: this cannot possibly be true. It feels as if this terrible event is unfolding in a parallel universe. The last time I felt like this was on 11th September 2001 when, after lunch with one

278

of my commissioning editors, I walked along a deserted Kensington High Street and into the offices of Associated Newspapers, just in time to see the second plane fly into the World Trade Centre. I read the article again to make sure I haven't imagined it. The accident happened shortly before 7.00 pm on Sunday, as I was walking Biff nearby. The sirens I heard on the way home were for Luis. Now I know why he didn't come to my house on Sunday evening, as I was so sure he would. Everything feels like it is happening in slow motion. With the phrase *grièvement blessé'*, playing over and over in my head, I make arrangements to return to France tomorrow.

*   *   *

I'm standing by the ticket machines in the Eurostar terminal when my phone rings. It's a radio station in Majorca, as arranged a week ago, to interview me about my book. I cringe at the thought of the possible questions.

'Luis sounds wonderful; is he still your neighbour?' the interviewer asks at one point.

'No, but he is not far away,' I say, wondering how I could possibly begin to tell the truth— that right now he's in hospital in Poitiers, and if the *Nouvelle République* is to be believed, fighting for his life. I picture him in intensive care with the very worst possible injuries. Then I think: it's The Lion; he can't possibly be in a bad way. He'll be sitting up in bed, bruised and bandaged but laughing and flirting with the nurses. The newspaper must have got it wrong.

During the train journey home, I replay the scene outside the café on Sunday over and over in my head, and I feel sick, so sick, at the thought of my behaviour that morning. As I sat in the sunshine, throwing my hair around and laughing, I wanted to hurt him and make him suffer by showing him what he could no longer have. Over and over, the image of The Lion, sitting so close that I could have reached out and touched him, comes unbidden into my mind. I remember the sudden, pressing desire to speak to him, and I torture myself with the fact that I didn't.

I thought I had all the time in the world to make peace with The Lion, to tell him that he was the star of my book. But I didn't. And when my mind is not torturing me with those images from the café *terrasse*, it is replaying the sickening picture of the mangled car in the *Nouvelle République*—the car that was once parked peacefully outside my house.

The train arrives at Poitiers station at 9.23 pm. I drive out of the multi-storey car park in something close to a trance. I have only a vague idea of how to get to the hospital, so I head to the *rocade* (orbital road) and follow signs for the CHU until they run out. It's hard to see in the dark and I must have missed a turn-off, so I pull over near the entrance to

280

an industrial estate, and search for Delphine's number in the dark.

''*Allo*,' says a cheerful voice.

'I only have one bar of battery on my phone,' I shout. 'So I'll have to be quick. How do I get to the CHU?'

'You're going to the hospital now?' says Delphine, who knows about Luis, as I called her from London. 'Are you sure that's a good idea?'

'*Please*, Delphine. I need directions.'

Calmly, she tells me how to get there and I set off again, eventually picking up signs for the hospital and arriving at *Urgences* (Accident and Emergency), which is a large, green, illuminated cube glowing eerily in the darkness. I run up to the steps and into a calm reception area, which seems remarkably free of accidents or emergencies. At a small reception desk to the right of the door, I explain that I've come from England—which, strictly speaking, is true—to visit Monsieur Luis Duarte, who was admitted following a car accident.

The receptionist is sympathetic and asks for the spelling of his name. She then stares at her computer for an interminable amount of time.

'I'm sorry but we have no one here by that name,' she says.

'Please try again,' I plead. 'He was admitted on Sunday, the eighth of August.'

She scrolls down the screen and shakes her head, but then, after another long wait, she says, 'Ah yes, we do have a Monsieur Duarte.'

'Where is he? Can I visit him now?' I ask.

'Just a moment.' She picks up the phone and I hear her explain that she is calling from accident and emergency, where someone is asking for information about Monsieur Luis Duarte. She nods and says *'D'accord'* (OK) half a dozen or so times before passing the phone to me. She tells me it is Monsieur Duarte's nurse in *neurochirugie*.

The nurse sounds very serious and tells me that he cannot give out any information over the phone. 'Are you a member of Monsieur Duarte's family?' he asks.

'I'm just a friend,' I say. *Just a friend.* How little of our history that explains. It does not convey the amazing moments that we shared, or the scintillating game of cat and mouse we have been playing for the past year. Nor does it convey that he had been trying to contact me and was standing outside my house staring at my bedroom window a week before the accident. His life froze at the moment he was thrown out of his car—at which point we weren't even on speaking terms.

'I've come from England especially,' I add. 'Is it possible to see Monsieur Duarte now?'

'He has a girlfriend and family,' says the nurse, his tone defiant and protective, while I reflect on the fact that had I answered Luis's calls in recent months, I would most likely have been that girlfriend now. It wouldn't

282

have made this terrible situation any better—if anything it would be much worse—but at least I would have the right to see him.

'*Please*. Can you please tell me what condition he is in? Is he conscious? Concussed? Can he speak?'

'I can't give you that information over the phone,' says the nurse. 'I strongly advise that you speak to his girlfriend or a member of his family before visiting.' *Speak to his girlfriend*. Even now, those words are like a slap in the face. I make one final, desperate plea for information and the nurse takes pity on me and tells me that he has had emergency surgery and his condition is 'stable but grave'.

Deflated and thwarted, I return to my car and sit in the darkness, staring at the glowing green cube, at the high, menacing tower behind it, and the other buildings nearby. The hospital seems like an impenetrable fortress to me. The Lion lies injured somewhere within and I have no way of getting to see him. I picture him in a darkened, windowless room, with his head in bandages, connected to a battery of beeping machines with flashing lights, a nurse stationed outside. There is so much that I don't know. Is he in a coma? Brain-damaged? Has he lost any limbs? If he was thrown out through the windscreen, he probably has horrific facial injuries. I push that thought out of my mind. If Magda were here, she would know the details via the

Portuguese community, but she is in Portugal. I have no one to ask, and no way of knowing until tomorrow morning. Dazed, I follow the winding road back to Villiers, my mind still in a dark room somewhere inside the hospital.

I wake up early the next day—Friday 13th—after a night of little sleep. Braced for the worst, I walk up to the café. The first person I see is Basile, who is outside smoking. He looks grave, almost embarrassed, when he sees me, because he knows what I am going to ask. He realises that it will fall to him to give me the grim details.

'It's not good, not good,' he says, shaking his head and avoiding eye contact, before rattling off the awful injuries. I only hear half of what he is saying. 'Life-support machine . . . in a coma . . . severe head injuries . . . brain trauma . . . spinal column . . . almost everything broken . . . punctured lung . . . hole in his back . . . hips broken . . . fractured ribs . . . legs shattered.'

My face is immobile but my lips respond with *'Merde . . . merde'*, to each terrible piece of news. Then Basile delivers the knockout blow: 'If he lives at all he'll be paralysed, and will need twenty-four hour care for the rest of his life; it's probably better if he dies.'

My emotions struggle to keep up with his words as he goes on to explain that the other passenger in the car—a young guy who had just arrived from Portugal to work for Supodal—was wearing a seatbelt and has walked away with only minor injuries. Luis, meanwhile, was thrown out of the car—it's not clear if it was through the windscreen or a side window—and his head took the full, violent brunt of the accident. *You stupid, stupid Lion*, I think to myself, wondering what macho impulse led him to not wear a seatbelt on that awful day. By not doing so, he has thrown his life away. Stupefied by the terrible information Basile has given me, I stand outside the café in the sunshine with the 'what ifs' proliferating in my mind. What if I'd taken his calls back in May? What if I had spoken to him that Sunday morning? In either case, I'm quite sure the accident wouldn't have happened.

'Listen,' says Basile suddenly, stubbing his cigarette out in an ashtray. 'If you need to talk, you can give me a call any time.' He hands me a card with his telephone number on and squeezes my hand, his kind, perceptive eyes looking directly at me. *'Il était un bon gars,'* (he was a good bloke) he says. 'Everyone liked him.'

I nod, unable to speak and walk back across the square. In front of the *mairie*, two young boys are kicking a ball around and a woman clutching a cake box comes rushing out of the *boulangerie*. It's jarring to see that normal life is carrying on, while The Lion is critically injured in hospital. As I walk back down rue St Benoit, I feel a strange calm radiating through my body—the calm of complete devastation. I thought my life had fallen apart when I found Luis with Sabine, but now it really has.

I get in my car and drive to Romagne to collect Biff, with the dreadful image of Luis being thrown from his little white Clio playing on a loop in my head. Unusually for mid-August, the sky has a grey-white pallor and there is a chill in the air, while the sunflowers that line the narrow road leading to Sarah's hamlet, hang their heads as if in mourning. As I drive along, it hits me that the reason why the nurse insisted I speak to Luis's family before visiting was not to protect them, but to protect me—the Lion's condition is so serious that visitors need to be pre-warned.

When I arrive, Biff comes running down the garden path to meet me. Sarah has had him clipped while I was away and he looks sweet and vulnerable, gambolling around the garden like a little black lamb.

'Is everything OK?' asks Sarah.

I explain that Luis has had a car accident and is in a very bad way and that I want to try and see him. 'Do you think I'm mad to even try?' I ask.

'No,' says Sarah. 'I would do exactly the same.'

I drive back to Villiers and head to the industrial estate on the outskirts of the village, following the maze of narrow roads until I draw up outside Supodal, the Portuguese construction company for which Luis worked. It's a big industrial unit in grey corrugated metal, surrounded by wire fencing. Ignoring a sign that says *Beware Of The Dog*, I push open the metal gate and enter the yard. A big Alsatian comes running towards me, but grief has rendered me fearless and I keep on walking as it barks at me. I remember Luis once telling me that he had spent the day building *une maison de chien* (a dog house) for it to live in. To my left, I see the kennel that he built and feel a wave of sadness at the poignant reminder of how much The Lion loved his job. It was one of the things that I most admired about him. Although he complained about the amount of tax he had to pay, he was the embodiment of the pride and self-respect that comes from hard work.

Next to the warehouse, there is a single-storey house where the boss and his wife live—Luis helped to build this too—and the door is open. *'Bonjour!'* I shout, knocking on the open door, but there is no reply. Fernando's black BMW is parked in front of the warehouse, so he must be at home. I wait a few minutes and enter the reception area. I have not been here before and I'm surprised at how neat and clean it all is. I'd imagined Luis working in some macho, messy work yard.

I call out *'Bonjour'* again and walk through an open door on the right, which leads into a modern kitchen where Fernando and his wife are sitting in shocked silence, perched on high stools on opposite sides of the kitchen counter.

Fernando looks like he has been crying.

'Madame Willer,' he says, looking unsurprised to see me.

'I'm sorry to disturb you,' I say, in French. 'I heard the news about Luis.'

Fernando indicates for me to sit down on the stool next to him. Nicole, his wife, who has always been a little wary of me—I think because I once had the temerity to shout at her husband—offers me a coffee from a Nespresso machine. She is wearing jeans with a crisp white shirt, a black tailored jacket and a lot of make-up. As she pushes a small white cup towards me, I'm grateful to her for looking so pulled together when others are falling apart. I know that I look a mess.

Fernando and I have always had a love-hate relationship, but I now regret the occasions when I marched across the square to yell at him about his noisy workers. The situation changed when I became *'la femme de Luis'* or literally, 'Luis's woman'. He would crack jokes with me and, on one occasion, invited me for coffee and a digestif with the all-male lunch party that had gathered in the house next door. But when I discovered The Lion's infidelities, I assumed that Fernando must have known—probably even had a laugh about it at my expense—and as a result, I could only respond with a withering look whenever he wished me a polite *'bonjour'* in the street. Now that he is my only hope of seeing The Lion, I really regret those disdainful looks, especially since he was always polite to me.

Speaking in heavily accented French, Fernando tells me that Luis and his friend had been drinking, but shortly before 7.00 pm on Sunday afternoon, they decided to go to St Secondin.

'To go swimming,' adds his wife.

'He wasn't wearing his seat belt,' says Fernando, shaking his head, his big brown eyes full of pain. He runs through the terrible list of injuries, confirming what Basile has already told me, and then turns to look at me. 'Madame Willer,' he says. 'It is better if he dies. If he lives, he will be handicapped from the neck down. For a man like Luis, this would be a fate worse than death.' He shakes his head again. 'It would have been better if he had been killed on the day of the accident.'

He tells me that he and his wife were on their way to Portugal for their summer holiday and had just crossed the Spanish border when they received the call telling them about the accident. He immediately turned around and drove back.

I tell Fernando how I saw Luis on the morning of the accident and had a really strong desire to talk to him, to invite him over to my house to pick up a copy of my book.

'If you had,' says Fernando, 'he probably wouldn't have been driving around the countryside drunk. He would have followed you back to your house without hesitation, I'm sure of it. Luis, as you know, had an unhappy childhood and a difficult life, but he was most happy and most stable when he was with you, Madame Willer.'

'Listen,' I say, annoyed at the hypocrisy. 'I know that Luis was unfaithful the entire time that he was with me. And I know that you all knew it.'

Fernando shakes his head. 'It's not true. I knew this man like my brother. He told me everything. He was faithful to you until he started seeing Sabine.'

'But she told me about the two other women—one of them who lived in Poitiers, and another who lives in the village.'

Fernando laughs. 'There was a woman in Poitiers, but only briefly and that was before you. Trust me Madame Willer, he worked very long hours. He didn't have the time to cheat on you.'

I remember how I'd thought exactly the same thing, and how Delphine had warned me that Sabine was probably lying in order to keep me away. The strategy worked: it's the reason I ignored The Lion's calls and couldn't bring myself to acknowledge him in the café. Now I feel a weird mix of emotions: angry that Sabine lied to me; pleased that Luis wasn't cheating on me the whole time; but unbearably sad that I have only discovered this because he is dying . . . although it's possible, of course, that

Fernando is just saying this to make me feel better and to save the reputation of a dying man.

'Trust me, Madame Willer. Luis had a lot of respect for you. He talked to me a lot about you—about all the nice things that you did and the dinners that you made for him.' The tears start to well up in my eyes. So those midnight dinners did mean something.

'I feel so guilty,' I say. 'I feel I could somehow have prevented this. He had been phoning me again in recent months, and last Sunday he came to my house and was waiting outside.'

'Something happened early in May,' says Fernando. 'He seemed to become very depressed; it was then that he started drinking heavily. No one knows the reason why.'

I think back to early May and how, en route to the tapas evening in Pierre-Antoine's car, Luis had crossed the road in front of us. He looked directly at me for a few seconds and I could see great pain and confusion in his eyes.

'Perhaps it was to do with his girlfriend?' I say. 'Maybe they had a fight?'

Fernando shakes his head. 'I've asked her and she doesn't recall anything. And anyway, they were always fighting. I asked Sergio and his other work colleagues if they knew of anything that had upset him but they didn't, either.'

'What about his family?' I ask.

'He wasn't close to them,' says Fernando. He tells me that when he tracked down Luis's mother in Portugal, she responded to the news of the accident with, 'He's grown up. I don't give a f***.' Fernando shakes his head. 'What a bitch,' he says. 'What a whore.'

Poor Luis. How can a mother be so callous?

'But I went to the hospital last night and they said he had family here,' I say.

Fernando shakes his head. 'His mother won't come and he hasn't seen his father since he was a small boy. It's possible that his brother is coming, but we don't know when.'

It dawns on me that the 'family' the nurse was referring to, consists of Piedro, Sergio and his other colleagues, whom he thought of as brothers.

'Monsieur Rodriguez,' I say. 'I have something to ask you. I would like to go to the hospital and see Luis. Is there any way that you could help me?'

He hesitates for a moment and looks at his wife. Then he gives a curt nod. 'We are going there this afternoon. Be outside the main entrance at 3.00 pm and I will take you to see him,' he says.

'The main entrance of which building?' I ask, overwhelmed with gratitude.

'The tall tower. But listen, José is bringing the girlfriend at 4.00 pm, so you must leave well before then so that you don't meet her.'

'I will, I will. I just want to see him one last

292

time to say goodbye. That's all.' I get up to go, in case Fernando changes his mind. 'Thank you so much,' I say, feeling a huge wave of empathy towards *le patron* and his wife.

I have less than an hour and a half to go home, get ready and get myself to the hospital. I jump into the shower and get dressed in my best Marni dress, the one with the pink tropical blooms, that I wore the last time I ran towards Luis, rushing through Stansted to catch my plane. I then drive to the hospital in a daze. The route from Villiers takes me past soulless beige housing blocks and circumvents many roundabouts. I take a wrong turn at one of them and get lost on the way. The closer it gets to 3.00 pm, the more I start to panic; I cannot miss my only chance of seeing The Lion.

Eventually—I don't know how—I arrive in a car park somewhere in the hospital grounds. I can see the tower in the distance and rather than negotiate the network of roads and car parks, I decide to ditch the car and head directly towards it on foot, running breathless and panicked under a hard blue sky and a hostile sun.

The tower is much further away than it looks, but I keep running, as I have to see The Lion. At this moment, it is absolutely the only thing that matters in my life. Across three or four different car parks and past several buildings I run, before finally arriving, breathless and sweating, at the steps to the entrance. I look at my watch: it's almost exactly 3.00 pm but there is no sign of Fernando. There are many people outside, sitting on the steps and smoking. Some are in wheelchairs and hospital gowns, attached to drips. These, I realise, are the lucky ones.

I run into the hospital in case *le patron* and his wife are waiting there and then back out again. I stand at the top of the steps, scanning the numerous car parks to the left and right of the entrance, and after five minutes or so, see Fernando, sunglasses on his head, and Nicole, coming up the steps.

'*Bonjour, Madame Willer,*' he says.

His wife nods a brisk hello and we both follow Fernando's snakeskin boots as he strides through the lobby at a brisk pace, past the café on the right and into an orange elevator, where he presses the button for the third floor.

I make a mental note that Luis is on corridor C as we arrive in front of a set of walnut-effect doors marked *Secteur de Réanimation* (intensive care). It sounds so horribly literal. There is a notice instructing visitors to ring the bell and wait for permission to enter. Fernando rings, while I worry that Sabine might arrive early, scuppering my last chance of seeing Luis. But I have faith in *le patron*. After a five-minute wait that seems like several hours, a nurse opens the door and, recognising Fernando, lets us in immediately. *Le patron* turns to his wife.

'You wait here in case Sabine comes,' he says. She nods, accepting her husband's brusque command without question.

We are admitted to a grey-blue corridor that almost glitters with cleanliness. Taking my cue from Fernando, I rub antibacterial gel into my hands and then follow him into a small antechamber, where pale blue gowns for visitors are folded neatly on a shelf. He pulls on one of the gowns and, without saying a word, turns around so that I can tie it for him. He then does the same for me. Minutes away from seeing The Lion now, my mouth is dry and I feel dizzy as I brace myself for severe facial injuries and worse. Fernando hasn't said so but it seems very likely.

Fernando leads the way into a calm blue and grey corridor, turning left and into the corner cubicle that houses the injured Lion. Outside his room, there are dozens of X-rays pinned to the wall. I have steeled myself for the worst but as I step into a room flooded with natural daylight—there are windows running the length of the room, as well as on the side that looks out onto the corridor—I am surprised to find that Luis is lying with his eyes closed, as if taking a siesta. Amazingly, there is not a bruise or a scratch on his handsome brown face. His chest is bare and his strong brown arms lie at the side of his body, which is covered up to the waist with a white sheet. His legs and feet are bandaged and I can see bruised, swollen toes sticking out at the end. There is a probe in the top of his head and a tube in his nose, but his lush black hair has not been shorn as I imagined, merely pushed back off his face. It's superficial, I know, given the extent of his internal injuries, but I just want to cry with relief that The Lion's handsome features remain intact. This scene that I have been dreading is nowhere near as grim or distressing as I had imagined. A wave of peacefulness washes over me. Looking at him, you would not know that he's broken almost everything in his body apart from those beautiful arms.

'Bonjour, Luis,' I say, kissing his forehead. Fernando and I stand either side of the bed in our pale blue gowns—a colour that does neither of us any favours—each holding one of Luis's hands. Fernando greets The Lion in his mother tongue, pronouncing his name *Loo-eesh*. His manner is gruff and macho, like that of all Luis's male compatriots.

We stand in silence for a while, then Fernando says, 'Look, Madame Willer! Did you ever see hands as big as these? Real worker's hands. I'll never find another like him.'

I look at Luis's hands, calloused and huge, covered in small cuts and scratches from the accident, and I'm overwhelmed by the

296

poignancy of the situation. These are the hands that built the kennel for the boss's dog . . . that painted the ceiling in my spare bedroom and opened oysters in my kitchen. They also held my face gently to his. I think of all the hard work those hands have done and the ludicrously long hours that Luis worked so that one day he could buy a house of his own. And I want to cry that it has all been in vain.

'Madame Willer, if this doesn't work,' Fernando is saying, pointing towards Luis's groin, 'there is no point in him living.'

The comment makes me angry. How dare everyone assume that Luis would be better off dead? How can anyone judge if someone else's life is worth living unless they are in that situation themselves? It might be selfish, but I want Luis alive, regardless of whether or not his wedding tackle is working. More than anything else, I want to talk to him again.

Fernando looks directly at me. 'I wish, Madame Willer, that he had stayed with you. Then this probably would not have happened.' He shakes his head. 'I told Luis that you might not be the most beautiful girl in the world, but that you had inner beauty.'

Even in my shock and grief, I'm not impervious to the insult behind the compliment.

'I told him, "Madame Willer is older but she is stable. She has a house and a car,"' he continues, making me sound like a business

297

package or a pension plan. At the same time, I want to laugh that Fernando thinks a house and a car would be enough to attract a man like Luis.

'How is Sabine?' I ask, in an attempt to stop any more insults being thrown across The Lion's broken body.

'She seems genuinely upset,' says Fernando. 'She has said that if he lives, she will stand by him, even if he is badly disabled.' He tells me that she wanted to go to St Secondin with him on the day of the accident, that they fought over it, but that he was going there to get away from her and so took his colleague instead. He looks at his watch.

'I am sorry, but you will have to go soon. We cannot risk her finding you here.' He nods towards the window overlooking the corridor and for a second, I panic that she might suddenly appear.

I kiss Luis on the forehead. I never imagined that I would kiss him again, let alone in circumstances like these. He looks so peaceful it's hard to believe that he is fighting for his life. I tell him that it's going to be OK and that I have confidence in him. It's difficult to say anything more in front of the boss, but this won't be the last time I see The Lion. Now that I know where he is, I will climb in through the third floor windows to see him, if necessary.

'Thank you again, Monsieur Rodriguez, for

bringing me to see Luis.'

He nods. 'Tell my wife she can come in now.'

As I leave, I glance through the window of a cubicle occupied by a man with bandages and a brace around his head, who looks in a far worse state than Luis. Typical of The Lion, I think to myself, to land the most private and peaceful room in the joint. (Later, it occurs to me that it's because he is the most serious case.) As I remove my gown, a male nurse arrives to mop the already squeaky-clean corridor. I feel a huge surge of gratitude towards him and the other nurses. I can see that Luis is getting the very best possible treatment here and I love France even more, having seen at first hand its medical system, and the care and dignity that it affords to the ill and injured. It's a small thing, I know, but I am just so grateful that they didn't shave The Lion's hair.

I thank Fernando's wife and take the elevator down to the ground floor alone, still fearful that I might bump into Sabine. Squinting in the bright sunshine outside, I realise that I have absolutely no idea where I left my car. Dazed and with a jagged headache, I wander around the hospital grounds for nearly an hour before I find it, my mind still in that small room on the third floor.

Sick to my soul, I wind my way back through the depressing concrete high-rises, towards the road that leads to Villiers. I pause briefly at a roundabout, not sure where I'm going and I'm shocked when the driver behind beeps his horn loudly. In my fragile state, it feels like a brutal assault. Would he have done that, I wonder, if he knew that I'd just been to visit someone in a coma? And then I think of all the times I've been just as impatient with dawdlers. I vow never to do it again, as who knows what pain and suffering there might be in the mind of a stranger?

Back home, I cry unstoppable tears for Luis and the life that he won't live. I cry for his difficult past, the fact that he will never buy his own house and renovate it, and that there will never be any little Lions. And I cry for myself—a bitter mixture of guilt and regret and lost opportunities. How foolish, how immature, that game of cat and mouse in the café now seems. I should have answered his calls, heard what he had to say, instead of listening to Sabine. I always told myself that if he knocked on my door I would invite him in. He came close to it on the Sunday before the accident. Just not close enough. I cry because I thought I had all the time in the world to make peace with The Lion. Instead, I followed Arnaud's advice and behaved—oh, the irony!—as if he was dead. The most hideous irony of all is that I put my house up for sale because I couldn't bear to carry on living in the same village as Luis. Now, I can't bear to live there without him.

Chapter 18
Sedated

I wake up on Saturday morning with no idea of what to do with myself. I am haunted by the image of Luis sitting behind me in the café last weekend. I wanted to create a firestorm on the terrace that day, to inflict on Luis a fraction of the hurt that he had caused me. I felt he should suffer for what he had done. I knew he would hear or see me laughing and chatting with Yvette as we crossed the road in front of his apartment, and I knew he would show up in the café a couple of minutes later. While he sat there alone and pensive, I laughed and chatted and put on a display for his benefit, the subliminal message being: 'You mean nothing to me now.'

The following morning I'd put my house on the market, specifically requesting a *For Sale* board in the hope that that, too, would inflict pain. And now all the pain that I wanted to cause him has come back to me a millionfold. I think of the Tuesday that I spent in Paris with Delphine and how sitting outside Les Deux Magots—still unaware of the accident—I told her about my decision to sell my house. She had pointed out that The Lion probably wouldn't be living in Villiers forever, and I had replied that my instincts told me that, too.

I can't help feeling that somehow I wished Luis out of the village, that I willed some kind of punishment on him. And now it feels as if I've been handed a life sentence of guilt and regret—the most destructive of emotions as the focus is inward, on what you could have done differently to bring about another outcome. And oh, the arrogance of thinking I was taking control of the situation by putting my house up for sale. How could I have known that fate would intervene so callously? Similarly, I assumed that Luis would always remember me, never imagining that one day his brain might be so badly damaged that it would be physically impossible. It's as if fate has stepped in to remind me that I am not the one calling the shots.

Alone with my torturous thoughts, I imagine what it would be like to drive over to La Rochelle and just wade into the sea. I think what a release it would be to be swept away by the strong Atlantic currents, to be engulfed, along with my immense emotions, by the powerful waves.

The doorbell rings. It's Delphine, looking worried. I invite her in and explain how Luis's boss took me to the hospital to see him yesterday.

'Oh my goodness. You must be devastated,' she says, as I recount Luis's injuries.

'I don't know what to do, Delphine. I feel like I can't cope.'

302

What she says next astounds me. 'If you feel you are drowning my friend, you just reach out and I will grab your hand,' she says, as if she has somehow tapped into my darkest thoughts. 'I will not let you drown, *Ka-renne*. And neither will your other friends.'

We sit in silence for a few minutes. 'Delphine, I'd like to visit Luis again and I was wondering if you would come along with me?'

'Yes, I will,' says Delphine. 'But we must be careful not to bump into the girlfriend. When would you like to go?'

'Tomorrow. The visiting hours start at 3.00 pm. Perhaps we could go early and try to see him before Sabine arrives?'

'OK. I will be at your house at 2.15 pm.'

Delphine has to attend 'a mayor party' later but tells me not to hesitate to call if I need to. I spend the evening sedating myself with a bottle of red wine, while Biff alternately lies on his back with his paws in the air, or faux-wrestles the snake draught excluder in an attempt to cheer me up.

The following morning, I wake up feeling a little calmer at the thought of seeing Luis again. I walk Biff around the lake in the local park and, without thinking, take the short cut around the back of Intermarché, which brings me out opposite Luis's building. Suddenly, it hits me that The Lion will never again sit in his spotless kitchen drinking whisky or sleep under his pink duvet, and all the pain comes flooding back. Back home, I sit at the kitchen table, not knowing what to do with myself. My thoughts drift again to the icy grey bulk of the Atlantic and I think how I would rather be crushed under the force of its waves than by all this grief. Biff, as if he has been reading my mind, climbs up on the bench beside me and delivers one well-timed consolation lick to my cheek. It's as if he is saying: 'You can't possibly do that. What about me?'

The phone rings. *''Allo, chérie, ça va?'* says a husky voice.

'Magda, you have no idea how pleased I am to hear your voice,' I say, feeling as if someone just rowed towards me in a lifeboat.

'*Lees-en,*' she says. 'I just get back from Portugal an' I hear the news about Luis. You wanna come and take a coffee with me?'

I get in the car and drive immediately to her *lotissement*. She opens the door looking browner than ever, and so crisp and freshly put together—white vest top, pale pink jeans and gold sandals, with her hair in a chignon—that it's hard to believe she has just stepped off an overnight bus. She throws her arms around me and I immediately burst into tears.

'Come 'ere, *chérie*,' she says, leading me through a door to her ground floor bedroom. 'It's better in 'ere because the girls, they are playing in the *salon*.'

Her bedroom looks like something from a Barbie house. Apart from a white melamine chest of drawers, almost everything in the room—carpet, curtains and walls—is pink. I sit down on her shiny pink quilt and proceed to bawl my eyes out. In the sitting room, I can hear the children slamming doors and running amok.

'If Luis dies,' I sob, 'I don't want to live.'

'*Lees-en*, you mustn't talk like that,' she says, pulling my head onto her tanned bosom. 'God has given you life, and life is very precious. You must not talk about throwing it away, when right now, someone, somewhere, is fightin' to stay alive, just like Luis.'

'I just don't know what to do with myself,' I cry, as she rocks me in her arms. 'I can't find peace anywhere. I don't want to live with all the regret.'

'Eets not your fault, *chérie*,' she says, stroking my hair, which is damp from all the tears. 'But God eez gonna 'elp you, and Luis eez gonna be alright.'

I stop crying for a second and look up, struck by the absolute certainty in Magda's voice. For the first time, I notice the collection of religious statues and pictures vying for space with the designer perfumes on top of the chest of drawers. A rope of pale green rosary beads hangs from one of the red handles.

'Do you really think he will survive?' I ask.

'I know so,' she says. 'Luis, 'e is not gonna die. God eez gonna keep 'im alive. I am sure of it.'

'I feel like I caused the accident,' I say, before telling her about the conversation with Delphine in Paris.

'But Luis, 'e already 'ad the accident by then,' says Magda, pointing out something that in my grief I hadn't realised. I didn't will the accident to happen, as it had already taken place.

'You probably think I'm crazy,' I say. 'Crying like this, over someone who didn't give a damn about me.'

'Shh,' says Magda. '*Lees-en*, I know Luis, 'e 'ad a lotta respect for you.'

'Why do you say that?' I ask, desperate for any insight into The Lion's mind.

'One Sunday, I was sitting outside the café with my aunt and Luis, 'e arrive and go in the café and come straight out again, looking sad. I call to 'im and say, "Luis, come an' have a coffee with us"—often, he was buying the coffees for my aunt and me—but 'e just shake his 'ead and walk away. I hask my aunt what eez the matter with 'im and she say iz because *l'Anglaise* iz in the café with her neighbour.'

'You mean that Luis left the café because he saw me with Arnaud?'

'Yeah, *chérie*. Arnaud was 'olding your hand. And Luis, 'e see this and 'e did not like it.'

'When was this?'

'I dunno, *chérie*. Maybe two or three months ago.'

I think of how Arnaud often picked up my

306

hand to emphasise a point. I must have been sitting with my back to the door at the time. My grief reaches new levels at this news. The story emerging since the accident is very different to the one that I'd written in my head. I start to cry again—great, racking, body-shuddering sobs.

'*Chérie*, I'm gonna give you something to calm you down,' says Magda, getting up and searching inside her quilted pink vanity case. She hands me a tiny white pill. '*Voilà, chérie.*'

'What is it?' I ask, accepting it with gratitude. I know it's dangerous to take someone else's medication, and I normally avoid drugs of any kind, even Nurofen, but right now I'll try anything to take the edge off my grief.

'It's a Xanax—a sedative,' says Magda. 'The doctor, 'e give them to me for when I 'ave panic attacks.'

'You have panic attacks?' I say. In the sitting room, one of Magda's children starts to scream.

'Sometimes, yes. But *lee-sen*, they are very strong and you mustn't take the alcohol with them. I will get you some water.'

She goes into the sitting room, yells at the children in Portuguese and returns with a glass of water. It doesn't take long for the pill to kick in, dulling my feelings and radiating waves of calmness in my brain. The effect is similar to three gin and tonics. As an added bonus, my

307

tear ducts seem to have closed down.

'I think it's working,' I say.

'Good. Any time you are feelin' sad, you come 'ere and we take a coffee,' says Magda. 'And if I 'ear any news about Luis from the Portuguese, I gonna tell you.' She hugs me goodbye and I think what an amazing thing it is to be strong enough to help someone else with their cross, when weighed down by your own, as Magda, with her sick daughter and money problems, is.

Back home, I'm surprised to find that I'm hungry. I make some pasta and then get ready to go to the hospital. Delphine arrives early and I immediately feel cheered by the sight of her in a floppy turquoise sun hat, purple gypsy skirt and sandals decorated with purple glass stones.

As we drive towards Poitiers in her sedate green Rover, I feel the calmest that I've felt since hearing of the accident—partly because of the Xanax, partly because I'm all cried out, but mostly because I'm going to see Luis again. Delphine tells me that we must be careful to be upbeat and only say positive things in front of Luis, in case he can hear us.

At the hospital, we park close to the entrance and I feel the familiar jittery sensation in my stomach as we take the lift to the third floor.

We ring the bell outside the walnut-veneered doors leading to intensive care; and so begins a terrible wait. Then, just at the moment the nurse comes to let us in, I hear the lift doors open and, without even turning around, I know who it is.

'She doesn't have the right! It's his ex,' a coarse voice shouts in French from the corridor behind. I turn around and see the skinny blonde approaching, her face twisted in anger.

'I think you should go,' whispers Delphine. 'I will stay, as she doesn't know who I am.'

Avoiding all eye contact with Sabine, I turn around and head to the lift. I know I should feel compassion for her, but the truth is, all I feel is contempt. As the lift doors close, I hear Sabine shouting at the nurse, and I dislike her even more for creating a scene in an intensive care unit.

Shaking and dry-mouthed, I buy a bottle of water in the ground floor café and sit at a table, hidden behind a pillar. I never imagined that one day I would be acting like a fugitive in a French hospital. I'm terrified that I won't get to see Luis again, but if anyone can argue my case with the nurses, it is Delphine. I text her to say that I'm waiting in the café.

After what seems like hours but is probably only ten minutes, Delphine reappears. I can see from her face that it's not good news.

'I'm sorry,' she says. 'I waited until the girlfriend had gone in and then I spoke to the nurses and explained the situation. I tried to find out how Luis is doing but they said they couldn't tell me anything, that I would have to speak to the girlfriend.'

'Sabine must have made a big fuss,' I say shaking.

'Yes, she did. I think we should go,' says Delphine. 'Before she comes down. Maybe we can try to come back later.'

Reluctantly, I agree, but as we are leaving the café I see José, second-in-command to *le patron,* coming towards us from the lifts. With him is another man and I'm forced to do a double take, as he is an almost exact replica of Luis, right down to his jeans and orange top.

'Bonjour, Ka-renne,' says José, a large, gentle man with kind eyes. According to Magda, his wife and children have gone to Portugal for their August vacation, while José has stayed behind because of the accident and is responsible for driving Sabine to the hospital each day.

'How is Luis? Is there any news?'

'Still the same,' he says, with a sad smile.

'I just tried to visit him again but I bumped into Sabine.'

'I know,' says José. 'I've just spoken to the nurses. But listen, she has no right to stop you. His brother is here from Portugal and since he is the next-of-kin, he is the one who decides who can see Luis, not her. We have spoken to him and he has given permission for you to visit.'

310

I'm so grateful, I want to prostrate myself at José's flip-flopped feet. José turns to speak to Luis's brother in Portuguese. He is younger than Luis—probably in his late twenties—and not so strongly built, but facially he could be his twin, with the same black hair and eyes. I shake his hand and thank him in French, but he looks embarrassed. José explains that he only speaks Portuguese.

'How will we know when is a good time to visit?' asks Delphine practical as ever.

'I will text you to let you know when she is gone,' says José, taking out his mobile phone. 'And I will give you my number so that you can check with me before coming to the hospital.'

After exchanging numbers and thanking José, Delphine suggests that we go into Poitiers for a coffee rather than hanging around the hospital and possibly bumping into Sabine again. And so, in the intense August heat, we get back into her Rover and drive into the town centre.

Poitiers is deserted, as it always is on a Sunday afternoon, but we order drinks at a café in front of the Hôtel de Ville. Then we wait for over an hour until José sends a text saying, *'La blonde est partie'*. The blonde has left.

'It's funny,' says Delphine, 'that José doesn't call Sabine by name or even refer to her as *la copine*. I get the impression that the Portuguese don't like her very much.'

Back at the hospital we take the lift up to intensive care and endure a long, nerve-racking wait at the doors until a nurse arrives.

'Are you family?' she asks, looking suspicious.

'No. We are friends. But we have permission to visit from the next-of-kin,' says Delphine, in a voice that brooks no argument. This seems to satisfy the nurse and, to my very great relief, she lets us in. We gown up, rub antiseptic gel into our hands and then head into the clean, light-filled room with its pale pink walls and faint but not unpleasant smell of throat lozenges, where The Lion lies sleeping. I feel a huge rush of relief at seeing him again.

'Hello, darling. It's Sunday, nearly 6.00 pm and the sun is shining outside,' I say in French, for as many people have pointed out, coma victims are often very aware of what is being said to them. I've been advised to talk to Luis, to tell him what time of day it is and what is happening in the outside world.

Delphine takes his hand. '*Ça va aller, Luis,*' she says softly. (It's going to be OK.) I think how reassuring it would be to have her at my bedside if I ever found myself in such a terrible situation.

'My goodness,' she says, turning to me. 'He still has all his lionly qualities.'

It's true. The Lion might be horribly broken on the inside, but on the outside he looks as magnificent as ever. He still has his beautiful jet-black hair, his thick black eyelashes, his big hands and broad chest.

'I've got confidence in you, Luis,' I say, in French. 'You're going to survive. You're strong. So strong. And you are handsome, Luis—so handsome, darling.'

The Lion always took pride in his appearance, so it feels important to let him know that his face has not been scarred by the accident. I notice that Delphine is smiling.

'You are talking to him just like you talk to Biff,' she says. And in the middle of this awful situation—standing at the bedside of someone who is holding onto life by a few tubes—she makes me laugh, lightening up the atmosphere in this little room immeasurably.

'Well, we all know how much I love Biff,' I say.

Then Delphine laughs too—light, clear laughter like ice rattling in an empty glass. I doubt that there has been much laughter in this room so far, so I hope that Luis can hear and that it will lift his morale.

'Je t'aime, Luis, je t'aime beaucoup,' I say, taking his hand and remembering how his taut brown arms once picked me up and carried me upstairs to bed.

I tell him that I've written a book about him—a beautiful love story. 'There are many people in this world who love you and who are praying for you, many of them you don't even

313

know, but they read about you in my book and on my blog,' I say.

And then something truly amazing happens: he moves both his arms, very slowly, lifting them several centimetres off the bed and moving them towards his body.

'*Oh, Mon Dieu!*' says Delphine, visibly shocked. 'Look at that! He can hear you, I am sure of it. He is responding.'

'You saw that, too?' I say, elated, for it feels like Luis is communicating with me. 'I didn't imagine it?'

'No,' says Delphine. 'He moved his arms in response to what you said. I am going to get the nurse.'

'Thank you, Luis,' I say, kissing his forehead. 'Thank you, so much. Now I know that you can hear me.'

And then, to my further amazement, he moves his lips as if he is trying to speak. I'm tempted to run into the corridor and call Delphine back so that she can witness this, too.

When she returns, she shakes her head. 'I spoke to the nurse and she says it is just a reflex action, that it doesn't mean anything.'

'Oh,' I say. 'But it didn't look like a reflex action. It wasn't a twitch. He did it slowly and deliberately, as if he was trying to communicate with us.'

'I know,' says Delphine. 'But medical staff are always very cautious. They probably tell you this so as not to build up your hopes.'

314

'But he moved his mouth, too. As if he was trying to talk to me.'

Suddenly, I hear male voices in the corridor and three doctors enter the room and stand at the foot of Luis's bed. Two of them are dressed in white hospital uniforms, the third—Professeur Martin, it says on his name badge—in a pale blue tunic and trousers.

'*Bonjour,*' says the shortest and most charismatic of the three men, Dr Jérome Durand, who appears to be the most up to speed on Luis's case. 'And you are?' he says, looking directly at me.

'I'm just a friend,' I reply, in French.

Delphine explains that she has come along to help translate for me, but that she also knew Mr Duarte personally. Dr Durand nods and launches into a rapid-fire monologue in medical French, updating his colleagues on Luis's condition. I catch only one phrase: 'If he lives, he will almost certainly be paralysed.'

'Well, actually he moved his leg this morning,' says the younger doctor and I want to jump across the bed and hug him for providing this thin thread of hope. Unprompted, Dr Durand turns to Delphine and proceeds to convey a lot of information. Delphine nods as she takes it all in, not once interrupting. I can't understand much of the medical jargon so I listen in respectful silence. The men standing before us are Luis's best hope of survival and as such, they are heroes

315

to me.

'Can I ask one question?' I say, when Dr Durand has finished. 'Is he going to live?'

'That we don't know,' he replies, switching to English and looking directly at me. 'What I would say is this: one mustn't be optimistic, and one mustn't be pessimistic.'

This time it feels like I've been flung a golden rope. If Luis were definitely going to die, surely he would have said so?

'My goodness,' says Delphine, after they have gone. 'They gave us such a lot of information. This is very unusual. I'm very surprised.'

She runs through what the doctor said. Much of it reaffirms what *le patron* told me. The most serious thing, it seems, is that The Lion's brain is covered in small lesions. Delphine also explains that Luis has been re-sedated as he was showing signs of pain.

'They say that they will not know anything conclusively until they can do an MRI scan of his brain. In order to do this, Luis must be able to breathe on his own and survive without the life-support machine long enough for the scan to take place.'

I nod, so grateful to Delphine for being here to speak with the doctors. But the medical information has taken second place to the simple, joyous fact that Luis moved. And before the visit is over, he does something else amazing. I tell him that I'll be back to see him tomorrow and that I'm so proud of him for moving his arms. As I bend to kiss his forehead, very noticeably, his eyelids and his mouth move.

'*Look!*' I shout to Delphine. 'He's trying to speak to me.'

'I saw it,' she says, shaking her head in disbelief.

As I leave, I look at the two photographs pinned on the wall next to The Lion's medical chart. The first is of Luis's brother and a stocky woman with short blonde hair and glasses, who I assume is their mother. I'm surprised, as I always imagined her to be raven-haired and exotic, like Luis. The Lion must have got his dark, magnetic looks from the father that he loathed.

The second picture is of Luis and Sabine in a drunken embrace. His arms are around her waist and he is leaning in towards her. It causes me a jolt of pain, as I have no pictures of Luis and myself together. He didn't like being photographed and I only have three pictures of him, all of them blurry as they were taken with my mobile phone. My favourite was taken one Saturday afternoon when he arrived with oysters; the others, in my bedroom on the night that he broke in through the skylight. I smile at the thought of it. Who needs pictures when you have such vivid memories?

'I'm so glad you were there to witness that,' I say to Delphine. 'Otherwise I would have thought that I dreamt it.'

'There is no way that was a reflex action,' she replies. 'He wants to come out of that coma, I can see it.'

As she drives us home through the Poitevin countryside—radiant in the light of early evening—we replay that small movement and its significance over and over.

'Don't worry, *Ka-renne*,' says Delphine softly. 'Luis is going to surprise us, I know it.'

The grief that threatened to overwhelm me is suddenly replaced by gratitude. I won't forget any of the kindnesses that I've been shown in the past forty-eight hours—by Fernando and José, who have made it possible for me to visit The Lion, by Magda and by Delphine, who stood with me at his bedside, like an angel in a pale blue gown. I am not sure if Luis derived any comfort from her calm, sunny presence today, or was even aware of it, but I certainly did. If there is an upside to suffering, it has to be that it brings you closer to others. I feel a huge debt of gratitude to the doctors for giving us so much information and to the nurses who are looking after Luis and cleaning the corridor outside his room so fastidiously. Above all, I feel grateful to The Lion for hanging on to life, and for that small movement that has given me hope— and such a huge high—in the midst of all this devastation.

Later that evening, I have an idea. Luis really loved the scent of the Jo Malone body oil that I wore for most of the time we were together—a sweet, almost edible scent that lingered on the skin and clothes for hours. As a beauty journalist, I've written enough fragrance features to know that scent has a hotline to the brain (something to do with the positioning of the olfactory gland close to the seat of the memory and emotions). Scared of the memories that it might trigger, I haven't worn the oil since breaking up with Luis, but if The Lion responds to my voice, he might respond even more forcefully to the scent of our shared past. I find the opaque black bottle of oil in a basket of discarded beauty products in the spare room. Unfortunately, it's almost empty, but as soon as I unscrew the cap, it triggers a vivid memory of The Lion in my bed, inhaling the scent of my clothes after he'd removed them.

I log on to my computer to buy a new bottle, only to find that it has been discontinued. So soon? It was only launched the summer that I got together with Luis. The following morning, I phone the press officer in London. She tells me that all stock has long gone— that there isn't a single bottle left at any Jo Malone store in the world—which only makes me more determined to find a bottle. I spend several hours trawling eBay and websites that specialise in discontinued beauty products, but without success. It seems that the scent of our two summers together, no longer exists.

Chapter 19

A Medal for Delphine

Magda arrives to clean, wearing a white vest top and grey marl leggings that leave little to the imagination. I'm cheered to see her, but alarmed by her stern expression, as I fear that it might mean bad news. I haven't been able to go to the hospital for three days because I have a cold and can't risk passing it on to Luis. But Magda lives next door to José and his wife, and so is well placed to hear of any developments.

'Come 'ere,' she says, taking me by the hand, so that we're standing in front of the mirror above the fireplace. 'Look at yourself, *chérie*.'

'I'd rather not,' I say, for I know that it's not a pretty sight.

'Look at your face, your eyes, they are all pink and *gonflé*.'

'Swollen?'

'Exactly! You look like a fuckin' mess. When are you gonna stop cryin'?'

'Magda, do you think I give a damn how I look when Luis is in a coma?'

'*Lees-en*, you cannot carry on like this,' she says.

'Do you have any news?' I ask, as she hangs up her pink tracksuit top in the hallway and marches into the kitchen.

She shakes her head and looks grave. '*Lees-en*, can I hask a leetle favour?'

'Of course,' I say, worried as to what it might be.

'Can you make me a coffee, *chérie*?' Her face breaks into a cheeky grin and I feel a sudden urge to hug her.

If it weren't for Magda, I would barely be functioning by now. Earlier this week, I left my bag containing my wallet and diary in the post office. Worse, it was two days before I noticed. Even then, it was only thanks to a neighbour who'd heard that the post office was trying to get hold of me. I've also lost Biff's lead and have taken to walking him around the village with a piece of pink string attached to his collar, traveller-style. I already have the dazed expression and crumpled clothes; all I need to complete the itinerant look is dreadlocks—and that can only be a matter of time.

Maison Coquelicot also feels like it is falling apart. The satellite dish isn't working and the bathroom sink has been blocked for several weeks. But none of this seems important set against the simple fact that The Lion is in a coma and connected to life by just a few tubes.

As I scoop coffee into the cafetière, I ask Magda how her daughter is doing.

'She is doin' fine, *chérie*. But I won't know for sure that the cancer has gone until they do the scan.' She goes into the courtyard and lights a cigarette. '*Lee-sen*, I do 'ave something to tell you.'

'What?' I ask, desperate for any information.

'The Portuguese, they are sayin' that Luis tried to finish with Sabine many, many times but she 'ad copied the keys to his flat.'

'She did?' I say, remembering how hurt I'd been that Luis had given her keys to his apartment.

'Every day 'e come home from work and find her there and he look for a reason to have a fight with her,' she says, echoing what Arnaud told me on a number of occasions.

I finish making Magda's coffee and sit outside with her while she drinks it. 'So you have no news at all about Luis?' I persist.

She sighs, as if reluctant to impart the information. 'People are sayin' that if 'e lives, Luis is gonna be a vegetable.'

I wince at the use of this word to describe The Lion. Magda looks at me with concern, as the tears start to roll again. 'Next time you visit 'im in the hospital, *chérie*, be careful. Everyone says Sabine, she is crazy.'

'But Luis's brother has given permission.'

'Yeah, *chérie*. But the brother, 'e az to go back to Portugal.'

She gets up and goes into the kitchen, where she starts to bang dishes around in the sink. I go upstairs on the pretext of doing some work and to check my emails. There is one from the editor of a British magazine for whom I've written a feature to publicise my new book.

'What does Luis think about the fact that you've written about him?' she wants to know.

I feel sick. I can't possibly tell her that he is in a coma and unable to think anything at all. Instead, I type back, 'Luis has always been very proud of the fact that I'm a writer,' which is the truth. I remember with affection the many times that he told me, *'Tu es beaucoup intelligente, chérie.'* (Literally: 'you are lots intelligent, darling.')

Magda comes clattering up the stairs. 'Just ignore the bathroom sink. I'm still waiting for a plumber to come and unblock it,' I say, knowing full well that the reason I'm still waiting is because I haven't actually called a plumber.

She gives me an exasperated look. 'Well, how much longer you gonna wait?' She rolls up her leggings to her knees and squats down to look under the sink. 'She [the sink] has been like this for many weeks now. Pass me that *truc*,' she says, pointing to a cloth.

'I've already unscrewed that pipe myself,' I say, not wanting to appear a complete fool.

'I know,' she says, looking at the complex arrangement of grey plastic tubing under the sink. 'But the blocked (she pronounces it 'block-head') bit eez 'ere.' She taps a pipe further up towards the basin and then, looking every bit like a professional plumber, unscrews

323

several parts of the plastic tubing. 'I cannot see where the water she goes,' she frowns.

'I'll turn the tap on, then we can see,' I say without thinking. The water gushes straight through the open-ended pipe and onto the tiled floor, splashing onto Magda's pale pink flip-flops and carmine-painted toes.

'Whatya doin'?' she shouts, jumping out of the way. 'Are you fuckin' stupid or what? The water, she is goin' everywhere. Look, she is all over the floor.' She looks at me with her sparkling green eyes as if awed by my stupidity. Then she starts laughing and before I know it, I'm laughing, too.

'Well, at least we now know where the water is going,' I say, throwing her a towel to dry her feet and using another to mop up the water.

'Laisse!' (Leave it!) she shouts. 'I do it. You can go and make me another coffee.' She shakes her head as if dealing with an imbecile. 'And we need the *truc* that the *plombiers* (plumbers) use,' she says, miming the act of pushing a rod through a pipe.

'I have exactly that,' I say, suddenly remembering the long metal contraption in the garage. I run downstairs to fetch it.

Magda looks impressed as I hand it over. *'Merci, chérie,'* she says, before manoeuvring the metal rod into the pipe with her toned brown arms. I can only watch in awe. She seems so capable. Eventually, she pulls out an unappetising selection of gunk: my hair mixed

324

with grey sludge from the washing machine, which is connected to this complex pipe arrangement.

'Get me a bowl, *chérie*,' she orders. *'Vite!'* (Quick!)

In my new role as plumber's mate, I run downstairs again to do as I'm told. I dash back up with the bowl and watch as she extracts globs of hair and laundry lint from the tubing.

'Magda, I'm so impressed. Where did you learn to do this?' I say as, biceps flexed, she fixes the pipes back into place.

'I 'ave to. I am a *femme toute seule*.' She shrugs. *'Allez, chérie!* Make me another coffee.'

In no time at all the sink is unblocked and the bathroom is so sparklingly clean, so dazzlingly white, that you could perform surgery on the floor.

'Magda, what would I do without you?' I ask, meaning it more than she knows.

She laughs. 'I dunno *chérie*.'

Before she leaves, she points out that she has saved me at least €35—the minimum hourly rate for a plumber.

'I know, *chérie*,' I say, handing her some extra money and a bag of expensive beauty products—sent to me for work—that I'd been looking for an excuse to give her for some time.

'Merci, Ka-renne,' she says, with such sincerity in her eyes that I am humbled.

'No, thank *you*, Magda.'

325

I watch as she ties her pale pink tracksuit top round her waist and struts off down the street. As always, the house feels empty once she has gone.

*   *   *

The following morning, I drive to Puysoleil for Delphine's medal ceremony. I volunteered some time ago to help prepare the canapés for *le cocktail* and I'm determined not to let her down. As I park my car by the ivy-clad church, I notice that a trestle table has been set up under the lime blossom trees.

It's the last week in August, but there's a nip in the air and it feels quite autumnal. Nature seems to have dimmed its lights prematurely this year. Rémi, the council worker, calls me over from the door of the *salle des fêtes*. He tells me that 'the boss', as they call Delphine, is still at the hairdressers, but he and Bruno have already started work on the canapés. Inside the village hall, I tie Biff to a table leg, wash my hands and join them at the kitchen worktop.

'I'm sorry to hear about your friend,' says Bruno quietly.

'Thank you,' I reply, grateful to be here with them, buttering bread in companionable silence. We cut each slice into four triangles, adding a little sliver of smoked salmon to each one. When we're done, Rémi adds a finishing

326

flourish to the platter: two green pickles in the shape of a smile, two silver onion 'eyes' and a nose made out of a carrot. He stands back to admire his handiwork and I can see that he is doing his best to make me smile.

Delphine has planned for three cocktail choices in red, white and blue—the colours of the French flag. I retrieve six bottles of sparkling Saumur from the fridge and hand them to Bruno to open. We add crème de cassis to a large glass jug and blue curaçao to another, and then top them up with the sparkling wine. The third cocktail, representing the white of the *tricolore*, is Delphine's universally admired *soupe de champagne*—a delicious but lethal aperitif consisting of Cointreau, fresh lemon juice and cane syrup, chilled in the fridge overnight and then topped up with sparkling wine.

When we have finished, we walk over to the *mairie* where many of Delphine's friends and family are already gathered. It's a one-storey building consisting of a main meeting room with an ancient flagstone floor, and a small office at the back, where Barack Obama beams down from a poster on the wall. It's obligatory to keep a photograph of the French president on display in the main room but Delphine, who is not a fan of Sarkozy, usually covers his face with her *tricolore* hat—a confection of red, white and blue netting made by her milliner in Niort when she first became mayor.

However, several local dignitaries, including the senator for the Vienne, will be attending today's ceremony, so Sarko smirks out at the room from the mantelpiece.

There are about forty people in total—Delphine's friends, family, councillors and colleagues from her 'mayor business' as she calls it. I take a seat next to Travis, who greets me with a nervous smile, no doubt worried that I might burst into tears at any moment. He tells me that the work on his kitchen is progressing and we both try to keep the conversation on neutral ground. Travis, I know, doesn't do grief or public displays of emotion. He is also very black and white about life: in his view, Luis cheated on me twice and should therefore be history, whereas I see the shades of grey. So we carry on as usual, chatting about granite worktops and pretending that I don't really have a friend in a coma. I don't blame Travis for this. Some people are just not very good at dealing with grief.

'*Bonjour, tout le monde.*' Delphine's crystalline voice cuts through the murmur of conversation. She is standing in front of the lemon fireplace in her *tricolore* sash, flanked by Stephan Barbe, the handsome mayor of Tauzé, Jacques Lefoy, the suave regional councillor, and one of the two senators of the Vienne. I'm a little worried that Biff might bark, but he seems to know that this is an important moment in our friend's life and lies under my chair, as quiet as a French Sunday.

Delphine has earned her silver medal and the right to be the centre of attention today. I think of how many people she must have helped in the twenty years since she became a councillor. She began serving her community when she was just fifteen, making the dessert for 'the oldies' dinner' as she affectionately refers to the annual event for the over-sixty-fives. (She has made the dessert every year since, without ever duplicating a dish.) As the senator launches into a long and rather dry speech about the importance of serving your community, I think of the many ways in which Delphine has enhanced the lives of others—taking the lonely and the depressed out to lunch, and listening to Brits moaning about everything from France Telecom to the French medical system, while responding with a graceful smile and often accompanying them to the relevant authority to sort the problem out.

Delphine embodies one of the most humbling lessons that Luis's accident has taught me: namely, that being of use to others and trying to pick them up when they're down—as so many people have done for me recently—is possibly the highest aim in life. It's really the only thing that guarantees you will feel good about yourself in the long run. Delphine is one of the most joyful people

I know, which suggests to me that there is a direct link between helping others and happiness.

Curled up at my feet, Biff gives a bored, doggy yawn. The senator has been speaking for a long time. I notice Bruno and Rémi slipping out to lay everything out for *le cocktail*. Eventually, the old senator— Delphine, I know, was hoping that it would be Stephan Barbe—pins the medal to her jacket, to a round of applause and shouts of 'Bravo!' She then poses for pictures for the local newspaper, positioning herself next to Stephan, with a big smile on her face.

We step outside to find that, after this morning's premature slide into autumn, high summer is back. Bruno and Rémi have poured the cocktails, arranging the glasses so that they look like a flag—three fat stripes of red, white and blue. As always at French gatherings, it is considered polite to hang back for as long as possible and pretend that the refreshments are a mirage. Then Delphine's little niece, Elodie, hands around a tray of canapés while Bruno and Rémi serve the cocktails.

By 12.45 pm, the gathering has dwindled to close family members—Delphine's parents have organised a lunch in her honour—so I say goodbye. Delphine tells me she will pick me up at 5.45 pm and I drive home through the blazing countryside, counting down the hours until I see The Lion.

Chapter 20

Confrontation

José has cleared for us to visit Luis after 6.00 pm. There is no wait at the walnut doors today. We are admitted straightaway. I'm shocked to find that since I last saw him, The Lion no longer looks invincible. He has a bandage around his head where they have removed the probe, and is now wearing a white cotton gown, which makes him look more vulnerable. His legs are clad in white surgical stockings and raised slightly at the end of the bed, and he looks noticeably thinner, his cheekbones more pronounced. My heart still flips when I see him but a look of concern flickers across Delphine's face and she goes off to ask a nurse for an update on his condition.

'It's Tuesday, 6.30 pm, *chéri*,' I say, stroking Luis's arm. 'Everything is quiet in the village and the weather is very weird. You're not missing much. All your friends in the café are thinking of you and waiting for you to come home.' As I say those words, I realise that Villiers really is Luis's home now. With the exception of his brother, the people who love him the most, are all here in France.

To my great joy, his lips move and his eyelids flicker as if he is trying to communicate with me again.

Delphine reappears, looking stern. 'The nurse won't tell me anything. She says I must ask the girlfriend; that the girlfriend knows everything.'

'It sounds as though Sabine has had a word with them,' I say.

Delphine grimaces. 'I'm afraid to say it, but yes.'

There are voices in the corridor and then Luis's doctors arrive, locked in an animated discussion. (It's weird, but every time I visit the hospital with Delphine—a total of three times to date—they appear almost immediately, as if by telepathy.) They stop talking when they see us.

'And you are . . . ?' says Dr Durand, looking at me.

'Just a friend,' I say, answering as I did the first time he asked. I think he has guessed that I am (or was) more than a friend. Either way, he seems sympathetic rather than suspicious, and proceeds to give us an update. They have done more tests, he says, and the results are not encouraging. But they won't know anything for sure until the MRI scan, or '*IRM*' as it is known in France, which they hope to do two weeks from now, by which time it will be a month since the accident.

It's gone 7.30 pm when we leave the hospital, stepping from the cool interior into the hot glare of the evening sun. In contrast to the cool stillness of Luis's room, the steps outside are buzzing with life—people coming and going, chatting and smoking. Driving home past fields ablaze with golden light, Delphine tells me she will continue to go to church to pray for Luis, and that she has already lit several candles for him. She turns to look at me.

'Each time, I say, "Please God, do the best thing for *Ka-renne* and the best thing for Luis."' The thoughtfulness behind her prayer suddenly hits me. I have simply been praying that The Lion lives and, for the first time, it occurs to me how selfish this is: the outcome that I am so desperately hoping for, might not be the best thing for Luis.

The following day, I send José a text to ask if I can visit Luis at 3.00 pm. A message comes back in the affirmative. Delphine has council meetings all day, so I must go alone, as I've done several times. I get ready in a floral print Moschino dress, dabbing my wrists with the rose and frankincense perfume that I sometimes wore when The Lion and I were together.

I set off for Poitiers in the suffocating heat that seems to descend every afternoon, sucking the life out of the village. Not far out of Villiers, I get stuck behind a tractor, crawling along, in what feels like a slow cooker, for several kilometres. Then, after the usual circuit of roundabouts and concrete housing estates, I see the tall tower that houses The Lion. I park the car, the adrenaline coursing as it always does, the closer that I get to him. I'm a little early, since visiting time doesn't start till 3.00 pm, and when I push through the first set of doors on the third floor, there is no one waiting in the small antechamber before the doors to the ward. I ring the bell and a nurse eventually arrives. I tell her that I've come to see Monsieur Duarte and she looks me up and down with suspicion, taking in my short dress and high shoes. She asks me to take a seat in the waiting room along the corridor.

After sitting in the narrow room for what seems like forever but is probably only ten minutes, I return to the short corridor between the two sets of doors, worried that the nurse has forgotten me. The first doors are open and I panic when I see a tall, thin figure talking to the nurse with her back to me. I immediately turn and walk away before she sees me, hurrying through the corridors towards the lifts. But it's too late. I hear her running after me and calling my name.

'Eh, *Ka-renne*, you have no right to come here,' she shouts in French.

Heart thumping, I push the button to call the lift. I'm as desperate to avoid a scene, as she is to create one. She rounds the corner just as the lift arrives and I step into it.

'I have nothing to say to you,' I say in French, avoiding eye contact and willing the doors to close on her angry face, which eventually they do. Shaking, I descend to the ground floor, gutted that I'm not going to see Luis today. But the irony that, even on a life-support machine he has two women fighting over him, is not lost on me. Standing behind the pillar in the cafeteria, I call José to find out what happened.

'I'm back at work,' he says.

'So how did she get to the hospital?'

'A friend brought her. But listen, *Ka-renne*,' he says softly. 'You have as much right to be there as she does. If you want to go and see Luis, you go. His brother has given the permission.'

I know this is true. I also know that if everyone is to be believed, Luis was trying to leave Sabine—which as a soon-to-be-dumped girlfriend, still gives her marginally more status than me. But I can't run the risk of bumping into her again. As the French would say, she wants to *faire du cinéma* or 'make some cinema', whereas I am horrified at the idea of creating a scene in a hospital. And while it's one thing to bump into her in a corridor, what if it happened at Luis's bedside? I can't go sprinting through an intensive care unit.

I'm upset to have been thwarted in my attempts to see The Lion, and I feel foolish to have got dressed up and driven over 25 kilometres in stupefying heat for nothing. There's no point in waiting for Sabine to leave today, as she will be determined to keep me out. If only The Lion knew the hoops I was jumping through to see him. I head back out into the car park—or rather, car parks—and, as usual, perform several laps of them all before I find my car.

I drive home to Villiers, my head throbbing with a migraine-in-waiting. As I pull into the square, I see Magda and her girls sitting outside the Café du Commerce. I park the car at the side of the *mairie* and join them.

'*Bonjour, chérie,*' shouts Magda, pushing her sunglasses back on her head. She is wearing white jeans and a floral print tunic top, her brown skin glistening in the sun.

I say '*Bonjour*' to the girls, expecting Janinha to eye me with the usual mix of contempt and suspicion. But instead, she nods at my dress and says, '*C'est jolie.*'

Coming from her, the compliment feels like a celestial gift.

'Can we take Biff for a walk?' one of the younger girls asks.

'Yes. But be careful with him,' I say, handing over the lead. I watch as the three of them take it in turns to walk him backwards and forwards in front of the *mairie*, shrieking with excitement when he cocks his leg against a tub of municipal flowers.

'You look good, *chérie*,' says Magda with approval.

'Don't sound so surprised.'

'I *am* surprised,' she says, laughing.

'You're saying I usually look a mess?'

'Yeah, *chérie*, I am sayin' that.' She laughs, her green eyes full of mischief. 'So why are you dressed hup? You've been to see Luis?'

'Yes. But I saw Sabine and left.' I don't tell her that I was chased out of the hospital.

'Is everything OK with you?' I ask, for Magda looks worried.

She shakes her head. 'Nah, *Ka-renne*.' She pulls a letter out of her bag and shows it to me. She has to go to Civray to attend the *pôle emploi*, which sounds like a lap dancing club, but is in fact the outpost of French bureaucracy that deals with employment issues.

'I 'ave to go there to show them a document in order to get a tax refund.'

'I'll take you, Magda. It's no problem,' I say. I've been leaning heavily on Magda since the accident, so I'm delighted to have the opportunity to help her in return.

'Really, *chérie*? When?'

'Whenever you like. What about tomorrow morning?'

'*Merci, Ka-renne*,' she says, with a big smile. We sit in silence for a while, watching the girls running around with Biff. At least it will help them to burn off a few of those pizza calories, I think to myself.

'Have you got a date for Janinha's scan yet?' I ask.

'Not for at least another month,' she says. 'But as soon as the doctors say she is OK, we are leavin', *chérie*. I'm going back to Portugal.'

'You are?' I say, surprised at how disappointed I am to hear this news. 'To live with your boyfriend?'

'That, I dunno, *chérie*. When I tell Roberto I'm goin' there, he doesn't seem that happy.' She shrugs. 'But I don't give a fuck. Me, I'm gonna get my own apartment and a job and 'e can do what he wants. I'm a *femme toute seule*, Ka-renne. If 'e wants to be with me, that's fine. If he doesn't want me, then fuck 'im. I'm just gonna get on with my life. It doesn't bother me.'

I narrow my eyes.

'I'm serious, *chérie*. I don't need no man for nothin'. Not even the sex,' she continues. 'If I never 'ad a boyfriend again, it wouldn't bother me.'

She says it with such sincerity that I believe her. And as I already know, she can do her own plumbing.

I look at my watch. I have to take Biff for a walk before Sarah and Steve arrive for a violin recital by Kya Groot, a talented Dutch violinist who lives locally. I invited them prior to Luis's accident, since they both like classical music—an act of great altruism on my behalf, as I mostly associate violin music with the shower scene in *Psycho*. And now there is the additional worry that the sad wail of the violin

338

will set me off crying again. Sarah already phoned to see if I wanted to cancel, but I'd like to see them. And rather than staying at home with my miserable thoughts, I might as well carry them to the market hall, where at least they'll be set to a soundtrack of Rachmaninov.

Just as I'm opening the door to Sarah and Steve, Fernando's black BMW draws up outside. He nods when he sees me on the doorstep and comes over to speak.

'*Bonsoir,* Madame Willer. I heard what happened at the hospital today,' he says in French.

'I'm sorry. The last thing I wanted was to cause a scene.'

'It wasn't your fault, Madame Willer. The nurses told me everything. I have spoken to them and I've spoken to Madame [he means Sabine], and I've told her that you have every right to visit Luis. You can go there whenever you want, Madame Willer.'

'Thank you,' I say, suddenly grateful for the patriarchal system over which Fernando presides, and the fact that no one, not even Sabine, dares to question his authority.

'*De rien.*' (It's nothing.) He nods his head and struts off down rue St Benoit, towards the building where Ruigi lives.

'What's all that about?' asks Steve when he has gone.

'That's Luis's boss.'

'He acts like he's the Godfather or

something.'

'Well, to the Portuguese, he sort of is.'

Half an hour later, we're sitting in the brightly lit market hall waiting for the concert to begin. The audience is a mix of French and British people, many of them Kya's friends. The violinist, who lives with her dogs in the middle of nowhere, in a barn that she renovated herself, is a no-nonsense kind of person, usually to be found in jeans, checked shirt and a leather waistcoat.

She and her accompanist, a delicate Russian pianist dressed in green silk, fill the summer night with a sad but beautiful lament. I had my doubts about the odd choice of venue—a soulless space with tiled floor and itinerant chiller cabinet—but as soon as the enigmatic Dutchwoman lifts her violin to her shoulder and raises her bow, the setting becomes irrelevant. There are no jarring *Psycho* moments; the music is fluid and calming. Even Biff seems soothed, curling up with his head on Sarah's feet, his tail on mine. In between the pieces, the audience applauds with real enthusiasm, and Kya bows her head modestly and makes self-deprecating jokes in French.

Afterwards, Sarah and Steve come back for a glass of wine and Steve tells me not to give up hope for Luis, as very little is known about the brain.

'He's young and fit. It's still possible that he'll come out of the coma, regardless of what the doctors say,' he tells me.

As I go to bed that night, I realise that I haven't cried for five hours—a record in recent weeks.

The following morning, I pick up Magda as agreed. She bursts forth from her concrete bunker in white jeans, platform heels and a low-cut violet top, yelling into her mobile phone. She's wearing red lipstick and big gold hoops, perhaps hoping to generate the same reaction as when we went to buy the bus ticket. I think back to the ticket clerk, straining every cell in his body to find her a good deal and hope we're allotted an equally vulnerable male at the *pôle emploi* today.

I am not looking forward to it. I picture a waiting room packed with demoralised people, each armed with a suitcase of forms and photocopies (the French love photocopies), waiting to be abused by a sadistic official. Since neither Magda nor I know where the *pôle emploi* is, I suggest that we stop first at La Grande Galerie, a British-run art gallery and tearoom in Civray, to ask for directions. We can also have coffee and cake in preparation for our assault on the *pôle emploi*.

'My aunt saw you at the hospital yesterday,' says Magda with a sidelong glance, as we drive towards Civray. 'You were running. In high heels.'

'Yes, to get away from Sabine,' I say, thinking that news travels fast in the

341

Portuguese community. 'But I didn't see your aunt.'

'She say you were running too fast to see 'er.'

'Was your aunt visiting Luis?'

'Nah, *chérie.*' Magda rolls her eyes sarcastically. 'My aunt, she often go to neurosurgery just for the fun of it.'

'Sorry. Stupid question. Of course she was going to see Luis.'

'My aunt, she say that Sabine is a beech. She az no right to stop Luis's friends from seein' 'im. I know the boss az sorted it out. But *lees-en, chérie,* maybe you shouldn't go to the hospital any more. Sabine is crazy.'

After yesterday's events, I've been thinking along similar lines. As badly as I want to see The Lion, and despite what *le patron* said, I've decided to stay away for a few days as I'm pretty sure Sabine will be watching out for me. But I have to keep finding a way to see Luis, as I'm certain that my visits are helping him.

At La Grande Galerie, we sit at a table outside and while Magda puffs furiously on a cigarette and checks her mobile for messages, I get directions to the *pôle emploi.* Several people ask about Luis and I'm touched when Eileen, the owner, comes over to say she is sorry to hear about the accident. She takes my hand and says, 'Have faith in Luis. He's going to come round from the coma.'

'Do you really think so?'

342

'Yes, absolutely I do.'

I leave the Galerie feeling buoyed. She is right; I must have faith in Luis. He *will* come out of that coma; he won't let me down.

Magda and I return to the car and find the *pôle emploi* without any problem. It's a makeshift-looking office on a main road out of town—so it's tough nuts to anyone lacking a car as well as a job, as it's pretty inaccessible without one. I drop Magda at the entrance, telling her I'm going to walk Biff around the car park (anything to delay the encounter with French bureaucracy). Just as I'm thinking that we should have come prepared for a long stay—with packed lunches, sleeping bags, that sort of thing—Magda re-emerges, beaming. I assume we've come to the wrong place, but no, it seems that everything is sorted and the *pôle emploi* will be in touch shortly by telephone. Job done.

'That was quick,' I say, as she lights a cigarette. 'Was it a man that you dealt with?'

'Yeah, *chérie*. A very 'elpful man. Why you hask that?'

'Just wondering. But that's great news. Well done.'

Who knew that going out of your way to help people could be this easy? Transporting Magda to the *pôle emploi* has also helped to take my mind off Luis. It feels like an amazing discovery: that when the cross you are carrying becomes too heavy to bear, the only thing to do is to put it down for a while and help someone else with theirs.

'*Chérie*,' Magda says, when we are halfway home. 'Can I ask a leetle favour?'

'Go on,' I say, ready to do more deeds.

'Can you take me to Aldi in Vivonne to do some shoppin' for *les enfants*?'

'No problem,' I say, realising that there is something that I need to do in Vivonne, too. As I drop her off outside the store, I tell her to call me when she is done.

'Why? Where you gonna be?' she asks.

'Not far away,' I reply.

I drive to the centre of town and park near the old stone church. It's too hot to leave Biff in the car, so I tie his lead to a railing in the shade. It's a long time since I've visited a church with religious intent, but as I enter the cool interior, the scent of incense, candle wax and old stone transports me right back to my Catholic childhood.

The church is empty except for a woman arranging flowers at the side of the altar. Feeling like an impostor, I head towards the little stand of flickering candles at the front of the church. I drop some euros into the metal box and light a tapered white candle. Then I kneel in front of the Madonna and apologise for the fact that it's been a while, pointing out that I'm here not for myself, but for a friend who needs help.

Then I remember something that Delphine

told me recently that really resonated: that you shouldn't just ask God for things, but thank him, too. So I tell Him how grateful I am that Luis is still in the world and express thanks for all the wonderful people in my life. Then, I make my plea: namely, that The Lion will survive the coma and one day walk out of the hospital, even if it is back into the arms of Sabine. I close my eyes.

'And if that's not possible, then please, God, do whatever you think is best for Luis.'

When I'm sure that I've pleaded Luis's cause as best as I can, I promise that I'll be back—and that I won't leave it a couple of decades this time. Then I return to Aldi to pick up Magda. She eventually emerges, wobbling under the weight of three fat shopping bags, stuffed with additive-packed food (a little surprising given that I thought she had no money). I stow the unhealthy cache in the boot, silently vowing that next time, I'll follow her around the supermarket and sneak some fresh vegetables into her trolley. As we drive home, I wonder how long the candle will flicker for Luis.

Chapter 21

Sad Saturday

I wake up feeling jittery and anxious. Luis had his brain scan yesterday. I'm hoping that Magda will have some news when she comes to clean for me this morning. Afterwards, I'm planning to go to the hospital, where I will try to talk to Luis's doctors. Magda rings the doorbell at 11.00 am—nearly two hours late. Dressed in black leggings and a grey vest, she frowns and throws her cigarette into the gutter as I open the door.

'Is everything OK?' I ask, seeing from her face that it isn't.

She walks into the hallway and hangs her bag on a peg.

'*Chérie*, I 'ave some bad news,' she says.

Oh God, oh God. I sit down on the sofa. 'What?'

She looks at me, her beautiful brown face riven with angst. 'All the Portuguese, they are going to the hospital this afternoon to say goodbye to Luis.' She pauses. 'The scan results have come back and 'is brain is dead, *chérie*. Nothin' is workin' at all.'

Oh God. Please don't let this be true. I've read enough about coma and brain trauma to know that the longer the patient takes to regain consciousness, the less chance there is of a meaningful recovery. And since Luis has now been in a coma for over a month, the prognosis is not good. But I have continued to have faith in him, to believe that he will do something when the time is right.

'Luis is completely paralysed, *chérie*,' Magda is saying. 'The doctors say 'e will never be able to speak or move again. He is blind and deaf.'

Blind and deaf. This piece of information sends huge, unstoppable waves of pain and grief crashing through my body. So I must have imagined it then, when I thought that he could hear me and was responding.

'Come 'ere, *chérie*,' says Magda, holding her arms out.

'So what happens now?'

'They gonna turn the machines off.'

'When?'

'I dunno, *Ka-renne*.'

'What time are the Portuguese going to the hospital?'

'4.30 pm, *chérie*.'

'Well, I'd better get a move on.'

I go upstairs to get ready, feeling once again the dead calm that descends when all hope has gone. But one thing is certain: they are not turning off the life-support before I say goodbye.

When I arrive shortly before 3.00 pm, a nurse lets me in straightaway, no questions asked today. After the usual angst and adrenaline surge—will I be allowed in or not?—I feel suddenly at peace, as I always do when I'm alone with The Lion. Grateful that there is no sign of Sabine, who is presumably coming at 4.30 pm with the Portuguese, I kiss his forehead and tell him that it is Saturday afternoon and sunny outside. As soon as I start talking, his eyes half open and he looks at me, as if drunk. I know that he can hear me and is aware of my presence, regardless of what the doctors say.

'Do you know how much it meant to me each time I saw you in the café?' I ask, speaking in French to him as I always do. 'I used to get dressed up every Sunday morning in the hope of seeing you there. It made me so happy just to be in the same room as you.'

He moves his mouth. He looks like he is trying to talk to me. I promised myself I wouldn't cry in front of him—that I would always keep up a positive front—but I can't help it. The tears start to fall and then they turn into loud sobs. I'm crying for Luis and a life wasted and I'm crying for me because I feel sure I could have prevented the accident and will have to live with that for the rest of my life. I stand there for a long time, tears running down my face and dropping onto his arm.

Eventually, a petite black nurse appears and asks if I would like a glass of water. I shake my head. Without saying anything, she brings a chair and places it next to me. It's quite low, so that when I sit down, I feel almost suppliant at The Lion's side, clutching his hand and sobbing. If the scan results are to be believed, it doesn't matter what I do now, as he cannot hear or see me. Yet every now and then, his mouth moves or an eye half opens and I'm sure it's in response to what I'm saying.

'We never had that baby, you and I, but with your black hair and your black eyes, it would have been the cutest, cleverest, most adorable baby in the world,' I say. This provokes an even stronger reaction. His eyes open almost fully for a second and he moves his mouth very noticeably.

The nurse reappears. 'He keeps moving his mouth,' I say. Before she can reply, Luis makes a noise, as if clearing his throat, which makes me jump.

'He's just coughing,' says the nurse, squeezing my hand. 'I know it's hard for you.' Very gently, she suggests that I go downstairs and get some fresh air, as they have to carry out some *petits soins* (little treatments). Reluctantly, I leave and head down to the café, where I buy a bottle of water and sit at one of the tables crying and dabbing my swollen, red eyes with a desiccated tissue.

Other people—some of them perhaps there for happy events such as the birth of a baby or to bring home a loved one—eye me with a mixture of sympathy and *schadenfreude*. I must make a strange spectacle, dressed as if

349

for a party in an oyster-coloured satin dress with pink and blue flowers at the hem, but my face a mess of tears and snot. I just don't know what I'm going do with all these emotions. It's not like I can just pack them away in a drawer. I'm going to have to carry them around with me for the rest of my life and right now, they feel too enormous to bear.

Through a blur of tears, I see *le patron* walking towards the café in black jeans and T-shirt and snakeskin boots, flanked by José, Sergio, Piedro and three other colleagues that I don't recognise, nearly all of them dressed in black. Sabine, I am relieved to see, is not with them. They walk across the lobby almost in a line, like a scene from *The Magnificent Seven*.

I stand up and the boss stops when he sees me, his eyes full of sadness. I feel compassion for him, keeping up this tough, macho facade when I know that he is as devastated as I am. I ask about the scan results, hoping that Magda has got it wrong.

Frustratingly, I can't understand much of his reply as he speaks French with such a thick Portuguese accent. But two sentences jump out with a horrible finality: '*Le cerveau est mort*,' (The brain is dead) and '*La vie de Luis, c'est terminée*' (Luis's life is over). The tears start to roll again with renewed vigour, accompanied by half-stifled sobs. Several of Luis's colleagues look away. I wish I had their quiet dignity but my soul is screaming in pain.

Fernando tells me that the doctors wanted to switch off the life-support immediately, but have been forced to wait until a member of Luis's family can come from Portugal to sign the papers, which will probably be early next week.

'But what if he continues to live after they've cut off the life-support?' I ask. Luis, I reassure myself, can be stubborn like that.

'I don't know, Madame Willer,' says Fernando with a shrug. I can see this is not the outcome that he is hoping for. He tells me that he's started to make arrangements to fly the body back to Portugal for the funeral, to the little village, near Leiria, where Luis was born. This is too much for me. Fearful that I'm about to start sobbing again, I thank him for the information and turn away.

'It's nothing, Madame Willer.'

Fernando and his men continue their sad journey up to intensive care. Dazed, I wait in the café for over an hour. Then I splash water on my red eyes in the (impeccably clean) washroom, and go back up to see Luis for the last time. In the narrow waiting room, Luis's colleagues are sitting in silence in a line against the wall, each lost in private thoughts. I wonder how many other grief-stricken people have sat in this small room in similar circumstances.

There is still no sign of Sabine, but Fernando's wife Nicole is there, dressed in jeans and a dark jacket with spike heels and too much make-up as usual. She greets me with a brisk *'bonjour'* and a brittle smile. Supervised by Fernando, Luis's colleagues appear to be going in two at a time to pay their last respects, while the rest wait in silence. Piedro and Sergio return to the waiting room looking wiped-out and then go downstairs for a cigarette, while another two follow the boss towards the ward. One of them is very thin with a moustache, a mop of dark hair and kind eyes; the other—who I later discover is Cristina's husband—strong and darkly handsome, like Luis.

Eventually, it is just Nicole and myself left facing each other. 'I feel so guilty,' I say, partly to break the silence and partly because I'm hoping she will contradict me. 'If I'd taken his calls or spoken to him on that Sunday, I could possibly have prevented this.'

She shakes her head. 'I always feared something like this would happen to Luis,' she says. 'I think we all knew deep down that he wasn't going to live to old age. He lived life to the full, but lately he'd been drinking too much and taking too many risks.'

Fernando reappears and nods brusquely at his wife, speaking in rapid French.

'We can go through now,' she says to me. I worry that Fernando is going to accompany us, but he tells Nicole he'll be waiting downstairs. We pass through the walnut-effect doors, which have been left open, and don the hospital gowns. I follow Nicole into the room where The Lion lies motionless. She takes Luis's hand in a proprietorial way, and addresses him in short, aggressive bursts—a style that she seems to have acquired from her husband.

'Luis, I'm here with your ex-neighbour,' she says, which annoys me, as she knows that I was more than that. 'Do you remember her?'

I take one of Luis's hands. 'Darling, can you open your eyes just a little to show us that you can hear what we're saying?' Immediately, he does so. 'Thank you, Luis,' I say. 'Thank you.'

'It's not the first time he's done that,' says Nicole, as if to imply that I'm not getting special treatment. 'He's opened his eyes many times when I've asked him to.'

'*Ah bon?* Then his brain must be working,' I say.

'Without doubt,' she replies, and in that moment, despite the *froideur* that exists between us, I warm to her, because she hasn't written Luis off either.

We stay with Luis for half an hour and then take the lift back down to the ground floor in silence. Outside Fernando and his men are sitting on the steps in a morose black line, smoking. Piedro has his head in his hands. At least they can grieve together, I think. After a moment's hesitation, I kiss Nicole on the cheeks—something I would not have done

353

before today—and return to the car park feeling very much alone. I cry all the way back to Villiers, until it feels like every drop of water has been wrung out of my body.

The doorbell rings shortly after I arrive home. Delphine is standing outside with a box of cakes from the *boulangerie*.

'I'm so sorry, *Ka-renne*,' she says, when I tell her the bad news. 'But my goodness, he is going to die in full glory, that is for sure. Can you imagine what the doctors thought, with all these women of different nationalities—French, English and Portuguese—coming to see him? Luis would have been very pleased with himself.'

I smile at the thought of Dr Durand and the other hospital staff trying to figure out our various roles in Luis's life. Delphine is doing her best to cheer me up and it's true what she says. Luis managed to survive being thrown out of a car window without so much as a scar on his face, he was fortunate not injure anyone else in the accident, and he still looked handsome, even in his hospital bed. In many ways, his will be the perfect death: young, handsome and in his prime, with all his friends gathered at his bedside and two women fighting over him in the corridor. He is leaving us at the end of the summer, in the month of the lion. He has retained his charisma until the very end.

The following morning, feeling numb, I take

354

Biff for a walk around the lake. The poor little chap hasn't had many walks of late and has been very patient, but this morning he decides to act up. Just as we're about to go home, he climbs up a steep earth bank, disappears into some scrubby bushes and starts digging. The slope is too steep for me to climb in flip-flops so I call his name with increasing desperation, while he continues to dig. After about twenty minutes of this, I lose the plot.

'BIFF! GET HERE NOW!' I yell, realising that I look and sound like a mad person—a wild-eyed, inwardly and outwardly screaming picture of grief. In my fragile state, even a disobedient dog is enough to tip me over the edge.

A boy in his early teens approaches, undeterred by my obvious distress.

'Madame, can I help you?' he asks in French, his tone gentle and respectful.

I nod, unable to speak. With enviable ease he climbs up the slope, gently pulls Biff out of the bushes and brings him back down to me. *'Voilà, Madame,'* he says, handing him back by his collar. I'm so touched by the action of this Good Samaritan in baggy jeans and a baseball cap that I struggle to find the words to thank him. When I do, he shrugs and says, 'It's nothing.'

He will never know it, but to me, at that moment, his random act of kindness was everything. I add it to the growing mental inventory of small but memorable kindnesses that I've experienced since Luis's accident. My faith in humanity, rocked several times over the past year, has been more than restored in recent weeks.

When I arrive home, there is a grubby white van parked outside Maison Coquelicot. Arnaud is preparing to leave. Dressed in jeans and with the sleeves of his shirt rolled up, he is carrying a pot plant from the house, while two men manoeuvre a bookcase into the van. He looks uneasy, embarrassed when he sees me but we both say *'Bonjour'*.

'I hope it doesn't bother you, the van parked in front of the house,' he says.

I shake my head. 'Are you moving out today?'

'Yes.'

'Well, good luck,' I say, thinking of my pilfered money pot. I now know exactly what I'm going to do with the small pile of coins and notes that the thief was kind enough to leave behind. The money will go to a charity that specialises in research into brain injury.

Later that afternoon, my neighbour drives away from rue St Benoit for the final time, without bothering to say goodbye. It's sad how things have turned out between us but despite everything, I hope that he will be happy in the Gers. And on the bright side, at least he didn't try and dump another load of socialist magazines on me before he left.

A few hours later, a feeling of emptiness overwhelms me. I ought to be packing for London, where I am due to give a talk on my new book later this week. Instead, I phone Magda and ask for two more Xanax—one to dull the immediate pain and a second to take to London 'for emergencies'. She tells me to come over for a coffee. Taking full advantage of the fact that I have her undivided attention—the girls are in Cristina's house next door—I sit in her cheerful orange kitchen for well over an hour, weeping and articulating all my feelings of grief, guilt and regret. Poor Magda! She is reluctant to give me more tranquilisers—if I were in her shoes, I'd hand them over just to shut me up—but eventually she caves in when I convince her that it won't become a habit. I swallow one pill and wrap the other in tissue and put it in my bag.

'If Luis dies,' I say, as the first waves of the sedative wash through my brain, 'I won't know what to do with myself.'

'*Chérie,* I tell you exactly what you're gonna do,' she says with absolute certainty. 'You're gonna write another book about Luis, and it's gonna be even more beautiful than the last one.'

And with that thought, Magda, though she doesn't know it, has just given me the best reason I can think of right now, to carry on living.

'*Lee-sen,* any time you are feelin' sad, you

357

come 'ere and take a coffee with me, OK?' she says, hugging me before I leave.

I nod, fearing that I'll start to cry again. 'You're an angel, Magda.'

She rewards me with a raucous laugh. 'Nah, *chérie*, I'm definitely not an angel.'

The following afternoon, I take Biff to the vet's for the obligatory worm and flea treatments before he travels. As Madame Beaupain, the vet, stamps his passport and asks how long we'll be gone, it hits me: by the time I get back, Luis will be dead. Driving home, I have a really strong urge to go and see him again. I try to convince myself that it's pointless—he won't even know I'm there—and like everyone else, I already said goodbye on Saturday. But the feeling persists.

When I arrive home the phone is ringing. It's Travis.

'Luis's life-support is going to be switched off,' I say, when he asks how I am.

'Oh God, I'm so sorry.'

I tell Travis that I have a gut feeling that I should go to the hospital one last time and tell Luis that if he wants to live, he has to do something.

The forcefulness of his answer surprises me. 'Oh, my God, then you *MUST*,' he says. 'You should go and tell him exactly that.'

I look at my watch. 'It's already gone 5.30 pm. Visiting finishes at 7.00 pm.'

'Go!' says Travis.

So I do, heading straight back out of the door and driving like a maniac to the hospital. It's 6.45 pm when I arrive—only fifteen minutes left of visiting time—but the nurse who opens the door today, looks at me with a mix of sympathy and resignation.

'Can I see Monsieur Duarte?' I ask.

'*Oui, tu peux,*' she replies softly. Yes, you can. I sense a noticeable shift in attitude, because we both know that, for Monsieur Duarte, the end is near.

I notice that none of the pale blue visitor gowns allocated to *Boîte 1*, Luis's room, have been used. He's had no visitors this afternoon. I notice, too, that the X-rays that once hung on the wall outside his room have been taken down. Everyone has given up on The Lion. The nurses are preparing to vacate the cubicle, ready for the next patient.

In his room, the TV is playing—a feature on how to revolutionise your aperitifs. It's unbearably poignant. I kiss his forehead and take his hand. He seems to be in a deep sleep.

'Listen Luis, I've come to see you one last time before I go to the UK, to tell you something really important,' I say, in French. He opens his left eye a fraction.

'I don't know if you can hear me but if you want to carry on living, you need to do something soon,' I continue. 'The doctors are going to switch off the machines. But I have confidence in you. I know that you will open

359

your eyes, darling. If you want to live.'

I look through the window at the fierce blue sky, at the cars moving on the orbital road below, at life going on as normal in the Poitevin sunshine, and I feel a profound sense of detachment. My world has shrunk to this small room, where a life lies in limbo. I think of all the things that I didn't know about The Lion, like the fact that he comes from Leiria. *Luis of Leiria.* Everything about him is somehow majestic. *Oh God, please don't let him die. Please let me be able to speak to him again.*

Calm and resolute, I stand at his bedside for just twenty minutes, repeating my message over and over. At one point, his entire face contorts—into what, I don't know. A yawn? An attempt to talk? An expression of pain? I tell him that I won't be able to come back again as I have to go to London to give a talk on the book I've written about him, but whatever happens, I will ensure that he is not forgotten. I thank him for the wonderful memories and the great times that we had together. Then I kiss his forehead for the final time.

'*Bonne nuit, chéri. Je t'aime.*'

It's difficult to pull myself away. Several times, I hover in the doorway or try to leave, and then turn around and go back to kiss his forehead again. Finally, I am about to take off my gown in the corridor when I remember something important about The Lion's personality. I return to the room one more time.

'Once again, darling, if you want to carry on living, you need to do something,' I say. And then, because Luis always liked to be in control, I add, 'But only if you want to, darling. It's up to you to decide.' I pause. 'And if you don't want to, I understand. I'll see you on the other side.'

I squeeze his hand and push his lustrous black hair off his forehead. Then I leave. With tears streaming down my face, I take the lift back down to the lobby and drive away from the tower and out of the hospital grounds for the final time. As I wait for the barrier to lift, an emergency helicopter lands on the green field in front of the hospital, bringing in a new casualty. The battle for them is just beginning; for Luis, it's nearly over. I think back to the afternoon when he first moved his arms and tried to speak to me. Those early weeks seem almost joyful in comparison to how I feel now.

Driving back through the maze of concrete roundabouts and tenements, I see a young couple greeting each other at a bus stop. He stoops down to kiss her, while she throws her arms around his neck. It's a happy sight but it makes me feel unbearably sad. Luis won't kiss or hold anyone in his arms again. Nor will he know the pleasure of sunlit fields as he drives home from work on a beautiful August

361

evening. I drive back to Villiers, crushed by the weight of my thoughts.

The house feels empty and desolate when I return, as if wrapped in an aura of melancholy. Even Biff seems too depressed to greet me and I have to coax him out of his bed for a walk. We head over to the château, and the green space overlooking the allotments and the curving road out of the village. The bench where I once sat in the mornings after a passionate night with Luis, is fenced off now, the ground annexed to a nearby school and locked up.

Above us the air vibrates to the twittering of birds and when I look up, the sky is dotted with thousands of black specks moving en masse. The swallows are gathering, getting ready to leave. Very soon, the skies above Villiers will become a lot quieter.

*   *   *

My departure the next morning surpasses even my usual standards of chaos and disorder. At roughly the time I should be driving past Tours, I'm still throwing armfuls of stuff into the car—clothes, work papers, toothbrush, laptop, Biff's bed and food. Biff then climbs into the back and we set off for Le Havre. I drive at 130 kilometres an hour for most of the way, thinking of Luis: Luis sitting outside the café in the sunshine; Luis lying on the ground

362

injured and waiting for the emergency services while I walked Biff nearby; Luis about to make his final journey back to Portugal alone.

At Tours, I find that a large section of the motorway has been closed and it seems almost certain that I'll miss the 5.00 pm ferry. By a miracle, I make it—but only just. At Portsmouth, Biff and I check into the Ibis, one of the few dog-friendly hotel chains, for the night. Then the following morning we drive to Clapham, south London, to stay with friends.

I spend a day wandering around London in a daze. On the evening of my talk in Waterstones, Kensington High Street, I consider taking my last Xanax. I'm dreading the questions that people might ask and worried that I might cry. But Delphine gives me a useful piece of advice. She tells me that whenever she has to give talks at funerals or sombre events, and is worried that she'll be emotional, she thinks of the most boring things that she can, such as bank statements or bills that need to be paid.

Some people in the audience know about Luis's accident. I have a blog on which I've written about a 'friend' in a coma and many readers have guessed who it is, sending me heartfelt messages which seem to arrive as if by magic, when I'm feeling at my lowest ebb. One lovely woman presents me with a box of Belgian chocolates and an uplifting card. I add the gesture to the growing list of unexpected kindnesses that have made life bearable in recent weeks, and that I will never forget.

In the end, I manage to do the talk undrugged and without incident. Only once am I forced to swallow hard and think of bank statements—when someone asks if I'm still with Luis.

'I can't answer that. I don't want to spoil the next book,' I say, knowing that the truth would spoil everyone's evening and mine. This is not the time or the place to reveal that Luis is almost certainly dead by now. (I haven't phoned Magda to find out for sure, as I don't want to hear it.)

I am booked on a ferry the following morning, but decide to postpone the booking until Monday afternoon as I am dreading going back. I spend a morose weekend in London, trying to look cheerful in the company of friends and then, on Monday morning I drive to Kensington High Street to run some errands. I leave the car in my secret parking place—a road just off the high street which appears to be private thanks to the security lodges at either end, but is in fact public. My old Golf, its wing mirror held together with brown parcel tape, makes for an interesting aberration among the gleaming Porsches, Ferraris and Range Rovers parked outside the row of multi-million-pound houses.

When I return to the car I somehow manage to lock both my keys and Biff inside. It's not particularly hot, the window is open a few centimetres and Biff looks quite happy, but I panic nonetheless. Tom, the kindly security guard—who I chatted to on a number of occasions when I lived nearby—comes over to help, inviting me into his lodge to call the RAC. Returning to the car to check on Biff, we are joined by two decorators who are working on the house opposite. One of them is certain that he can open the door and goes off in search of a wire coat hanger.

Biff, meanwhile, is sitting in the driver's seat looking surprised but not unpleased by the crowd that has gathered around him. The decorator returns with a bent coat hanger and eventually manages to pull up the lock. We all clap as Biff jumps out of the car, wagging his tail at this exciting reception. After thanking the decorator, I go back to the lodge to cancel the RAC. As I'm returning to the car, a smartly dressed man emerges from one of the houses.

'Did you manage to get the dog out of the car, Tom?' he asks.

'Yes, we did.'

'Good. Well done,' says the man, who must have been watching from a window.

I set off for Portsmouth feeling uplifted by these kind people who have shown such concern for my predicament, unaware of the inner turmoil that led me to lock my keys in the car in the first place. I miss the ferry, arriving at the port ten minutes before it is due to depart, but it hardly seems to matter. I have no pressing desire or reason to be anywhere at all, right now.

The ticket clerk suggests that I take the fast ferry departing for Cherbourg in an hour. I don't know where Cherbourg is, but I nod and hand over my credit card. Waiting to board, I realise that I haven't bothered to stock up on organic vegetables or Biff's gourmet dog food, but again, it all seems irrelevant compared with the simple fact that Luis will be gone when I get back.

Mindlessly playing with my phone while sitting in the queue of cars, I see his number in my address book, reminding me of the thrill I would get when it flashed up, along with the special salsa ring tone I set for him. I figure I should delete his details, but something stops me.

On board, I stare through the window at the grey, churning sea. If it wasn't for Biff curled up in the car below deck, I'd be tempted to throw myself into it. What a relief it would be to have all this emotional pain taken away by the icy, numbing embrace of the water.

Instead, I buy a coffee and flick half-heartedly through a magazine. I find myself reading Scorpio's horoscope for September. I have done this several times since the accident and discovered that there are few things sadder than reading the astrological

366

predictions of someone who is in a coma. But the final line of Luis's horoscope jumps out at me: *Like a phoenix, you will rise from the ashes.*

It's 7.00 pm and the light is already fading when I roll off the ferry at Cherbourg. The sky is a shocked-white and the fields are a leaden-green. The drive back to Villiers is the saddest journey of my life. I think of the summer evening not so long ago, when I sped south, deliriously happy because I knew that The Lion was waiting for me at the other end. This time, I'm returning in the almost certain knowledge that Luis is no longer in my village, no longer in France, no longer under the same sky. Perhaps for this reason, I manage to make what should be a six-hour journey last most of the night, stopping at countless service stations where I sit in the darkness with a coffee and my despair, consoled only by the thought of the little dog curled up behind me.

Chapter 22

Hope

It's nearly 5.00 am when I arrive back in Villiers. Before going to bed, I check my emails and find an alert from eBay telling me that a bottle of Jo Malone oil has come up for sale. But it's too late to be of any use now. I climb into bed and stay there until midday, only getting up because Biff needs a walk. I can't put off the inevitable any longer.

As I'm walking past the café, Cristina calls over to me in French. 'Eh *Ka-renne*, have you heard the news?'

'What news?' I ask, bracing myself for the worst.

'About Luis. He has come out of the coma.'

I look at her, hoping that this is not some cruel joke. 'You mean he's still alive?'

She nods. 'He pulled the tubes out himself.'

'When?'

'On Saturday. He can speak and recognise people.'

My first instinct is to laugh—I should have had more faith in The Lion—and then I want to punch the air and scream with happiness. In my head, champagne corks pop, balloons are released into the sky and a rain of confetti and champagne descends on the bar. This is a moment I will remember for the rest of my life. I throw my arms around Cristina and thank her for the news. And then, of course, I cry—tears of the purest joy. Never have I experienced such a mixture of relief, shock, surprise, elation and gratitude, all distilled into one euphoric moment. Despair is often described as 'a bottomless pit', but joy as I now know, is an equally deep well.

I have to see Magda, to hear from another person that Luis is alive. Driving over to her house, I realise that if I had acted on my darkest thoughts while crossing the Channel yesterday, I would have missed out on the most unexpectedly amazing moment of my life.

Magda opens the door with a grin. 'You've 'eard the news, *chérie*?'

I fling my arms around her. 'Is it really true?'

'Yeah, it's definitely true. The boss, he tell the Portuguese everythin'. Luis's father 'ad come from Portugal to sign the papers and Luis, 'e wake up.'

I shake my head. It's almost too wonderful to take in. I'm so happy for Luis that his father travelled to his bedside to say goodbye. This was probably what motivated him to pull out of the coma. And how typical that The Lion chose such a memorable day, the anniversary of 9/11, to do it.

'*Le patron* was there when it 'appened and 'e say to Luis, "Do you know who I am?" and Luis 'e say, "Of course I know who you are. You are Fernando Rodriguez, my boss."'

I start to cry again, overcome with love and admiration for The Lion. He has pulled off the impossible. The doctors had written him off—his brain was not supposed to be working on any level—but from the moment he woke up he has been able to speak and recognise people. Like a phoenix, he has indeed, risen from the ashes.

I follow Magda into the kitchen, where she is slicing up flabby-looking pizzas for the girls' lunch. 'Is he speaking French, too?' I ask.

'He is just spikin Portuguese for the moment. And he doesn't say very much. He is sleepin' a lot because he is very tired. Apparently, when Sabine went to the hospital, she was cryin' and tellin' him that she loves him and Luis, 'e just look at her and say nothin'.'

'I knew all along that his brain was working,' I say. 'But what about his other injuries?' (I dare not ask directly if he is going to be paralysed.)

'Tha' I dunno. All I know is that he is breathin' without the machines.'

'He's just amazing. I'm so proud of him.'

'But *lees-en*, *Ka-renne*,' says Magda, suddenly serious. 'Sabine, she is going to the hospital all the time now. And the Portuguese, they are all spikin with her again. Only last week they were sayin' she was a beech and a drunk, but now they say she really love Luis and is gonna take good care of 'im. They're fuckin' crazy if they think that. They are changin' their minds all the time. But I don't think it is a good idea for you to visit anymore.'

'I know. I understand.'

'You do?' says Magda, looking surprised.

'Yes. I told you. All I want is for Luis to live and one day walk out of the hospital.'

I know that Magda is right. It's not a good

370

idea for me to 'force the door', as the French would say. I'm certain that I helped to bring Luis out of the coma, but now that he is conscious, the last thing I want is to create stress at the hospital. He must be allowed to start his recovery with Sabine at his side. More than anything, I want to see him, to speak with him again. But for now, I must take a back seat.

As Magda goes to call the girls in from the garden to load up on carbs, I get up to leave. I have things to do and suddenly the energy to do them.

Firstly, I call Delphine. 'You're not going to believe this,' I say. 'But you were right. Luis has surprised us, just as you predicted.'

'I knew it,' she says, overjoyed. 'I knew he would come out of that coma. And I'm sure he is going to go on surprising us.'

Afterwards, I log on to eBay and make a ridiculously high bid for the Jo Malone oil.

*   *   *

In the days that follow, I feel as if I too, have been given a second lease of life. I feel more alive, more grounded in the present, than at any other point in my life. I no longer sigh at the thought of doing the washing-up or having to walk Biff in the rain. Instead, I'm grateful for the simple fact that I can. I know that the battle for The Lion is just beginning and that

371

he might not make it, but while he is still in the world, there is hope.

One morning, I drive over to the church in Vivonne to light another candle and thank God for delivering a miracle. Afterwards, I have to fight the overwhelming urge to drive on to Poitiers to visit The Lion. But thanks to Magda, who makes it her mission to gather as much information as possible from her Portuguese neighbours, I am able to follow his progress from afar. One Saturday, she comes to clean and tells me that Sabine has instructed the medical staff not to let me visit, and that *le patron,* having decided that Sabine is the best person to look after Luis, is supporting her in this.

'What a pig!' declares Magda, who despises Fernando and is not impressed by his BMW, his money or the macho posturing. 'I told you not to trust him. He thinks he fuckin' controls everyone in this village,' she says, flicking a wet cloth against the sink with such violence that Biff flinches. 'I see him last week and I say to him, "Who do you think you are: the God of fuckin' Villiers? You 'ave no right to stop Luis's friends from seein' 'im".'

'You really said that?' I say, unable to suppress a smile.

'Yeah, I did. He look like he fuckin' wanna kill me. Then 'e walk right up to me and 'e say, "One day Magda. You and I, we gonna talk."'

I picture the scene: macho Fernando

pitched against fearless Magda. I know which of the two I'd place my money on. Surprised though I am by Fernando's *volte-face*, the only thing that matters to me is that Luis is alive.

*   *   *

September rolls into October and the countryside looks exhausted. The maize, the last crop to be harvested, has gone, leaving only blonde stubble behind. The weather meanwhile, is weird. It's winter in the morning, when I walk Biff around the village muffled up against the cold, but in the afternoon, thick layers of clothing are cast aside and red parasols go up outside the café as the sun comes out.

I meet Magda for a coffee there most days. She is teaching me Portuguese so that when I do eventually visit Luis, I'll be able to regale him with a few tortured sentences in his mother tongue. But what I really want is information about Luis's recovery. The news is maddeningly sparse. Often a week goes by and Magda has nothing to report. But when news comes, it always affects me deeply. Gradually, I learn that Luis has had an operation on his broken legs, that he has told his boss that he is determined to work for him again—this makes my eyes well up—and that Luis always looks really bored and says nothing when Sabine visits.

373

I ask Magda over and over if Luis will walk again, but each time I get the same response. 'It's too early to tell, *chérie,*' she says. 'The doctors, they don't know yet.'

*   *   *

As November approaches and with it The Lion's birthday, the urge to visit him becomes stronger. One morning, Magda arrives to do the ironing. (I'm still looking for ways to give her work, and since Luis regained consciousness I have been quite prolific on the freelance front, which means I can afford to pay her.) She looks very serious, so I brace myself for bad news.

Luis, Magda tells me, needs a dressing gown, because he is now sitting up in a chair. The Portuguese are apparently very cross with Sabine because she has not yet bought him one, preferring to spend the money on alcohol and partying.

'What did I tell ya? She's a beech,' concludes Magda, pulling off her jacket and walking through to the kitchen.

'If Luis needs a dressing gown, I will buy him one,' I say.

'I think it would be a good idea,' she replies. '*Lee-sen*, can I hask you a question?'

'Of course.'

'Why you eat all these weird *trucs*?' She points to a bowl of orange lentils soaking

374

in water. I seize the moment, explaining to her the principles of healthy eating and the damage done by hydrogenated fats, additives and foods like pizza. As soon as I've got my message across and Magda's eyes are glazing over, I go upstairs and Google 'dressing gowns'.

November 3 arrives, Luis's birthday, and I cannot stay away any longer. He needs a dressing gown, I've bought him one off the Internet, and I want to see with my own eyes how he is doing, rather than hearing it second-hand. I've also secured the Jo Malone perfumed oil from eBay and spent hours downloading his favourite songs onto an iPod. And so in the afternoon, I drive to the hospital under a steely grey sky. From the ground floor reception, I discover that Monsieur Duarte is no longer in intensive care but has been moved to the eighth floor. As I take the lift up, I experience the familiar feeling of giant moths leaping about in my lower stomach. I have no idea how Luis will react when he sees me and I'm worried that Sabine might be there.

Fortunately, I don't have to ring a bell or wait for admittance. The doors to this ward are wide open and when I ask a nurse for Monsieur Duarte, she tells me that he is in room number 834, further along the corridor. The door is closed, so I hesitate for a second, listening for voices on the other side. But all is quiet. When I enter the dimly lit room, I'm disappointed to find that The Lion is sleeping. He is thinner than when I last saw him two months ago, but still handsome. Taking his hand, I speak to him softly in French.

'Luis, I've come to wish you happy birthday.'

Despite the fact that he's asleep, I talk to him for nearly an hour, telling him how I cried with happiness when I heard the news that he had come out of the coma, and how proud I am of him.

'I had faith in you,' I say. 'What you have done is amazing.'

At one point he opens his eyes momentarily. When two young nurses arrive to take his temperature, I say *'Bonjour'* and ask how Monsieur Duarte is doing. They tell me that he has been given strong medication for a chest infection, which is why he is in a deep sleep. They ask who I am.

'Just a friend,' I say, grateful when they don't ask any more questions. After hanging his new navy dressing gown on a hook, and explaining to the nurses how to work the iPod, I kiss his forehead and tell him that I'll be back tomorrow.

When I return the next day, the door to his room is open and I am surprised to find that The Lion is out of bed, sitting bolt upright in a chair in front of the TV, as if he were waiting for me. I cannot believe the improvement. Even in his pale blue hospital gown, with his head supported by a neck brace, he looks proud and majestic, his presence dominating the room.

'*Bonjour,* Luis,' I say, kissing his forehead.

He doesn't reply, but nor does he look surprised to see me. I have the distinct feeling that he was expecting me. The moths in my stomach migrate upwards, as if they are now dancing around my heart. I perch on a little stool by The Lion's chair, feeling like I've come to pay homage at the court of a medieval king.

'*Luis, c'est Ka-renne,*' I say, pronouncing my name the way that he used to. 'I hope you don't mind, but I really wanted to come and see you.'

I'm painfully aware that as a very proud man, The Lion, in his current condition, might not welcome a visit from me, and that by wandering in here with no warning and without asking, I'm taking a very big liberty. I must proceed, as the French say, 'with velvet paws.'

I take his hand and ask him in French if he recognises me. He murmurs something that I can't hear. In my bag, I have a little notebook filled with the phonetic spellings of Portuguese phrases that Magda has given me, because so far, Luis has only spoken in his mother tongue. But I'm certain that he understood me when he was in the coma and I'm certain that he can understand me now.

'*Ça va aller, Luis,*' I say over and over. It's

377

going to be OK. And very noticeably, very firmly, he squeezes my hand in response. Two or three times he communicates with me in this way, sending waves of joy into my heart. 'Would you like to hear some music?' I ask.

'*Si,*' comes the surprisingly definite reply. I place the iPod and speaker on a shelf nearby, and turn my back momentarily while I search underneath it for a power socket. In the process, I manage to pull the iPod off the shelf, catching it just before it hits the floor.

And then I freeze at the sound of the deep, macho voice behind me.

'*Ne fais pas de gaffe!*' he says. (Be careful! Or literally, 'Don't make a blunder!') It's a phrase that he used all the time when we were together, often with a playful wag of his finger. I turn around and feel a huge surge of love for him. He is teasing me. *And he is speaking to me in French, because he knows I don't speak Portugese*. He is amazing.

I close the door to his room so as not to bother anyone and turn the music up. He recognises the track, *Closer*, by the Kings of Leon, and starts to hum along. I open the bottle of Jo Malone oil and apply the thick, gloopy oil to his arms, the fragrance taking me right back to the nights that we spent together. As I massage the oil into his temples and forehead, he closes his eyes and pulls a comic face, just as he did back then. He is trying to make me laugh.

'You know, many people are thinking about you and saying prayers for you,' I say in French, noticing an expression of real interest in his dark eyes. The Lion always did like to be the centre of attention.

He says very little in return—just a few inaudible words. I've been told by Magda that sometimes he speaks a lot and sometimes not at all, even when his work colleagues visit. But I can see by subtle changes in his facial expression that he is following, and is interested in, what I am saying.

When I tell him that many people love him and are missing him, he replies *'Merci,'* in a low, deep voice. That he can understand— and that he has replied in French—gives me a feeling of profound joy. It means that his brain is working well enough to recognise that I don't understand Portuguese.

One of Luis's favourite U2 tracks, *Moment of Surrender*, starts to play. 'It's the sort of song that really makes you think,' he once said of it, and I wonder what he is thinking now. What thoughts go through the mind of a man once so strong, so full of life and energy—a proud man who liked above all else to be in control—who suddenly finds himself confined to a wheelchair and entirely dependent on others? And what is it like for him to have his ex-girlfriend, who hadn't spoken to him for nearly a year, breeze back into his life at such a vulnerable moment?

There are so many questions that cannot be answered. Should I feel guilty for coaxing The Lion back to consciousness, when maybe he would have preferred to go peacefully? Perhaps, as Fernando said, it would have been better for Luis if he had died on the day of the accident. But on the other hand, it took spirit and determination to emerge from the coma, which makes me think that Luis must have wanted to live on some level. His current situation is most people's idea of a living hell. And yet, as several people have pointed out to me, a very high number of people with locked-in syndrome—a condition worse than Luis's, whereby the brain is fully aware but the body paralysed and the victim is only able to communicate by blinking their eyes—are still happy to be alive.

According to an article that I recently read by a US doctor, studies show that many people afflicted with this syndrome prefer to be here, even if they can only observe the world, rather than engage in it. In the article, Dr Matthew Edlund points to a poignant paradox of life: 'People with lives we would not wish to live want very much to survive as long as they can, while others who appear to have "everything" want nothing better than to end it all.' It's a humbling thought.

The reason, it seems, is that victims of paralysis redefine their idea of happiness. Rather than looking at what they can no longer do, they focus on—and are grateful for—the simple fact that they are still in this world. By contrast, most of us overlook the blessings in our lives. The more we have, the more we upscale our definition of happiness, to the point where we expect to be walking around in a state of permanent nirvana.

As I watch Luis listening to U2's *Beautiful Day*, it's clear that he's enjoying the music and still able to derive some pleasure from life. He can't eat, drink or move, or do anything for himself, but he can see and communicate with his friends. He can speak and understand two languages. Even in this terrible situation, I can see positives for Luis. The accident will have shown him how very much he is loved— in some cases by people that he might not have imagined. Had he died on the day of the accident, he would never have been reunited with his father, or known that the man who abandoned him at birth cared enough to come to his bedside at what seemed like the end.

From the eighth floor window, I watch the afternoon light fade into evening. I stay with The Lion until 7.00 pm, the end of visiting time.

'Luis,' I say. 'I've got to go now but can I come back and see you tomorrow?'

He is silent. I repeat the question. 'I will only come back if you want me to.'

There is a pause and then a quick, '*Si, si, si.*'

'OK, I'll see you tomorrow, darling. *Bonne*

nuit.'

I leave him listening to *You've Got The Love* by Florence and The Machine, and then walk back along the busy corridor, where nurses are preparing meals for the other patients. I exit the brightly lit hospital tower and walk out into the darkness, feeling elated. The Lion understands French as well as Portuguese and he wants me to visit again. I know that I probably shouldn't—that really I should take a step back—but I can't bear the idea of The Lion spending his afternoons alone. I want to help him.

I drive back to Villiers on an incredible high and go straight over to see Magda. Cristina lets me in and I follow her through to the bonfire-orange kitchen, where Magda is chopping up red bell peppers while, several small, scrubbed-looking children run around in their pyjamas. Janinha lies on the sofa playing a noisy computer game.

'That smells good,' I say, looking at the pot simmering on the stove.

'You wanna try some?' says Magda, offering me a spoonful. 'It's a Portuguese dish—chicken with red peppers and chick peas.'

It's delicious. And so much better for the children than Lidl's spring rolls.

'I've been to see Luis,' I say, sitting down opposite Cristina.

'Did he recognise you?' asks Magda.

'Yes. And he spoke to me in French, but not

very much.'

'*Voilà!*' says Magda, triumphantly, as if she'd known all along that he could speak two languages. She makes me a coffee and I stay and chat with my two Portuguese friends until it is time for Magda to give the children their dinner. I'm tempted when she invites me to stay and eat with them—her house is so full of life and energy—but I have to feed Biff. I drive home on a high, my heart filled with gratitude and love, and hope for Luis.

Chapter 23

Leaving

The next day I go back to the hospital, taking my laptop and a copy of *Toute Allure*. The door to Luis's room is closed, but I'm delighted to find him sitting up in his chair again in front of the television, on which a football match is playing.

'*Bonjour,* Luis,' I say. 'I hope this won't be too painful but I'm going to try and speak to you in Portuguese today. Magda has given me some lessons so that I can talk to you.' Then, using the phrases that Magda has spelt out phonetically for me, I ask him if he remembers me. He doesn't reply, so I repeat the question in Portuguese.

I see a small smile form on his lips and then suddenly he says, *'Bien sûr.'* Never have two words made me so happy. Encouraged, I try a little more Portuguese. *'Toe dough, vy fee-car bang,'* I say, referring to my notebook and the phonetic spelling of 'It's going to be OK'.

In response, he squeezes my hand.

I open my laptop, hoping to jog his memory with some pictures. 'Do you remember this?' I ask in French, showing him a picture of the wrought-iron table in the courtyard, where we ate many meals together.

He looks at it for a few seconds and says, *'Si.'*

'Here's my little dog, Biff. Do you remember him?'

'Si,' he replies again.

'And here you are on my bed, the night you jumped into my house via the skylight,' I say, showing him a picture of himself falling back on my bed, laughing. Again, he studies it intently. I wonder if this is bringing back painful memories. I take his hand and ask him to squeeze mine if he wants me to keep coming to the hospital. He squeezes and he doesn't let go.

Touched, I show him a copy of my book, telling him that people all over the world have read about him.

'That's you on the cover,' I say pointing to a small figure in the illustration. Again, he looks engaged, interested, as if scrutinising the

384

drawing of himself.

The door opens and two young nurses enter. I ask if they want me to leave, assuming that they are going to carry out some medical checks.

'Madame, can you tell us who you are?' one of them asks, in a tone of voice and with a look of concern that immediately makes me feel like some crazy hospital stalker.

'I'm a friend,' I reply. 'An English friend.'

'Actually, Madame, it has been asked that you do not visit the hospital any more,' one of them says, delivering what feels like a sharp slap in the face.

'By the girlfriend?'

'No. It is Monsieur Duarte himself who has asked.'

'Did he tell you that?'

'No. He can only speak Portuguese. Apparently he said it to his cousin on the telephone.'

'Really? Monsieur Duarte is able to speak on the telephone?'

'Apparently yes.' I can see from their faces that they don't believe it, either.

'And the cousin told you that he doesn't want me to visit?'

'No, it was one of his colleagues, a Portuguese man, this morning.'

Fernando, I think. *The bastard*. I nod at the nurses.

'OK, I understand what you are saying.' I

get up to leave.

'You don't have to go straightaway,' one of them says. 'You can say goodbye.'

They leave the room, closing the door behind them.

'Luis,' I say, taking his hand. 'The nurses have told me that I cannot come and see you any more. But if ever you want me to visit, just tell them and I will come immediately.'

It feels like I've already said goodbye to him so many times. Maybe this really is the last time. *'Bon courage, chéri,'* I say and kiss his forehead. He doesn't respond.

In the corridor outside, the nurses are hovering by a metal trolley. They look wary as I approach them and I can understand why. Who knows what Sabine has told them?

'Did Monsieur Duarte give a reason why he doesn't want me to visit?' I ask.

One of the nurses shakes her head. 'We have just been told that he does not want you to come here.'

I have nothing to lose, so I tell them the truth—that I'm Monsieur Duarte's former girlfriend. I explain that he had attempted to contact me in the weeks before the accident, which is why I came to see him, and that his brother gave permission for me to visit. I can see the nurses softening towards me.

'But I won't come back again as I don't want to create any stress in a hospital,' I conclude. 'I just want him to recover.'

'I'm sorry,' one of them says. 'It's not our decision.'

I nod and thank them for looking after Monsieur Duarte. 'And just one more thing,' I say, before I leave. 'Please don't ever underestimate him. He understands more French than you think.'

I take the lift down to the ground floor and walk past the café and away from the hospital where I've experienced such unimaginable highs and lows over the past few months. I feel humiliated. If what the nurses are saying is true, I've been forcing my love and attention on someone who doesn't want it. But my instincts tell me that this is not the case. And at least I got to see The Lion again, to speak to him and thank him for all the good times. I got to say all the things that I wanted to say. And for that, I will always be grateful.

As I drive into Villiers, I see that the lights are on in Sabine's apartment and she has company: one of the unemployed guys who hangs out in the local café is sitting in the window, smoking. Later, as I take Biff for his evening walk, I hear very loud music and male laughter coming from her bedroom. Not for the first time I ask myself, 'Oh Luis, what *were* you thinking?'

Magda is outraged when I tell her what has happened. 'The bastard!' she says, referring to Fernando. 'Do you really think Luis is able to spik on the telephone? No, Fernando is behind this, I'm sure of it. What did I tell you about him? He likes to control everyone.'

Delphine agrees. 'How cruel,' she says, when I tell her. 'But one thing is sure, you have acted only from kindness and the best possible motives. You did everything you could for Luis.'

In my heart, I know this is true. I've pushed doors, skulked like a spy in the hospital café, and been chased along corridors in my efforts to see him. I am certain that I helped to bring him out of the coma. It pains me greatly to think that The Lion might be sitting alone a hospital room when I could be talking to him, playing him music, helping him through the long afternoons, but I can't argue with the nurses. If ever he calls for me, I will go. But the moment has come to accept that I have done as much as I possibly can and that my role in his life is over. I take solace from knowing that I have made peace with Luis, and in so doing I've made peace with myself.

*　　　*　　　*

A few nights later, I drive over to Travis's house for a cocktail party to celebrate the completion of his kitchen. Ever the optimist, he has chosen 'Summer' as his theme, even though snow is forecast before the end of the week. As I pull up in his gravel driveway, I see blue fairy lights twinkling in the window and the orange glow of the fire within.

Travis opens the door holding a jug of sangria, dressed in cut-off denim shorts and flip-flops, with a pair of Oakley sunglasses on his head. Behind him I can hear Wham's *Club Tropicana* playing on the sound system.

'Darling! I'm so glad you decided to come.'

'I figured it was time to dust down my sombrero and show my face to the world again,' I say, handing him a bottle of wine.

'And about time too. Come on in!'

I step out of the cold night air, into his warm kitchen, which is filled with the sound of friendly chatter. Biff runs straight through to the sitting room, where most of the guests are, and performs several high-energy circuits of the room—along with a few barks and bunny-hops—to let everyone know that he's arrived.

'Wow!' I say, partly referring to my fellow guests—a mix of French and British locals, who have all gamely embraced the summer theme, in a colourful selection of Hawaiian shirts, straw hats and sundresses—and partly referring to Travis's new fitted kitchen. Not for him the rustic look of free-standing cabinets and cheerful clutter displayed on open shelves. His pale maple cabinets and granite worktops, the bar-style counter and stools, are pure London bachelor pad.

'Really Travis, all you're missing is a DJ booth and you'd never need to go out again.'

'Well, like I say, life is all about being your

own party,' he grins, handing me a glass of punch and leading me into the sitting room. It's clear that he has gone to quite a lot of effort to turn winter into summer for his guests. He points to the Lilo and two sun parasols suspended from the ceiling. 'It took most of the afternoon to get them to stay up there,' he says.

'That's all very well, but Biff was expecting a beach.'

Travis pulls a face of mock exasperation. 'Well, Biff will just bloody well have to pretend like everyone else,' he says, looking over at the smiling black terrier who's stretched himself out on a beach towel by the log fire.

'Honestly! Just look at him,' says Travis. 'It's as if he's waiting for someone to bring him a cold beer and a choc ice.'

'Please, don't give him ideas.'

I look around the room—at Tania, the petite brunette hairdresser, dressed in a leopard chiffon kaftan and Bert the electrician, wearing baggy shorts and a Hawaiian garland. Everyone is having a good time, pretending it's summer and drinking sangria, oblivious to the thick frost forming on their windscreens outside. Travis really has created his own bubble of fabulousness here in the middle of the French countryside.

I spot Delphine in her floppy turquoise sun hat, chatting to Jean-Françoise the goat farmer, dressed in a tropical print shirt. Both of them give me a cheery wave from their deckchairs. With them is Gabriella, a feisty ninety-four-year old who lives in my village (Delphine must have driven her here, since I only decided to come along at the last minute.)

Gabriella beckons me over to ask about Luis, or 'that poor young man' as she refers to him. I tell her the good news—that he can speak and understand two languages—but that the nurses have asked me to stop visiting.

'Then you must accept that. Life is like a wave. You can't fight it,' says Gabriella, the former wife of a diplomat, and a very wise soul. She takes my hand. 'You know, my dear, I always say that life is like a cake. Some people have very few ingredients and manage to make something wonderful; others have eggs, sugar, flour and butter, *everything* in abundance, and yet they create something lousy.'

While I'm reflecting on the truth of this, Travis calls everyone into the kitchen to make an announcement: he was offered a job this morning and will be returning to London in the New Year.

'But I want to thank each and every one of you for making my time out here so much fun,' he says, before asking everyone to raise their glasses to *'la belle France'*.

As people cheer and wish him 'Congratulations' I realise how much I'll miss Travis and the long chats and bottles of

Sauvignon around his log fire. But I'm also happy for him, as I know he was worried about money.

'Of course, you won't be getting rid of me completely,' he continues. 'I'll still be coming out to visit. It's not so much *'Au revoir,'* as *'À bientôt.'*

At the end of the evening, it is just Travis and myself left, sitting by the fire in his lounge as we have done many times before. We chat about Travis's sojourn in France and his future plans. Suddenly, he reaches forward to squeeze my arm and says, 'Listen, I hope you realise that you did everything you could for Luis. You mustn't have any regrets.'

'I know,' I say. 'But it's hard.'

'The thing about regret,' he continues, 'is that people always assume that the alternative outcome would have been rosier. The truth is that it could have been much worse.'

'How do you mean?'

'Well, imagine if you *had* got back together with Luis. The accident might still have happened and had you been his girlfriend, it would have been much worse. Or what if he'd fallen off your roof and seriously injured himself the night that he climbed in through your skylight? You would have blamed yourself for not opening the door and you'd have been even more devastated. The point is this: you just don't know where the alternative path might have taken you, but you might have

392

liked the destination even less.'

I nod. All this is true. As I get up to go, Travis gives me a hug.

'You should be so proud of everything you've done for Luis,' he says. 'I don't think you could have done more.'

As I drive home through the calm, clear night, the despair of the past few months is replaced by a new determination. I have been blessed with some really good ingredients. And now I owe it to Luis to make something wonderful with them.

*   *   *

A white sky day in early December, punctuated by spats of rain and sudden bursts of wind. Shortly before 3.00 pm, I drive over to Magda's house for the last time. She is waiting outside with Cristina, chatting and smoking. There is a surprising amount of luggage stacked up by the front door. Magda assured me that everything 'apart from a few bags' had been shipped back to Portugal by a lorry driver 'friend' a few weeks ago, but those 'few bags' I notice, equate to three cupboard-size suitcases, two bulging nylon holdalls and at least half a dozen smaller bags.

Magda is wearing jeans tucked into stiletto boots and a slim-fitting white shirt. 'You never know who you gonna meet on the bus, *chérie*,' she winks, when I comment that she hasn't exactly dressed for an overnight journey. Somehow, we manage to get all three suitcases into the car, although the rear window is completely obscured. Magda then calls Janinha—the other two girls are already back in Portugal with Magda's mother—who waddles out of the house in grey marl leggings and matching hoodie. The doctors gave her the all-clear just two weeks ago and Magda wasted no time in finding an apartment to rent in northern Portugal.

Janinha barely acknowledges my friendly *'Bonjour'*. Instead, she looks at me as if I am an escaped lunatic, as she always does, and climbs into the back of the car. We pack the barrel-shaped bags in around her. Magda then hugs Cristina goodbye and slides into the passenger seat with another big bag on her lap.

'I'm going to miss you, Magda,' I say as we drive out of Villiers in the hard winter light.

'I gonna miss you too, *chérie*. Are you gonna be OK?'

'Yes. I'll be fine.'

Magda's phone rings. I assume from the way she is yelling that it is her boyfriend.

'Everything OK?' I ask, when she has finished.

'*Nah, chérie*. Roberto, 'e just tell me that 'e is not gonna leave his wife.'

'*WHAT*? He's married? You never told me that.'

She shrugs and looks crestfallen for a

second. 'I know, *chérie*. I told you I ham no angel.' Then she rallies. 'But fuck 'im. I don't need him.'

'Maybe you'll meet someone on the bus,' I say. Looking the way she does, I'd say the odds are stacked in her favour.

I ask Magda the question I must have asked a hundred times over the past few months: 'Is there any news of Luis?'

She shakes her head. 'Nah, *chérie*. Still the same.'

Shortly after my last visit, The Lion was moved to a small hospital and nursing home in the nearby town of Lusignan and by all accounts, his progress has stalled. I've been told that he hardly speaks and doesn't move at all. But it's still early days and I haven't given up hope that one day he will surprise us again.

We drive into the multi-storey car park at Poitiers station. I run and get two trolleys and between us we heave the bags and suitcases onto them. Magda is early for the 5.00 pm bus, so we push the heavy trolleys into the small café next to the station. While I queue for two coffees and a Coke, Magda sits at a small table arguing with Janinha, who wants pizza. She tells her daughter that she only has €5 to last all the way to Portugal. Horrified, I give her the contents of my wallet, which is not much more than €10. Rifling around in the pocket of my bag hoping to find more loose change, I find the 'emergency' Xanax that I have been carrying around for several months, still wrapped in tissue.

'So I will see you in Portugal in the New Year?' says Magda, as we push the mountain of luggage back into the bus station.

'Yes,' I say. 'You will. Thank you, Magda, for everything. I don't think I could have got through this year without you.'

'It's nothin',' she says. 'You have been a very good friend to me also.'

I hug her goodbye as the bus draws up. Then I walk away, smiling at the eager way in which the driver jumped out to help Magda with her luggage. With Biff trotting along at my side, I take the lift back up to the car park, thinking how it is often the people who come into your life for a short time, who leave the strongest impression. Spotting a bin by the payment machines, I throw the Xanax into it. I don't need it any more. Luis coming out of the coma was the emotional equivalent of electric shock treatment for me.

Some things, like the stars in the midnight sky, you only see in the darkest hour. In some of the worst months of my life, I have learned more about the path to happiness than ever before. Luis has taught me that life is a miracle, not a chore—a source of constant wonder and surprise. I've learnt that nothing and no one that is here today will necessarily be here tomorrow, and that you should tailor your actions accordingly.

Our time on earth is made up of all types of experiences, good and bad and the secret of happiness, I have realised, is to accept both with good grace. A life without pain and suffering is a life not fully lived. It is the bad times that make it possible to appreciate the good.

We are each of us moving through a series of acts or scenes and evolving all the time. My next act, I hope, is going to be a joyful one. I'm done with crying and leaning on others for support. I now want to be the one who does the propping up, because the kindness and compassion of other people after Luis's accident—some of them complete strangers—has shown me that the most important thing, the sum of your existence, is what you bring to the lives of others.

I will never tire of replaying scenes of my life with Luis in my head. I can picture him now, sitting against the bright pink wall in my kitchen, running his hand through his lush dark hair and looking too big for the space. He came into my life fleetingly, like a field flower—a thing of short-lived beauty that dies when you try to own it. We shared two summers and a winter, but I think I always knew that The Lion would never be tamed or owned . . . that we would never sit by the fireside together in our sunset years. But Luis taught me what it is to really love another person, and I am grateful to have experienced such passion.

In addition to the wonderful memories of our time together, I'll never forget the jolt of excitement I experienced when I saw him in the bar on Sunday mornings. Or the euphoria on hearing that he had survived the coma. This, I think, was his greatest gift to me: he taught me that amazing things are possible when you least expect them, that everything can change in an instant and that even in utter despair, joy might not be far way. The euphoric moment in the café when I discovered he was still alive—and that I might be able to speak to him again—is one that I will treasure for the rest of my days.

When times are bad, I have realised, you have to march on in the hope that happiness is waiting further down the road. That's what I'm planning to do now: march on. And whatever happens from this point, I will always be grateful that one summer, in a small village in rural France, I found myself living next door to The Lion.

Afterword

Luis Miguel Jorges Duarte died on Wednesday, 29th June 2011, aged thirty-three, in the hospital in Lusignan. The birds were singing, the sunflowers were in full bloom and the sky was a vibrant blue. Andy Murray had not yet been knocked out of Wimbledon and the temperature on the pharmacy clock read 31 degrees.

The news, when it came, was unexpected. I last saw him at the end of February—for, despite everything, I still contrived, with the help of some of his Portuguese friends, to visit him several times after he was transferred to Lusignan. I stopped only because Sabine informed the hospital staff very forcibly, that I was not to be allowed to see him.

The Lion finally laid down his arms after succumbing to a fever and, according to the medical staff, it seemed like he wanted to go. He was buried in his hometown of Amor—it means love in Portuguese—in Leiria, Portugal, on Saturday, 2nd July 2011. His estranged mother and father both attended his funeral, along with his brother, Fernando and several of his work colleagues. Sabine also went, which meant that I couldn't. Instead, with the help of my Portuguese friends, I sent three roses—one red, one white, one pink. There was no card. I figured that this book would say it all.

It's selfish, I know—for who can guess at the suffering The Lion endured in the ensuing months?—but I will always be grateful to him for coming out of the coma. It meant that I had a chance to say goodbye. He lived on, I'm sure of it, because we asked him to and because he knew that some of us weren't ready to let him go. He was being strong until we could imagine a world without him.

Shortly after his death, Delphine and I went to L'Auberge de L' Écurie, near Usson-du-Poitou, for dinner. It was a beautiful summer evening and as we sat on the terrace, in the middle of the French countryside, surrounded by palms in terracotta pots, it occurred to me that we could just as easily be in Spain or Portugal. Halfway through the evening, one of the group at the neighbouring table produced a guitar, and they all started singing in Spanish. The song was about a girl with golden hair, who loved a man very much, waving goodbye from a harbour.

Suddenly, the most amazing thing happened. I looked up and saw the orange sail cloths strung above the terrace to provide shade, and I immediately thought of Luis—orange being the colour that I most associate with him. Then I noticed the vivid orange nasturtiums growing by the wall, the orange napkins, and the orange vase on our table. In the fading light of a summer evening, bright, shining orange was leaping out at us from every turn.

'My goodness,' said Delphine. 'It's as if Luis has arranged this to cheer us up. I am sure that he is up there smiling down at us.'

It was a reminder that life beats on, full of colour and music and moments of potential happiness, even at times of great sadness. The painful image of him in the café, in his orange T-shirt, hours before the accident on that awful Sunday, was suddenly replaced by a more joyous one.

As I stood up to leave, I noticed a painting of two wild, orange-red poppies on the wall behind me. And once again, I felt a huge surge of gratitude to The Lion. Even in death, he was providing me with unforgettable moments. Despite everything that has happened, I will always associate Luis with music and laughter, love and joy. He left footprints in the well of my skylight and all over my soul. For which I can only say, *obragada, chéri*.

Acknowledgements

I read dozens of books on the subject of happiness while writing Tout Soul, but it was a relatively unknown work that spoke to me at the most profound level: *Evolutionary Outlook on Life*, by Swami Ramananda. The short tract contains some sublime thoughts on dealing with sadness and loss, including the very simple advice that the solution to all life's problems lies in marching on.

A Google search reveals that there are many Swami Ramanandas on the Internet, but this Swami Ramananda is not one of them. He died in 1952 at the age of 33 and deliberately left no formal organisation behind him. His works have been passed on by word-of-mouth. It is thanks to Dr Barbara Sarter and Babaji that I discovered them, and I'd like to thank them both for some excellent practical advice on coping with 'the daily rosary of misery', and for the light that they shone into my life at a dark moment. I owe a great debt of gratitude to their friend and mine, the indomitable Gabriella Mellen, in whose wisteria-swagged garden I met them, in the summer of 2011.

I am also very grateful to Dr Matthew Edlund, and his website www.therestdoctor. com for allowing me to quote from his thought-provoking piece on the ability of paralysis victims to redefine their idea of a new definition of happiness, and in so doing, to continue to value their lives.

Finally, I'd like to thank my friends in France and my readers around the world for their enthusiasm for my books and their kind messages in the months following the accident. Those messages always seemed to ping into my in-box when I most needed to read them, and spurred me on with the writing of Tout Soul. There are too many people to name individually, but I'd like to say a big collective—and heartfelt—thank you.